D.H. Lawrence and Cornwall

Also by Philip Payton and published by
University of Exeter Press

Cornish Studies (ed.) (a series of twenty-one annual volumes, 1993–2013)
New Directions in Celtic Studies (ed. with Amy Hale) (2000)
A.L. Rowse and Cornwall: A Paradoxical Patriot (2005)
Making Moonta: The Invention of Australia's Little Cornwall (2007)
John Betjeman and Cornwall: 'The Celebrated Cornish Nationalist' (2010)
Regional Australia and the Great War: 'The Boys from Old Kio' (2012)
The Maritime History of Cornwall
(ed. with Alston Kennerley and Helen Doe) (2014)
Cornwall: A History (revised edition) (2017)
The Cornish Overseas: A History of Cornwall's
'Great Emigration' (revised edition) (2020)
Cornwall in the Age of Rebellion, 1490–1690 (ed.) (2021)

D.H. Lawrence and Cornwall

In Search of Utopia

PHILIP PAYTON

UNIVERSITY
of
EXETER
PRESS

First published in 2024 by
University of Exeter Press
Reed Hall, Streatham Drive
Exeter EX4 4QR
UK

www.exeterpress.co.uk

Copyright © 2024 Philip Payton

The right of Philip Payton to be identified as author of this
work has been asserted by him in accordance with
the Copyright, Designs and Patents Act 1988.

All rights reserved. Apart from short excerpts for use in research or
for reviews, no part of this document may be printed or reproduced,
stored in a retrieval system, or transmitted in any form or by any means,
electronic, mechanical, photocopying, recording, now known or hereafter
invented or otherwise without prior permission from the publisher.

https://doi.org/10.47788/HKJR8984

British Library Cataloguing in Publication Data
A catalogue record for this book is available from the British Library.

ISBN 978-1-80413-132-9 Hardback
ISBN 978-1-80413-133-6 ePub
ISBN 978-1-80413-134-3 PDF

Cover image: Poster, Southern Railway, North Cornwall, Pentire Head near Padstow
by Norman Wilkinson, 1947. National Railway Museum/Science Museum Group.

Typeset in Goudy Oldstyle Std by BBR Design

For Elise

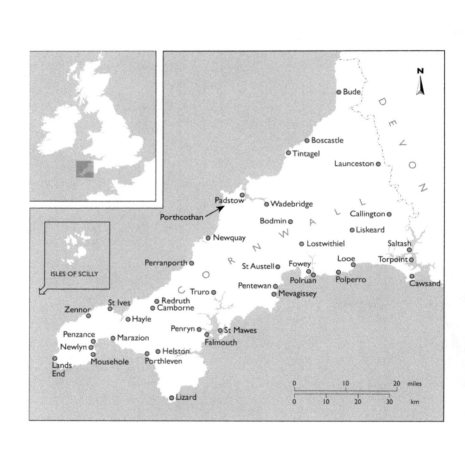

Contents

Acknowledgements		ix
Prologue		1
Chapter 1	Dreaming of Rananim	10
Chapter 2	Dreaming of Cornwall	22
Chapter 3	Rananim Found and Lost: Lawrence at Porthcothan	39
Chapter 4	Rananim Regained? Lawrence at Zennor	61
Chapter 5	War in Cornwall: 'The Nightmare'	99
Chapter 6	'So on to Australia!'	125
Epilogue		143
Notes and References		150
Select Bibliography		172
Index		180

Acknowledgements

As ever, I am indebted to numerous friends and institutions for a variety of assistance, but I am especially grateful for the support of colleagues at Flinders University, especially Gillian Dooley, Heidi Ing, and Valerie Munt. I am likewise indebted to former colleagues at the University of Exeter, notably Jane Costin (who read the draft text in its entirety, making numerous important suggestions), Bernard Deacon and Ella Westland. At the Australian National University, Matthew Spriggs and Stephen Wilks have been endlessly helpful and supportive.

Cornwall Heritage Trust has assisted in the identification of certain research material, and the D.H. Lawrence Society has also been most generous in pointing me towards relevant sources. At University of Exeter Press, Nigel Massen and Anna Henderson, who so enthusiastically endorsed this project, have been patient and tactful as they have steered this book from genesis to publication. So too David Hawkins, production editor at UEP.

The authors and publishers of the numerous books and articles cited in this volume also deserve particular acknowledgement, for their major contributions to knowledge from which studies such as this are fortunate to draw. Extracts from works by D.H. Lawrence are reproduced by permission of Pollinger Ltd.

I am also hugely indebted to my companion, Elise Ruthenbeck, whose love and ceaseless encouragement have carried me through the writing of this book. I could not have done it without her.

Prologue

In January 1981, Cornish local historian P.A.S. Pool, well known for his intimate and meticulous studies of the West Penwith district of far-western Cornwall, penned a short work entitled *The Life and Progress of Henry Quick of Zennor*.[1] Henry Quick (1792–1857), an obscure nineteenth-century doggerel poet, little known beyond Cornwall or, indeed, outside his native parish of Zennor, was a keen commentator in verse on local and occasionally national events. He wrote about the Irish potato famine, a train crash in Berkshire (in which a Cornish clergyman was killed) and the coronation of Queen Victoria. But, as P.A.S. Pool observed, much of Quick's versifying was about disasters in and around Zennor, from mine accidents to shipwrecks, with sudden death a constant theme.

As Pool noted, Zennor was situated about six miles north of Penzance and five miles west of St Ives. The parish consisted of a narrow coastal strip of cultivated land, with ancient field systems, bounded on the north by precipitous cliffs and on the south by granite hills rising to over 700 feet, with granite-strewn moorland beyond. This was Henry Quick's milieu, scene of the tragedies he recorded in verse and home to kinfolk whose lives he understood in intricate detail. He knew the tenant farmers and smallholders, and the family relationships between them, including all the usual genealogical complexities of ancient lineage, intermarriage and illegitimacy. He was immersed in local society and its culture, including, perhaps, the lingering remnants of the Cornish language still on the lips of at least some inhabitants, alongside a vibrant Cornu-English dialect spoken in Zennor which had incorporated many words from the old tongue.

'Our Cornish drolls are dead, each one'

There was a sense of 'timelessness' in Henry Quick's Zennor, of families rooted in the parish for generations, of a way of life slow to change, seemingly remote, even impenetrable. Quick fancied himself a 'droll-teller', an itinerant storyteller wandering the locality who, as folklorist Ronald M. James put it, 'skilfully animated narratives to brighten the world, performing at the hearth, at a fair, or wherever the drudgery of life needed to be eased'. Such droll-tellers, according to James, were 'heroic artists who preserved traditions from one generation to the next'. Henry Quick himself became a familiar figure in his native Zennor and neighbouring parishes, as well as in Penzance and St Ives, selling broadsheets of his verse and telling stories. But in perpetuating tradition, as James also notes, Cornish droll-tellers were prepared to innovate, addressing contemporary events and including well-known local personalities in their stories. Quick's verses amply illustrate these tendencies, with subject matter such as 'John Uren of Bescrowan, 1847', 'The Death of John Martyns, 1836' and 'The Death of Pascoe Semmens, 1826', each describing the fate of local characters but also reinforcing traditional morality:

> O sinner should the Lord in vengeance frown,
> Where wilt thou run if justice cuts thee down?
> Thy soul will drop into a burning hell,
> Where none but damned souls and devils dwell.[2]

Henry Quick recognized that he lived on the cusp of modernity, reinforcing his desire to innovate and to describe contemporary happenings. As he acknowledged, despite the aura of 'timelessness' in Zennor and its environs, there had been significant changes in the parish during his lifetime. The application of steam power to deep mining, the triumph of Methodism and the emergence of overseas mass emigration deeply affected Zennor, as they did other parts of Cornwall. Remoteness was now tempered by technological advance and by a sense of the global where Zennor folk found themselves in destinations as far-flung as the goldfields of Australia, sometimes to return home, sometimes not. Quick understood the profound implications of these changes, not least for himself:

> Our Cornish drolls are dead, each one;
> The fairies from their haunts have gone;

Prologue

> There's scarce a witch in all the land,
> The world has grown so learn'd and grand.[3]

P.A.S. Pool applauded Henry Quick's insights and his status as one of the last of Cornwall's droll-tellers. Ronald M. James has offered a more nuanced appreciation. 'If Quick was indeed part of the final episode of the droll tellers', James writes, 'his example shows how much the profession had been transformed. Quick made a meagre living selling broadsheets of his poems … [he] earned his way with the turn of phrase and like many professional storytellers, he conveyed the news of the day'.[4] Indeed, James points out, while previous generations of storytellers had earned their livelihoods 'telling tales, reciting poems, singing songs and bringing news from distant lands', Quick 'sold his printed wares to an increasingly literate population', underscoring the 'nature of the new world in which he lived'. As James concludes, the 'loss of the old droll tellers … was a major blow to the survival of traditions in the face of modernization'.[5]

The paradox of tradition versus modernity is at the heart of Cornish identity, as much today as it was then, and it was perhaps no coincidence that Henry Quick's experience was mirrored in uncanny ways by that of D.H. Lawrence half a century and more later, when Lawrence lived briefly at Porthcothan in North Cornwall and then at Zennor itself during the Great War. Lawrence had recognized the inexorable creep of modernity, exemplified in the mechanized industrial warfare that erupted in Europe in August 1914, and longed for an escape, for an opportunity to create his own utopian community, his 'Rananim'. His journey took him to Cornwall, and at Zennor he thought himself beyond England's reach, beyond the demands of war and its destructive power, and able to participate in the simple lives of local families, most of whom were immune to the war-fever apparent elsewhere. But, as in Henry Quick's time, the remote 'timelessness' of Cornwall proved a chimera. Not only was the reach of England's relentless war machine felt increasingly west of the Tamar but Cornwall itself, especially West Cornwall, became a vicious maritime battleground, one that Lawrence was able to see and hear from his temporary refuge at Zennor. Modernity had intruded with a vengeance on his Rananim and Lawrence's own idealized vision of traditional Celtic Cornwall. The consequences for D.H. Lawrence would be catastrophic, and far-reaching.

Despite these intriguing possibilities for comparison between the two writers, Henry Quick and D.H. Lawrence, the local droll-teller and the international novelist, P.A.S. Pool was indignantly insistent that Quick's 'parish has more reason to be proud of him than of its fleeting and unhappy association with D.H. Lawrence'.[6] Really?

'Cult of the Celt'

At this distance, Pool's assessment seems surprisingly ill-considered. But if his dismissive attitude was the general opinion in Cornwall in the 1980s, when he published his booklet, then it reflected a much wider discomfort apparent elsewhere in the literary and cultural world and among the general reading public in Britain and abroad. Almost universally reviled, D.H. Lawrence was then at the nadir of his reputation.

Earlier, in the heady 1960s, according to the journalist Mia Levitin, writing in the *Irish Times* in June 2021, Lawrence had been 'hailed as a mascot of the sexual revolution'.[7] Sylvia Plath, for example, had confessed that Lawrence was among her greatest literary influences, especially the inspirational character of Lady Chatterley who 'identifies herself with life. She chooses the spontaneous, intuitive expression of her own woman's nature'.[8] John Bayley, the literary critic, thought that 'D.H. Lawrence worship was getting into its stride in the mid-fifties, reaching a sort of climax in 1963', some three years after the Lady Chatterley trial, and 'to the post-war generation Lawrence appealed less as a writer than as a cult figure, like the newly famous Beatles, a symbol of enlightenment and modernity'.[9]

Yet only a decade later, Levitin explained, Lawrence was repudiated comprehensively for his perceived misogyny and reactionary phallocentrism. Feminist critiques of Lawrence and his work had been spearheaded by Kate Millett in her book *Sexual Politics*, published in 1970, and by 1978 Anne Smith could observe wryly that: 'It is not so long ago that hidebound old ladies were carrying copies of *Lady Chatterley's Lover* out of bookshops with tongs, to burn it on the pavement, and now liberated young women are all but doing the same'.[10] In her own edited collection, *Lawrence and Women*, Anne Smith gave free rein to her contributors' critiques. Faith Pullin, for example, argued that Lawrence was 'a ruthless user of women' and that his 'main object was always to examine the male psyche and to use his women characters to that end'.[11] Indeed, Pullin continued, 'Lawrence isn't concerned with women as themselves … he has a marked tendency to undervalue individuality in women (clever women he distrusted and hated)'.[12] There was, Mark Spilka alleged in the same collection, a deep-seated Laurentian 'hostility to wilful women'.[13]

However, even in Smith's collection, there were signs of ambiguity and hesitation, a sense that it was not possible to categorize Lawrence with certainty, that outright condemnation was dangerously simplistic. Lydia Blanchard, for example, examined Lawrence's fictional treatment of the relationships between mothers and daughters, concluding that Lawrence was capable 'of responding sensitively to the problems that women face together'.[14] Smith herself warned that 'the last thing we should expect to emerge from an overall view of Lawrence's attitude to women is consistency, or even a steady, forward development'. Such an expectation would be 'something of an insult to women', she added, 'for it would imply that they do not change, that all the years of Lawrence's life the women he knew stood still'. Likewise, it 'would be an insult to Lawrence, who believed so utterly in spontaneity'.[15]

Of all the contributions to Smith's collection, the ambiguity of Lawrence's complex approach to women (and much else) was perhaps best exemplified in Julian Moynahan's seminal essay 'Lawrence, Woman, and the Celtic Fringe'.[16] Moynahan observed that it 'is a truism of Lawrence studies that the novelist, in his continuing quarrel with urban-industrial civilization, especially English civilization, tends to exalt those groups—the Amerindian, the southern European peasant, Gypsies come immediately to mind—whose life is disadvantaged and marginal to that civilization'.[17] As 'outsiders', these groups, though materially deprived and frequently oppressed, retained a purer, 'less ravaged heritage' of 'instinctive virtue' that prevented them from suffering the 'corruption, moral, spiritual and psychological' that characterized modern urban-industrial society. As Moynahan added, such exaltation explained Lawrence's 'cult of the Celt' and the 'continuing attraction he shows in his artistic productions and in life to characters, themes and scenes drawn from the "Celtic fringe" of Scotland, Wales, Cornwall and Ireland'.[18]

Moynahan pointed out that in the nineteenth century there were two (largely English) constructions of 'the Celt', one of which saw the Celtic peoples as feckless, hysterical, unruly, untrustworthy, ethnically inferior. The other offered a more subtle appreciation, again based on prejudiced assumptions, but now admitting positive characteristics that might recommend the Celts to their English neighbours. This was the project of the Celtic Literary Revival, exemplified in Matthew Arnold's long essay 'On the Study of Celtic Literature', published in 1867. Arnold (Cornish on his mother's side; she a Penrose from Constantine) stressed what he saw as the sensitivity, emotionalism and vivid imagination of the Celtic peoples, which, he agreed, verged sometimes on the irrational. However, he viewed these attributes as complementary to the dull pedestrian stolidness of the English, with Celtic genius contributing much to the vigour and vitality of English literature and of England itself. Significantly, Arnold recognized a supposed feminine dimension in the Celtic temperament, arguing that 'no doubt the sensibility of the Celtic nature, its nervous exaltation, have something feminine in them, and the Celt is thus peculiarly disposed to feel the spell of the feminine idiosyncrasy; he has an affinity to it; he is not far from its secret'.[19]

During his time in Cornwall, D.H. Lawrence's view of the Cornish vacillated considerably, ranging from one extreme to the other, from fulsome admiration to outright disgust, and back again. He had arrived with the usual array of English colonialist assumptions about 'the Celts', some favourable, some not. As we shall see, when Cornwall proved to be less immune to England's influence than he had hoped, with the Cornish seemingly passive in the face of coercion, he was angry as well as disappointed. But at length, he empathized with the Cornish in their predicament, joining their community and beginning to see the Celtic peoples as his natural allies, quietly subversive and duplicitous in their subtle attempts to undermine England's hegemony.

The Celt-woman nexus, with its own subversion and duplicity, was similarly apparent in Lawrence's writing. Indeed, for Lawrence the Cornish, men as well as women, 'are most unwarlike, soft, peaceable, ancient'.[20] In *The Fox*, one of Lawrence's several short novels, March, the heroine, marries a Cornishman, Henry Grenfel, and together they go to live in the far west of Cornwall, 'to his own village, on the sea'. There March experiences a strange self-emptying liberation, becoming 'de-anglicized', a Celt-woman looking, like the Cornish themselves (shades of global emigration), ever westwards: 'sitting in a niche of the high wild cliffs of West Cornwall, looking over the westward sea, she stretched her eyes wider and wider. Away to the West, Canada, America'.[21] Even more 'deeply implicated with Lawrence's theme of woman and the Celt',[22] as Moynahan put it, is *St Mawr*, a novella set in the Welsh border country of Shropshire, where, according to Lawrence, 'the spirit of aboriginal England still lingers, the old savage England, whose last blood flows still in a few Englishmen, Welshmen, Cornishmen'.[23]

St Mawr is at one level a metaphor for the ancient struggle between Celt and Saxon, the story of a strong-willed and wayward stallion. According to Moynahan 'St Mawr is probably the stoutest blow Lawrence ever struck for women's liberation', and the women in the story—Mrs Witt and her daughter Lou—are guided in their liberation by the behaviour of the horse. St Mawr, the horse in question, refuses to perform the roles expected of him. He refuses to be a safe, reliable riding horse; he will not service mares; he will not pass a viper when one appears in his path. Alongside the evidence of his name and the geographical location of the novella, the horse exhibits typical 'Celtic traits', being anarchic and undisciplined, and Mrs Witt and her daughter 'feel a deep complicity with St Mawr's nature and behaviour', likewise adopting a refusal to conform to society's expectations. As Moynahan concluded, 'it does not seem paradoxical to claim that Lawrence, in perceiving and working with the Celt-woman link, was working for women's liberation and [thus] the liberation of all from the fettered past'.[24] Among those whom he sought to free from their 'fettered past', of course, were the Cornish.

This growing recognition of Lawrence's inherent ambiguity, exemplified in Anne Smith's collection and amplified in Carol Siegel's later work *Lawrence Among the Women: Wavering Boundaries in Women's Literary Traditions* (1991), which details Lawrence's struggle to speak for women, appears to have underpinned the gradual rehabilitation of D.H. Lawrence that by the early twenty-first century had become so clearly apparent.[25] Indeed, as Jonathan Long has observed, in 'the twenty-first century, Lawrence Studies has moved beyond defensiveness against allegations by ... Kate Millett, and others, and instead is beginning to come to terms with "inconvenient" aspects of Lawrence's life and work'.[26] A major international conference in (fittingly) St Ives, Cornwall, in 2016 attracted attendees and contributions from Lawrence scholars across the globe, evidence of rekindled enthusiasm for the writer and his achievements. In the same year, Andrew Harrison's *The Life of D.H. Lawrence: A Critical Biography* appeared, a masterly reassessment, replete with new insights and fresh perspectives, further proof of Lawrence's return to the academic mainstream.[27]

Then, in 2021, Frances Wilson's *Burning Man: The Ascent of D.H. Lawrence* went further in its attempts to rescue Lawrence from what Levitin called 'his post-feminist infamy'.[28] Wilson herself cautioned that 'Lawrence is still on trial', recalling that when she was growing up in the 1980s her 'mother wouldn't have his novels in the house', while 'my (female) tutor at university refused to teach him'.[29] But she found much to admire in Lawrence, in all his paradoxes and ambiguities, from 'his rants' and 'the heat of his sentences' to 'his identification with animals and birds' and 'his enjoyment of brightly coloured stockings'.[30] Although Wilson's book was not without its critics (including a hostile review by Jonathan Long in the *Journal of D.H. Lawrence Studies*), the volume's role in placing Lawrence centre-stage once more, and in presenting him as a legitimate and safe subject for contemporary scholarly enquiry, opened up new possibilities for research and debate.[31]

'Persistence of difference'

And if D.H. Lawrence was now ripe for further study, then so too was Cornwall. At much the same time that Lawrence was being rehabilitated as a writer fit for serious study, so new perspectives were forming on the history and identity of Cornwall, including its complex ethnic and cultural dimensions. By the 1990s a 'new Cornish historiography' had emerged, one which attempted to locate Cornwall within the wider discussion of the recently established 'new British history', where the interrelated but separate experiences of the component territories of the British and Irish Isles—the 'Atlantic archipelago'—were considered individually in context. Here Cornwall found a hard-won place alongside England, Ireland, Scotland and Wales, not least in discussion of the early modern period where Mark Stoyle's *West Britons: Cornish Identities and the Early Modern British State* in 2002 initiated an extended reassessment of the role of Cornwall in state formation in these islands, culminating in *Cornwall in the Age of Rebellion, 1490–1690* in 2021.[32]

Similarly, there were determined attempts to explain the distinctive history of late modern and contemporary Cornwall—especially the experiences of industrialization and deindustrialization—including the 'persistence of difference' so evident in the twentieth and twenty-first centuries. This endeavour produced several new full-blown histories of Cornwall, each written from an uncompromisingly Cornish perspective, together with a number of allied subject-specific studies, notably Ella Westland's edited volume *Cornwall: The Cultural Construction of Place* (1997) and Alan M. Kent's *The Literature of Cornwall: Continuity, Identity, Difference 1000–2000* (2000).[33] More recent interdisciplinary volumes in this genre have included Rachel Moseley's *Picturing Cornwall: Landscape, Region and the Moving Image* (2018) and Gemma Goodman's *Alternative Cornwalls: Literature and the Invention of Place* (2024).[34] Added to this wealth of activity has been a redoubled interest in Cornwall's nineteenth-century 'great emigration' and the creation of a transnational Cornish identity, including elucidation of 'the myth of Cousin Jack', where the Cornish routinely asserted their supposedly innate superiority as hard-rock miners on the international mining frontier.[35]

Biography has formed an integral part of these new directions in Cornish studies. Here the focus has been on the relationship between person and place, especially the impact of Cornish identity on an individual's life and work. *A.L. Rowse and Cornwall: A Paradoxical Patriot* (2005) and *John Betjeman and Cornwall: 'The Celebrated Cornish Nationalist'* (2010) were both conceived and written in this vein, producing two comparable but contrasting biographical studies (demonstrating, among things, the blurring of 'insider' and 'outsider' categories) and establishing an approach that might usefully be applied to other writers on Cornwall.[36] Luke Thompson's *Clay Phoenix: A Biography of Jack Clemo* (2016), indeed, is an exhaustive examination of the poet Jack Clemo's intimate connection with his native mid-Cornwall clay-country.

It is surprising, perhaps, that D.H. Lawrence has not yet received such treatment. Although Lawrence's sojourn in Cornwall has as a matter of course attracted the attention of his various biographers, none, as Jane Costin has argued, has appreciated the enduring impact on Lawrence's life and work of his summary expulsion in October 1917.[37] Put another way, Lawrence's time in Cornwall has yet to receive the full explanatory attention that it so patently deserves. Indeed, interpretations from a specifically Cornish perspective have been negligible, restricted to Jane Costin's own work, and to Ella Westland's path-finding article 'D.H. Lawrence's Cornwall: Dwelling in a Precarious Age' (2002), together with the surprisingly little-regarded but important twin volumes *Lawrence at Tregerthen* (1988) and *The Cornish Nightmare* (1996), both by C.J. Stevens.[38] There is also my booklet *D.H. Lawrence and Cornwall*, published in 2009 by Truran Books as part of their 'Cornish Lives' series, elements of which inform this present study.[39]

It is in the spirit, then, of both the recent new directions in Cornish studies and the rehabilitation of D.H. Lawrence, that this book looks with fresh eyes at Lawrence's all-important Cornish episode during the Great War. In doing so, it offers a discussion and conclusion that contrasts radically with P.A.S. Pool's curt dismissal and his unfavourable comparison of Lawrence with Henry Quick, the droll-teller. It tells a different story altogether.

Chapter 1

Dreaming of Rananim

'We go to Cornwall, on Thursday. There is the beginning.'[1]

So wrote D.H. Lawrence on Monday 27 December 1915, in a letter to his friend Lady Ottoline Morrell, the celebrated aristocratic hostess of Garsington Manor in Oxfordshire. It was wartime, and although there would be yet worse to come—the Somme, Passchendaele and other cataclysmic struggles all lay ahead—it was apparent already that the Great War was not going well for Britain and that, even if it could be won, the cost in lives and human misery would be huge. The world would be changed for ever; no doubt for the worse, Lawrence was convinced. Now was the time to reach out for something new, he believed, something bold, something that would offer a real alternative to urban-industrialized England, where like-minded and equally committed people of good will could work together to create a living utopia. This would be the new beginning. Cornwall, it turned out, would be the place where Lawrence would try to make this happen.

Lawrence had already made a name for himself in the literary world, and moved in influential circles, his friends and correspondents including society figures such as Ottoline Morrell and Lady Cynthia Asquith. Several of his poems had appeared in the prestigious *English Review* in 1909, and his first novels *The White Peacock* (1911), *The Trespasser* (1911) and *Sons and Lovers* (1913) had all been well received, even if they were not yet making him much money. Yet behind this veneer of success and a fast-growing reputation, Lawrence was not a happy man.

'This industrial-mechanical-wage idea'

For Lawrence, the Great War was a tragedy beyond measure, and it was this that drove him to Cornwall—and 'out of England'. There was also the complication of his recently acquired German wife, Frieda, cousin of Baron Manfred von Richthofen, the 'Red Baron' ace shortly to acquire a fearsome reputation for the shooting down of Allied airmen. Ottoline Morrell thought Frieda 'aggressively German', as she noted in her journal in June 1915, with Lawrence 'crushed and unhappy' as a result of her rages and outbursts. 'Poor Lawrence', Ottoline wrote, 'what a distraught creature he is underneath'.[2]

But Lawrence's anguish ran deeper than his sometimes tempestuous relationship with his wife. The war was the culmination of his disappointment with England. Born into a working-class family in the coal-mining town of Eastwood, Nottinghamshire, in 1885, Lawrence wrote at length in his short stories and novels about the lives of ordinary people, professing not only to understand them but to love them too. Yet he also thought working-class life 'dark and violent', as he told Ottoline Morrell in his letter of 27 December. The working classes were 'passionate enough', he said, 'sensuous, dark— God, how all my boyhood comes back—so violent, so dark, the mind always dark and without understanding. It makes me sad beyond words. These men, whom I love so much.' Pausing for a moment, he added: 'I love them like brothers but, my God, I hate them too'.[3]

The only thing the working people understood now, he complained to Ottoline in his letter, was 'industrialism, only wages and money and machinery. They can't *think* anything else … They are utterly unable to appreciate any pure, ulterior truth: only this industrial—mechanical—wage idea'.[4] Lawrence was not alone in his disillusion with the modern industrialized, urban world. In many ways, for example, as Richard Aldington noted, Lawrence resembled John Ruskin.[5] Ruskin, the great polymath of the Victorian era, was anti-industrial as well as anti-capitalist, a conservationist before his time (he foresaw the 'green-house effect'), and a lover of the countryside and traditional craftsmanship. He loathed materialism, and despised 'the barbarians who know the price of everything and the value of nothing'.[6]

Likewise, William Morris, architect of the Arts and Crafts movement, had emerged by the mid-Victorian period as an arch critic of industrial society, devoting himself to craftsmanship and design, and postulating an ideal, utopian world in which 'people lived in little communities … and had few wants, almost no furniture for instance, and no servants, and studied … what they really wanted'.[7] William Morris encouraged the establishment of Arts and Crafts 'colonies', such as those that sprang up in Sussex, with communities at Amberley, South Harting, Storrington and, most famously, at Ditchling, the latter founded by the sculptor Eric Gill.[8] Gill argued that industrial society had corrupted working people. The system made 'good mechanics, good machine-minders', he acknowledged. But it also moulded 'men and women who in every other respect are morons, cretins, for whom crossword puzzles, football games, watered beer, sham half-timbered bungalows and shimmering film stars are the highest form of amusement'.[9]

Gill's concerns were shared by Father Vincent McNabb, a Dominican friar, who had first encouraged Gill to set up his community at Ditchling and was an advocate of the 'back to the land' movement. McNabb was also close to Hilaire Belloc, who lived in Sussex, not far from Gill, and wrote extensively about his adopted county. Belloc was similarly anti-industrial—as well as anti-capitalist and anti-socialist—in 1912 publishing his *The Servile State*, which set out his critique of current society and offered ideas for a better future.[10] Like McNabb, he looked to the land itself for redemption, with his dream of 'three acres and a cow' for 'Everyman', and hoped that in the Sussex countryside it might be possible to achieve his utopian aspirations. 'Utopia', it seemed, was high on the agenda of English intellectuals.

By the Edwardian era, England had already absorbed much of this anti-industrialism, and there was everywhere a demand for progressive change—votes for women, Home Rule for Ireland, the growth of the Labour Party. Yet the spirit of industrialism was by no means dead, and there were significant material and technological developments which matched this progressive Edwardian mood, not least the growing sophistication of the motor-car and the invention of the aeroplane. Such innovations, paradoxically, helped make possible the greatest industrial nightmare of all—the Great War of 1914–18.

The slaughter and destruction of the Great War redoubled the efforts of pre-war critics and utopians, drawing into their ranks new writers such as J.B. Priestley and H.V. Morton who in the post-war period popularized an alternative vision of England. As his biographer, John Baxendale, has noted, 'Priestley loved the English countryside … [and] deplored the effects on it of nineteenth-century industrialism and twentieth-century suburbanisation'.[11] Like William Morris, Priestley was a radical, and he too admired the skills and creativity of craftsmen such as the Cotswold stonemasons whose buildings radiated warmth and seemed to grow organically from the landscape. Writing in 1926, Priestley recognized that many now were 'in revolt against the ugly mechanical things of today', acknowledging as a simple truth the healing power of country life, a realization 'from which there is no escape except into brutishness'.[12]

H.V. Morton's *In Search of England* appeared in 1927. He admitted that the book was 'pitched in a much lighter key' than most other critiques of industrialism, but his intent was serious.[13] As Simon Jenkins has explained, Morton regretted 'the loss of country innocence, the decay of country values and the final triumph of the urban cosmos over what is most true to the national character'.[14] Morton was no political radical but it was significant that, in his journey to discover an older and more authentic England, his first encounter was with a bowl-turner, 'a craftsman, the lover of his job, the proud creator of beautiful, common things; a voice that is now smothered by the scream of machines'.[15] Here was more than an echo of William Morris and the Arts and Crafts movement, as there was in what Morton termed the increasingly popular 'Back to the Land' cry.[16]

John Betjeman (a founder member of the William Morris Society) was in some sense a successor to Morton, Betjeman's cosy 'teddy bear to the nation' persona disguising a subversive streak that could take on the Establishment and win in matters of planning and conservation, including his later support for the anti-nuclear movement. For Betjeman, 'England stands for the Church of England, eccentric incumbents, oil-lit churches, Women's Institutes, modest village inns ... branch-line trains, light railways, leaning on gates and looking across fields'.[17] A.L. Rowse warned against misreading Betjeman: there was 'much ambivalence about him, much that was paradoxical, ironic, not easily penetrable ... idiosyncratic—all was not as meets the eye'.[18] Behind the apparent light-hearted nostalgia, Betjeman too had been seared by the events of the Great War, as a schoolboy suffering taunts as a result of his German surname (then spelt Betjemann) and, doubtful of his own 'Englishness', seeking instead an alternative Celticity which took him inexorably to Cornwall.[19]

Significantly, for both Morton and Betjeman, their search for an 'authentic' England led to an embrace of Cornwall as 'other', its allure being the fact that it was decidedly un-English in culture and ambience. 'There is a strangeness about Cornwall', Morton wrote: 'You feel it as soon as you cross Tor[point] ferry'.[20] When, finally, he said a farewell to Cornwall, crossing into Devon, his tour complete, Morton thought himself 'In England once again' and reflected again that Cornwall was a 'different country'.[21] Musing on his recent experiences, Morton recalled speaking to an old man he had met in Tregony who, anticipating an imminent journey to neighbouring Plymouth, had 'told me that he was "going up to England next week"'.[22] Likewise, insisted John Betjeman, 'Cornwall is a Duchy … it is separated from England by the picturesque Tamar Valley, and has more sea coast than anywhere else in Britain'.[23] One 'realises', he said, 'that Cornwall is still a foreign country as remote from England as Ireland'.[24] There was a romantic yearning inherent in both Morton's and Betjeman's imaginings of Cornwall, perhaps a recognition that, in its distinction from England, Cornwall offered the possibilities of utopia—or at least escape and retreat, a kind of cultural asylum.

'A war of machines'

For Lawrence, the debasement of humanity by the forces of industrialization had reached its climax in the Great War. He had witnessed the formidable German Army exercising in Bavaria before the outbreak of hostilities, and knew at once that any future conflict would be murderous and destructive on a grand scale. As he observed in the *Manchester Guardian*, this would be industrial warfare: 'a war of machines, and men no more than the subjective material of the machine'.[25] He went on to explain:

> I remember standing on a little hill one August [1913] afternoon. There was a beautiful blue sky, and white clouds from the mountains. Away on the right, amid woods and corn-clad hills, lay the big Starnberg lake. This is just a year ago, but it seems to belong to some period outside of time.
> On the crown of the hill were three quick-firing guns, with the gunners behind … and then the sharp cry 'Fire!'. There was a burst, something in the guns started back, the faintest breath of vapour disappeared.
> What work was there to do?—only the unnatural suspense and suppression of serving a machine which, for ought we knew, was killing our fellow-men, whilst we stood there, blind, without knowledge or participation, subordinate to the cold machine. This was the glamour and glory of war: blue sky overhead, and living green country all around, but we, amid it all, a part in some iron insensate will, our flesh and blood, our soul and intelligence shed away, and all that remained of us a cold, metallic adherence to an iron machine. There was neither ferocity nor exaltation nor even quick fear: only a mechanical, expressionless movement.[26]

A year later, and war did break out. Lawrence saw Reservists at the local station, 'leaving for London by the nine o'clock train'. They were all young men, some of them drunk and rowdy, and there were a few women, 'seeing off sweet-hearts and brothers'. As the train moved away, one of the women shouted to her boyfriend: 'When you see 'em let 'em have it'. 'Ay, no fear', replied the young man. Grimly, Lawrence 'thought what it would really be like, "when he saw 'em"'.[27] They would find out soon enough, he knew, as they did at Mons, the Marne, Loos and Gallipoli, and any illusion that it would be a short or easy war was soon shattered. And so, as Lawrence was to write later in his novel *Kangaroo*: 'It was in 1915 the old world ended. In the winter of 1915–16 the spirit of the old London collapsed ... and became a vortex of broken passions, lusts, hopes, fears, and horrors.'[28]

Lawrence's disillusion with England was made all the more complete in 1915 by the banning of his latest novel *The Rainbow* on the grounds of obscenity, leaving Lawrence low in spirits and short of cash. Philip Morrell, Ottoline's husband and a Liberal MP, spoke in the House of Commons in support of the book's publication, to no avail. By now, Lawrence had already begun to think of abandoning England—at least metaphorically, and if possible physically too—by creating somewhere an alternative utopian society of like-minded spirits, an experiment in communal living divorced from the norms of what passed as everyday life. Here people would live in a co-operative manner of intimate friendship and harmony—mutually supportive, tolerant, creative.

This would be Lawrence's Rananim—a whimsical, romantic name, apparently of Hebrew origin, that he had borrowed from one of the lyrical 'Russian' songs on the lips of his friend Samuel 'Kot' Koteliansky, a Jewish-Ukrainian émigré whom Lawrence had met just before the outbreak of war in 1914. Lawrence had first heard this captivating song on a walking tour with Koteliansky and friends in the Lake District in late July and early August 1914, on the very eve of war. As Lawrence explained it:

> The war finished me. It was the spear through the side of all sorrows and hopes. I had been walking in Westmoreland, rather happy, with water-lilies twisted around my hat—big, heavy, white and gold water-lilies that we found on a pool high up—and girls who had come on a spree and who were having tea in the upper room of an inn, shrieked with laughter. And I remember also we crouched under the loose wall on the moors and the rain flew by in streams, and the wind came

rushing through the chinks in the wall behind one's head, and we shouted songs and I imitated music-hall turns, whilst the other men crouched under the wall and I pranked in the rain on the turf in the gorse, and Koteliansky groaned Hebrew music—Ranani Sadekim Badanoi.[29]

This, it turns out, was a rendering of the first line of Psalm 33—in English, 'Rejoice o just / righteous ones in God'.[30] Although Lawrence and Kot had been unaware that war had actually been declared on that very day, Kot's choice of Psalm 33 was uncannily appropriate, even prophetic: 'it teaches that no king can be saved by his great army, and no warrior can be delivered by his great strength or be victorious through the might of his horse'.[31]

'Ranani', suitably recast by Lawrence, became his cherished Rananim, a sometimes nebulous notion that, in the years ahead, sat alongside his other varying conceptions of what a utopian community might be like and where it could be located. John Turner and John Worthen have mused on Lawrence's fluctuating plans for such a community. The term Rananim, they explain, has been used by Lawrence's biographers as a convenient byword or catch-all for each one of Lawrence's schemes, which has had the unfortunate effect of obscuring differences between them. From this more nuanced perspective, Rananim as initially conceived was already in doubt by February 1915, when Lawrence introduced his new 'Island' variant, with its widening repertoire of who might be invited to join. This, in turn, became his short-lived Florida project, so rudely interrupted by the war. Later, Lawrence had thoughts of creating a community in the Andes, and after the Great War set off for Ceylon, Australia and the Americas. In 1923 he sought companions to join him in New Mexico. But now he simply needed supportive friends, argue Turner and Worthen, and had long since abandoned any thoughts of an idealized utopian society. From this perspective, they conclude, Rananim was effectively dead by the end of 1918.[32]

Adding further to this debate, we should observe that, if there was any practical prospect of Rananim ever being achieved, then it was surely in Cornwall during the Great War. Lawrence certainly thought so. For example, he wrote to Jack Middleton Murry and Katherine Mansfield from the far west of Cornwall in March 1916, telling these two prime candidates for his utopian community that Zennor was 'such a lovely place: our Rananim'.[33] Later, Frieda recalled the intense discussions at Zennor with 'the Murrys' (as Lawrence dubbed them). 'By the hour', she wrote, 'we could talk Rananim'.[34]

Dreaming of Rananim

Stanley Hocking, one of the Cornish farmers befriended by Lawrence, was also subjected to such lectures: 'Lawrence had an imaginary place which he was calling Rananim ... Lawrence talked a lot about this'.[35] It is possible, as David Game has suggested (see p. 136), that in 1916 Lawrence had also briefly considered Australia as a candidate for Rananim, although this possibility appears to have faded by the time he actually arrived in that country in 1922. It was in Cornwall, then, that Lawrence had tried to make Rananim a reality, the prospect finally extinguished by his sudden expulsion in October 1917. In this way, Cornwall occupies a distinctive place in any consideration of Lawrence's utopian schemes, the one locale where Rananim was almost within his grasp.

Koteliansky—or 'Kot' as he was known to Lawrence and other close friends—was extremely supportive of Lawrence during those difficult Great War years. It was a constancy that Lawrence thought to be bravely emblematic of the Rananim ethos, and he and Kot kept up an intimate correspondence that lasted until just weeks before Lawrence's death in March 1930. As Galya Diment has observed in her biography of Samuel Koteliansky, 'Lawrence's "little colony" [Rananim] was his own idea but it owed its name to Kot', something that Lawrence never forgot.[36] The exciting prospect of a utopian future, suggested unwittingly by Kot in his 'Hebrew' song at the outbreak of war, was firmed up by Lawrence and close friends over Christmas 1914. Yet by early 1915, Lawrence's 'Island' variant had already emerged, and it was this model that would engage his thoughts for much of the ensuing year, until the enticing possibility of a move to Cornwall suddenly appeared.

After five months of living in a cottage near Chesham, in Buckinghamshire, at the end of January 1915 Lawrence and Frieda had moved to Greatham, near Amberley, in Sussex. Here they had been given the use of a cottage by the novelist and poet Viola Meynell within the Meynell 'family settlement' (as Paul Delany has described it).[37] The cottage was well appointed—it even had hot water—with a timbered ceiling and oak furniture, somewhere where Lawrence could feel secure and entertain friends. This was the beginning of what Delany has called Lawrence's 'Messianic phase', when he thought he could save England and 'build a new Jerusalem on the ruins of the old', a period when Lawrence was close to both Ottoline Morrell and Bertrand Russell, who were themselves conducting an intricate amorous affair.[38] But the messianic phase lasted only nine months, from arrival at Greatham until October 1915, and Lawrence's relationships with both Ottoline and Russell would prove increasingly bumpy and strained.

Russell and Ottoline visited Greatham together in early February 1915, and Lawrence spelt out for them his ideas for his new 'Island' project. However, as Lawrence was to explain to Kot, his distinguished visitors, having listened patiently to what he had to say, were able to persuade him that his imaginary 'Island' should involve the rebuilding of England, not an escape from it. Thus, as Lawrence put it, 'they say the island shall be England, that we shall start our new community in the midst of the old one'.[39] It was this decree that prompted Lawrence to develop his messianic voice, although by March he was already suffering from ill health and feeling depressed. He complained now that the Greatham cottage was damp and the 'colony' plagued by too many casual visitors.[40] By mid-April, Lawrence was planning to move to Ottoline's Garsington estate, where Philip Morrell had offered to undertake the renovation of a building—a three-bedroomed gardener's cottage—for the Lawrences' use. Lawrence offered to pay six per cent of the costs of renovation, which would include installation of a bathroom, heating, a large workroom and furnishings. Thus equipped, Garsington would become the centre of the 'Island' project. However, Ottoline baulked at the cost, and offered instead a habitable monastic building adjoining the main house. Now it was Frieda's turn to require alterations and new fittings, and an exasperated Philip Morrell told Lawrence that the bill would be so vast that he, Lawrence, would have to meet the expense himself. The 'Island' variant of the Rananim project had already faltered beyond retrieval. As Miranda Seymour has observed, at that point 'the dream of Rananim at Garsington fizzled out'.[41]

In May 1915, to add to his woes, Lawrence was made bankrupt. He was unable, he said, to afford the costs of Frieda's divorce from her first husband, and was angry and distraught when he received his summons. As he wrote to Bertrand Russell:

> I cannot tell you how this reinforces my utter hatred of the whole establishment—the whole constitution of England. I wish I were a criminal instead of a bankrupt. But softly—softly. I will do my best to lay a mine under their foundations. I am hostile, hostile, hostile to all that is, in our public and national life. I want to destroy it.[42]

War news continued to be deeply depressing, and on 19 October 1915 Lady Cynthia Asquith was told that her younger brother, Yvo Charteris, had been killed. Aged nineteen, he had gone straight from Eton into the Army.

He was dead within three weeks of reaching the front. Although Lawrence had never met Yvo, the shock of a young life cut short so precipitously was enough to tip him over. There was to be no messianic desire to reform England from within. He wrote in anguish to Lady Cynthia:

> I am sick in my soul, sick to death. But not angry any more, only unfathomably miserable about it all. I think I shall go away to America if they will let me ... Perhaps you will say it is cowardice: but how shall one submit to such ultimate wrong as this which we commit now, England and the other nations? If thine eye offend thee, pluck it out. And I am English, and my Englishness is my very vision. But now I must go away, if my soul is sightless for ever. Let it then be blind, rather than commit the vast wickedness of acquiescence.[43]

'A monotonous wilderness of phallicism'

Thereafter, with this ever-increasing desire to turn his back on England, Lawrence did indeed look further afield, becoming ever more expansive in his ambitions. As Ottoline noted in her journal, he 'said he must leave England, and go to a country that has a future before it, a country that is in the spring of its life. Here in England the autumn has set in, life is dead, the land dead, the people are dead sapless sticks'. And so, she wrote: 'He is determined to go off to America and write for Americans'. She could hardly agree with his pessimistic assessment but concluded that 'it will be better for him to go to fresh fields than to stay here bemoaning and wailing the decay of England, especially as his health is very bad'.[44]

By now *The Rainbow* crisis was also coming to a head. The book had been published on 30 September, to be followed the next day by an equivocal review in the *Standard*. The newspaper thought the book good but wondered what lay in store for a work that seemed likely to excite consternation and offence.[45] The *Daily News* gave a taste of such a reception when it found *The Rainbow* 'nauseating' and opined that it represented 'a monotonous wilderness of phallicism. It is the sort of book which many an artistic schoolboy desires to write, but, on growing to maturity, he refrains.'[46] Similar reviews followed in other papers and magazines, with the suggestion that the book's supposedly degrading contents were somehow an affront to the high-minded sacrifices being made at that very moment on the battlefields of the Great War. Such arguments struck a chord, and on 3 November 1915 the police issued a warrant under the Obscene Prints Act 1857 requiring the publishers, Methuen & Co., to surrender all copies of the book. That Lawrence had made his anti-war views public, and that he had a German wife, may have influenced the decision, but it does seem that the book's contents—especially the references to lesbianism—were enough to precipitate the action. Subsequently, Methuen was summoned to appear at a magistrate's court. The company's representative duly turned up, only to be surprised that the matter was to be heard in open court (Methuen had been advised otherwise), with the press in attendance. Predictably, the magistrate ordered that all copies of *The Rainbow* be destroyed. Philip Morrell did what he could, asking questions in Parliament, but the Home Secretary was in no mood to intervene. The books were duly destroyed—the story went around that they had been burned by the public executioner.[47]

Among those outraged by this high-handed and summary action was Richard Aldington. As he wrote years later:

> But consider. The book was condemned without the author being told, let alone heard. No attempt at a proper investigation was made by the magistrate. Though in all other cases what the soldier said is not evidence, here what journalists said was so accepted. In this kind of case the hair-splitting law, so pedantic in its lucrative jesuitical distinctions, makes no attempt to distinguish between the crudely ithyphallic and vulgar productions of the clandestine press and a serious work which happens to enrage the Chadbands of Slobocracy.[48]

'Cornwall and Florida—the germ of a new idea'

Lawrence and Frieda by now had the offer of a cottage at Fort Myers in Florida, and were scraping together the funds to make the journey. Lawrence had also made friends with a young musician, Philip Heseltine, whom he hoped would join his planned utopian community, and Heseltine was at that very moment in correspondence with the composer Frederick Delius about the possibility of settling on his ramshackle estate, also in Florida.[49] The plans seemed to be coming to fruition. But then Lawrence made a mistake. To be given permission to go to America, he would need a medical certificate exempting him from military service on the grounds of ill health. Given his weak chest, this was surely a formality, and Lawrence attended a medical board in London in December 1915. He waited his turn for hours but, just as he was nearing the head of the queue, he panicked and fled. He felt that this was a moment of triumph, that he had defied the state and expressed some sort of solidarity with his fellow countrymen. Yet without his exemption, he could not cross to America, and so Florida was put on hold.

However, Lawrence wanted desperately to get out of London. His friend Dollie Radford had offered her cottage in Berkshire but more attractive was the offer (negotiated by Jack Middleton Murry) from a literary acquaintance, J.D. Beresford, that he and Frieda rent his cottage at Porthcothan on the wild Atlantic coast of North Cornwall, near Padstow. It was only available for two months, but Lawrence jumped at the chance. Jack Middleton Murry and Katherine Mansfield, close friends of the Lawrences, had stayed there on holiday in September 1914 and greatly enjoyed the experience. Besides, it was far removed from London and metropolitan England.[50]

Lawrence already considered Cornwall beyond England, a Celtic land of Arthurian associations that promised not only a sort of immunity from England's reach but also an environment in which it might be possible to plant the seed of a utopian future. Gratefully, Lawrence accepted Beresford's offer, and plans were made for the move to Porthcothan. He felt sure now that Cornwall would be the first real step on the road to Rananim, a prelude perhaps to a more permanent utopia in America one day in the future. As Lawrence wrote in his letter to Ottoline Morrell, announcing his imminent departure for Porthcothan: 'Cornwall and Florida; the germ of a new era'.[51]

Chapter 2

Dreaming of Cornwall

D.H. Lawrence was dreaming of Cornwall as early as 1910, half a decade before his dramatic move during the Great War to Porthcothan and later Zennor in search of his utopian Rananim. Cornwall had emerged already in Lawrence's mind as a potential refuge, an alternative to the industrial-urban England that he found increasingly corrosive, stifling and depressing.

In December 1910, Lawrence became engaged to Louie Burrows, just six days before his mother's death (the betrothal survived until November of the following year, when Lawrence broke it off). Lawrence explained to Louie that he wished to apply for a teaching post at a school in North Cornwall. She was not keen. Even Laurence's romantic image of them communing together 'by the brawling ocean in a land of Cornish foreigners blowing out our lonely candle as the clock quavers ten' did not persuade her. Nor did his more direct threat: 'If I should get the school to Cornwall you shall go, or to the Devil'.[1] Subsequent attempts at compromise came to nothing, and the idea was dropped. The application for the Cornish teaching job was never submitted. The engagement did not last.

'May Tintagel be our centre'

North Cornwall, as Lawrence knew, was especially redolent of the King Arthur legend, the imposing castle ruins on the clifftops at Tintagel said to have been Arthur's fortress, the hinterland roundabout full of Arthurian associations. Slaughter Bridge, on the river Camel, near Camelford (shades of Camelot!), was supposedly the site of Arthur's last great battle, while Bossiney Round, an earthwork near Tintagel, was reputed to conceal Arthur's Round Table. Another earthwork, in St Breward parish, was 'King Arthur's Hall'. As Ella Westland has observed, 'Lawrence was familiar with the literary creations of Arthur's legend which had inspired many Victorian visitors—certainly with the versions of Malory, Swinburne and Wagner'.[2]

Lawrence was also aware of Tennyson and his explicit linking of the Arthurian cycle with Cornwall. Although Tennyson liked to think of Loe Pool, near Helston, as the site of the Passing of Arthur and the Lady of the Lake, when, as Arthur lay mortally wounded, Bedivere was finally persuaded to throw the mighty sword into the lake, the tale was well suited to desolate Dozmary Pool in the heart of Bodmin Moor—not far from the river Camel and St Breward:

> So flash'd and fell the brand Excalibur:
> But ere he dipt the surface, rose an arm
> Clothed in white samite, mystic, wonderful,
> And caught him by the hilt, and brandish'd him
> Three times, and drew him under in the mere.[3]

Tennyson's Arthur was also bound up with the Isle of Avalon, Arthur's final resting place, and Lyonesse (sometimes Lyonnesse), a mythical land somewhere off the south-western tip of Cornwall, itself an echo of the lost land of Atlantis, drowned beneath the ocean. All this and more was common knowledge in Victorian and Edwardian literary households, part of the everyday canon of English literature. To this was added the poetic outpouring of the Revd Robert Stephen Hawker, vicar of Morwenstow in North Cornwall from 1835 to 1875. Hawker had honeymooned at Tintagel with his first wife, Charlotte, in 1835, and thereafter had been a constant devotee of the Arthurian legend. He met Tennyson during the latter's visit to Cornwall in 1848 when, Hawker later recalled, 'We talked about Cornwall and King Arthur'.[4]

Arthurian allusions peppered Hawker's own poetry, but it was not until after Charlotte's death in 1863 that in his grief he embarked upon his greatest work 'The Quest of the Sangraal', the legend of the Holy Grail and the quest of the knights of Arthur's Round Table. As Hawker explained it: 'Ho! For the Sangraal! Vanished Vase of God!'.[5] It was a powerful composition, and a humbled Tennyson admitted that 'Hawker has beaten me on my home ground',[6] an assessment echoed later by John Betjeman who argued that 'on this theme Hawker was the finer poet', his 'Quest for the Sangraal' outclassing Tennyson's 'Idylls of the King'.[7] Together, Tennyson and Hawker had reinforced popular enthusiasm for the Arthurian legend and rooted it even more firmly in the landscape of Tintagel and North Cornwall. Lawrence was among those suitably enthused.

As Betjeman would also observe, the 'first whorls of the Celtic Revival' had risen at Tintagel with Tennyson's *Idylls of the King*, adding that the 'Cornish Celtic Revivalists, poetical and artistic, took an interest in the old Cornish language which was akin to Breton and Welsh ... and in the legends of the Celtic saints'.[8] As Betjeman implied, the Celtic Revival was multidimensional, in part a movement in the Celtic lands themselves and partly an external phenomenon, not least among those English enthusiasts who had begun their radical reassessment of the Celtic world. In Cornwall, the Celtic Revival occurred against the background of rapid deindustrialization—the crash of the Cornish copper-mining industry in the 1860s, and the faltering of Cornish tin a decade later—a principal aim being the re-creation of 'Celtic-Catholic Cornwall'.[9] This involved looking back over the debris of the industrial period to a Cornwall of Celtic crosses and holy wells when, as Betjeman noted, the Cornish language was still widely spoken.

In the nineteenth century, folklorists such as William Bottrell and Robert Hunt had drawn attention to Cornwall's Celtic past, the latter insisting that in the west of Cornwall at least, 'long years must pass before the Englishman can banish the Celtic powers who here hold sovereign sway'.[10] Such ideas had become commonplace by the end of the century, and in 1901 a Cowethas Kelto-Kernuak (Cornish-Celtic Society) was formed by leading revivalists who managed to attract the support of prominent public and literary figures such as the scholar and writer Sir Arthur Quiller-Couch. The Society's other leading lights were L.C. Duncombe-Jewell and Henry Jenner.

Duncombe-Jewell's intervention was short-lived but powerful.[11] A romantic anti-industrialist, Duncombe-Jewell's vision was quintessentially Celtic revivalist. 'I enjoy, with all its drawbacks the Celtic heritage', he protested, 'the love of poetry and colour, the pilgrimage of dreams, the pageant of nature, the devotion to a fixed star of a principle, the desire to pursue ideas to their logical conclusion, no man withstanding'.[12] He was anxious to build links with other Celtic lands, drawing inspiration from the 'Celtic Twilight' of W.B. Yeats's Ireland, and as well as encouraging Cornish sports (notably wrestling) and the Cornish language, advocated the introduction of a Cornish national dress which would include a black kilt and conical hat.

Despite his initial impact, Duncombe-Jewell soon faded from the scene. Henry Jenner's influence was far more enduring. Born in 1848 in St Columb

Major, where his father was rector, Jenner was in fact of English and Scottish parentage. As Robert Morton Nance noted later, it was open to Jenner 'to choose any of three nationalities. He chose from the first to be Cornish'.[13] His interest in the Cornish language culminated in the publication in 1904 of his *A Handbook of the Cornish Language*, a guide to the history and structure of the language but also an introductory means to learning it. Jenner considered the language the foremost badge of Cornishness, arguing that the 'reason a Cornishman should learn Cornish' was because it was 'the outward and audible sign of his separate nationality'.[14]

In 1904, the same year that his book was published, Henry Jenner addressed the Celtic Congress at Caernarfon in Wales on the subject of 'Cornwall: A Celtic Nation', a passionate and persuasive speech which clinched Cornwall's application to join the Congress and be accepted by its peers as a Celtic country. This institutional approval was met with jubilation, Hambley Rowe, one of the revivalist enthusiasts, sending Jenner a congratulatory telegram, composed in the Cornish language. 'Tintagel byth agan cres fenten an breeder!', he exclaimed: 'May Tintagel be our centre, our fountain of the brothers!'[15] In this way, the newly emergent Celtic-Cornish movement was wedded neatly to the already well-established Arthurian tradition and its association in particular with North Cornwall. When Hawker, the arch-Arthurian, expressed his ardent anti-industrialism in his rhetorical question—'What angel could arrive with duties to perform for that large Blaspheming Smithery, once a great Nation, now a Forge for Railways?'—he was prefiguring the post-industrial sympathies of the Cornish-Celtic Revival.[16] He was also, of course, anticipating exactly the sentiments that would eventually lead D.H. Lawrence to Cornwall.

'I could not but think of you in Brittany'

In looking to the other Celtic nations for their inspirations and models for the future, the Cornish revivalists were drawn especially to Brittany. Aware of the long historical entwinement of Cornwall and Brittany, and the closeness of the Cornish and Breton languages, the revivalists viewed with satisfaction the comprehensive 'reinvention' of Celtic Brittany that had occurred by the turn of the twentieth century. In the aftermath of the French Revolution, many in France had viewed Brittany as a backward periphery, steeped in reactionary and superstitious belief. According to one report, in Brittany 'ignorance perpetuates the yoke imposed by the priests and nobles ... The inhabitants of the countryside only understand Breton', the language a 'barbaric instrument' used by 'intransigents [to] hold them under their sway, direct their conscience, and prevent citizens from knowing the laws and from loving the Republic'.[17] Hostile to central government, outlandish in their dress, and primitive in their behaviour and speech, the Bretons represented an unsavoury and sometimes dangerous underclass.

However, even as such prejudices were being expressed, new attitudes were already in the making. Intrepid travellers, many of them English, now found Brittany 'picturesque' and 'quaint'. Thomas Trollope, brother of the famous Anthony, for example, toured Brittany in 1839, in the following year publishing his *A Summer in Brittany*. No longer to be condemned, the Bretons were an attractive curiosity: 'with all the faults, which result from backwardness in the race of improvement and civilization, the natural character of the Breton has much in it to admire. Honest, frank, loyal, hospitable, and religious ... He is idle, it is true, but contented with the small produce of his easy labour'.[18] By the 1860s, the French rail network was beginning to penetrate Brittany, making it accessible in its remoteness. Brittany became a holiday destination, with a plethora of travel- and guide-books such as *Rambles in Brittany* and *Summer Holidays in Brittany* promoting a rapidly developing tourist industry. Alongside the trippers were the archaeologists, drawn now to the remarkable stone monuments at Carnac and other megalithic sites (believed then to be 'Celtic') scattered across Brittany, together with novelists and artists who found in Brittany material in abundance for their creative endeavours. The English continued to be prominent among these visitors, artistic 'colonies' or 'schools' springing up at Concarneau and elsewhere, but the French were increasingly drawn to Brittany too—among them Paul Gaugin, who first visited in 1886 and was intrigued especially by Breton peasant dress, particularly that of the women.[19]

As Barry Cunliffe has observed, such visitors 'crafted a vision of the land and its people that set in high relief their distinctive characteristics. This inevitably fed back into the consciousness of the people themselves, providing them with a vision to which to aspire.'[20] As Cunliffe concluded: 'Thus it was that the fascination of foreigners encouraged the Bretons to become even more Breton.'[21] Revisiting their myths of origin, for example, the Bretons re-emphasized the migration from Cornwall to Brittany in the fifth and sixth centuries, accounting for the similarity of the Cornish and Breton languages and the many shared place-name elements and saints' dedications, as well as an assumed common ethnicity. As early as 1859,

Matthew Arnold had penned a telling letter from Paris to his mother (a native of Constantine, in Cornwall): 'I could not but think of you in Brittany, with Cranics and Trevennecs all about me, and the peasantry with their expressive, rather mournful faces, long noses, and dark eyes, reminding me perpetually of dear Tom [his brother] and Uncle Trevenen, and utterly unlike the French.'[22] In 1900 a Breton Gorsedd was formed, based on the Welsh model, which aimed to perpetuate the Celtic bardic tradition, its members meeting annually in a bardic circle, suitably dressed in flowing bardic robes more or less reminiscent of Victorian estimates of Druidic attire.

A similar Cornish Gorsedd was founded in 1928, evidencing again the links—modern as well as ancient—between Cornwall and Brittany. In many ways, the 'reinvention' of Celtic Cornwall had mirrored that of Brittany, not only in the emergence of Brittany as a model for the Cornish revivalists but in the changing attitude of outsiders, principally the English, to the Cornish themselves. But it was a slow process. In 1910 D.H. Lawrence, in his letter to Louie Burrows, described the Cornish as 'foreigners', an 'othering' inherited from the high Victorian period when the Cornish, like the Celts in general but particularly the Irish, were often deemed to be racially inferior. As late as 1898, Herbert S. Vaughan, in his touring guide for cyclists *The British Road Book*, could observe that in Cornwall there 'are thatched mud cabins here and there that might have been transplanted from Galway; hedges of stone, logs and peat-stacks, pigs galore and a general aspect of dirt and happy laziness truly Irish'. Also, he added, 'the people are very excitable and very kind-hearted, and their dress often remind one of the Irish peasantry'.[23]

The comparison between Cornwall and other Celtic countries, particularly Ireland, was frequent, a device to label the Cornish as 'other' while simultaneously requiring them to reject the comparison. This paradox was made explicit in the short story 'Inconveniences of Being a Cornishman', which appeared in Charles Dickens' periodical *All Year Round* in 1861. As Simon Trezise has noted in his treatment of the story, the fictional narrator, called Pendraggles (itself a pejorative play on Cornish surnames), 'is made to deny Cornwall's genuine links with other Celtic countries' but at the same time 'finds it impossible to resist the stereotypes thrust upon him by his English companions'.[24] A tormented and exasperated Pendraggles complains:

> I wonder how often, and in how many varieties of ways, I have had forced upon me that stale, flat insipid joke about the wise men having from the *east*. I wonder how often I have had to declare to well-meaning

people, that Cornwall is *not* a queer country, that we do *not* speak the language of Wales and Brittany, that we are only one day's post from London, and that we regularly read the Times.[25]

'A rare thing in a Cornish peasant'

Even in the early twentieth century, prejudiced opinion was still readily apparent in some quarters. In 1908 W.H. Hudson, the noted ornithologist, published his *The Land's End: A Naturalist's Impressions in West Cornwall*, a volume marred by its sustained racist diatribe against the Cornish. 'The Cornish people', he averred, 'are Celts with less alien blood in their veins than any other branch of their race in the British Islands.'[26] But lest this be taken as a compliment, Hudson was quick to add that there were few 'Englishmen in Cornwall who do not experience that antipathy or sense of separation in mind from the people they live with, and are not looked at as foreigners'.[27] Comparisons with the Irish were common. He met individuals whose physical features were 'of that intensely Irish type so common in West Cornwall', on one occasion encountering a tenant farmer who worked a smallholding of a dozen or fifteen acres, and who despite his fifty-odd years had never ventured more than ten miles from his house.[28] According to Hudson, the farmer 'was a curious-looking undersized man with a small wizened face, small cunning restless eyes of no colour, and reddish-yellow eyebrows, perpetually moving up and down. He reminded me of an orang-utan and at the same time of a wild Irishman of a very low type.'[29]

Hudson attempted to engage the farmer in a discussion about ravens. But his speech was 'utterly unintelligible; the strangeness was in his manner of delivery. He grinned and he grimaced, swinging his long thin sinewy monkey-like arms about, jerking his body, and making odd gestures, interspersed with … clicks and inarticulate sounds'. He was, Hudson concluded, 'hardly like a human being'.[30] Hudson encountered similar types arguing among themselves on the beach at St Ives, 'discharging a torrent of wild gibberish at each other'. Affecting not to understand a word, he turned to a younger Cornish onlooker for help, to see if 'the jabber really meant anything'. '"I can understand him very well", said the young man: "he is talking *proper Cornish*"'.[31]

At Sennen Cove, Hudson came across yet another example of this behaviour: 'he too was in a dancing rage when I first saw him, chattering, screeching and gesticulating more like a frenzied monkey than a human being'.[32] On the plus side, he discovered a woman who appeared to share his interest in the natural world; she was 'a lover of all wild creatures—a rare thing in a Cornish peasant'.[33] Rambling across the countryside, Hudson was struck by the rudimentary nature of the dwellings. The farmhouses, he said, 'were pretty much all alike in their dreary, naked and almost squalid appearance. Each, too, has its own ancient Cornish name, some of these very fine or very pretty, but you are tempted to rename them in your own mind Desolation Farm, Dreary Farm, Stony Farm, Bleak Farm, and Hungry Farm.'[34] Hudson was also taken aback by Cornish hedges, great ramparts of stone and earth. 'Everyone in England knows what a hedge is', he exclaimed, 'a row of thorn or other hardy bushes … It consequently comes as a surprise when we first visit the remote and most un-English county of Cornwall to discover that a hedge there might mean something quite different.'[35]

'A common charge against the Cornish is a want of solidity or stability of character', Hudson continued: 'You cannot rely on them. You are constantly deceived by their manner: they are the readiest of any people on earth to fall in with your views and do exactly what you want. *But they don't do it.*'[36] As in Wales and Ireland, Hudson added, so in Cornwall it 'is really not so much a vice as a custom of the country, perhaps of the race … that illicit intercourse usually ends in marriage. It has been said that in Cornwall matrimony is the result of maternity.'[37] He also noted that it 'is said of the Cornish, as it has been said of the Irish and of Celtic people generally, that they are cruel … it may be that Celtic cruelty, like the Spanish, is due rather to a drop of black blood in the heart—an ancient latent ferocity which comes out in moments of passion.'[38]

Irish comparisons continued to colour Hudson's narrative. 'Walking to a village one day', he wrote, 'I fell in with a man who had, like many West Cornishman, a strikingly Irish countenance, also an Irish voice and flow of spirits.'[39] Later in the day,

> I walked by a footpath which led me through what is called the 'town-place' of a small farm-house. Here I found two men engaged in an animated discussion, and one, in ragged clothes, with a pitchfork in his hand, was the very type of a wild Irishman; in all Connemara you would not see a more perfect specimen—rags, old battered hat, twinkling grey-blue Irish eyes.[40]

Exploring Cornwall, 'I could hardly avoid falling into the illusion that I was in Ireland', Hudson admitted.[41] Especially characteristic of the Cornish was a 'curious child-like simplicity of mind', something 'almost painful'.[42] Indeed, 'the Cornish peasant appeared to me easier to understand than the English ... because he was nearer, mentally, to the child.' Among the Cornish, Hudson said, 'man and child are nearer in mind than is the case with English people'. Like children, the Cornish 'are subject to petulant and stubborn fits, and will brood in sullen resentment for days, meditating revenge, for some trivial imaginary slight'.[43] Moreover, 'emotional outbreaks ... when produced by religious excitement are painful to watch', although in this respect 'the Cornish are no doubt very much like other Celts in Britain'.[44]

In the realms of art and literature, Hudson insisted, 'Cornwall has given us next to nothing. Compare it in that respect with the adjoining county, divided from it by a little river, but distinct racially: what lustre Devon has shed on the whole kingdom! How many of her sons are so great in arms and arts, above all in literature'.[45] To those who pointed to 'Hawker of Morwenstow' in answer to the question 'Has Cornwall ever produced a great poet?', Hudson conceded that Hawker was a 'great man' but dismissed him as 'a very small poet'.[46] Besides, despite Hawker's passionate devotion to Cornwall, he was, as Hudson pointed out, actually born across the border in Devon.

That such sustained vitriol from the pen of a respected scientist could find its way to publication as late as the Edwardian era is perhaps surprising. It demonstrates that in pondering Cornwall, traditional disdain for 'the Celts' could linger side by side with the new English enthusiasm for all things Celtic, a schizophrenic or Janus-like complexity that could create confusion and uncertainty in the minds of educated and sensitive observers—as in the cases of D.H. Lawrence and Philip Heseltine, as we shall see in this book. However, as in Brittany, overwhelmingly negative portrayals of the Cornish gave way little by little to more romantic estimations of the 'Cornish Riviera' and the 'Delectable Duchy'. In this way, the Cornish were given licence to be more self-consciously 'Cornish', although England became more proprietorial in promoting and 'owning' its new-found playground.

By the turn of the twentieth century, Cornwall was becoming a favoured destination for holidaymaking, and even the acquisition of holiday homes, desirable locations such as Trebetherick on the North Cornwall coast already sought after by well-heeled aficionados. Among their number was a smattering of 'the artistic and the discriminating', as John Betjeman would later describe them, 'who sketched, etched, and painted the scenes we know so well, finding in Cornwall and North Devon a second Brittany'.[47] The Betjeman[n] family, indeed, were among those fortunates who holidayed habitually in North Cornwall. John Betjeman himself, born in 1906, as a small schoolboy played on the beaches and clifftops of Polzeath at much the same time D.H. Lawrence was at nearby Porthcothan.

From the 1880s, painters had begun to settle in Newlyn, drawn by both its picturesqueness (people as well as place) and the particular quality of the Penwith sunlight, which gave clarity to shape and form and made colours strong. An early arrival was Stanhope Forbes who saw in Cornwall a striking physical and cultural kinship with Brittany. He, like many other young artists of the time, had trained partly in Brittany—in his case, in Concarneau. Indeed, he often painted Newlyn as though it were Brittany, expressing— perhaps to a degree creating—in his art a powerful visual similarity between the two. Cornwall looked like Brittany, and the Cornish and the Bretons were physically alike, at least in Forbes' imagination. He was, however, but one among many artists attracted by the particular qualities of West Penwith. In Newlyn itself, significant names included Frank Bramley, Thomas Cooper Gotch, Norman Garstin, and Dod Shaw and Ernest Proctor. Sail lofts were converted to artists' studios, and even as early as the 1880s purpose-built studios had been constructed—such as the celebrated Trewarveneth Studio. At nearby Lamorna Cove, another artists' 'colony' (and they were 'colonies', almost all the artists incomers) grew up. Here the driving force was John 'Lamorna' Birch, who had lodged at Boleigh village in 1890 before moving to Lamorna in 1902. Notable amongst the Lamorna set were Harold and Laura Knight, who had first arrived at Newlyn in 1910. Across the Penwith peninsula at St Ives, similar colonies had also emerged. In 1883–84, Whistler and Sickert had spent several weeks there, and before long one after another of the sail lofts along Porthmeor beach at St Ives were being converted into artists' studios.[48]

'Over that fairy bridge of Brunel's'

As in Brittany, the growing number of visitors intent on discovering 'Celtic Cornwall' was facilitated by the expansion of the railway network. Cornwall had long been promoted as a quasi-Mediterranean resort, and the intimation of the exotic and the foreign was a successful marketing ploy which advocates of the new Cornish tourism hoped to develop in the closing years of the nineteenth century. As Mary Elizabeth Braddon put it in 1880: 'There are some travellers who think when they cross the Tamar, over that fairy bridge of Brunel's, hung aloft between the blue of the river and the blue of the sky, that they have left England behind them on the eastern shore—that they have entered a new country, almost a new world.'[49] The conversion to standard gauge in 1892, and the opening of the 'Westbury cut-off' in 1906, shortening the mainline from London, made Great Western Railway journeys to Cornwall quicker and more convenient, rendering Cornwall more accessible in its 'remoteness', just as the French rail network had done for Brittany.

The Great Western had formed its own advertising department as early as 1886, an unrivalled propaganda machine that produced its own sophisticated construction of Cornwall and was to stay in place until nationalization in 1948.[50] In 1904 the Great Western published *The Cornish Riviera*, written by the prolific topographical author A.M. Broadley, in which Cornwall was portrayed as balmy, foreign, exotic.[51] The first edition ran to a quarter of a million copies; there were a further four editions. In the following year, 1905, the Great Western introduced the Paddington (London) to Penzance 'Cornish Riviera Limited', a train that shot to international fame as a result of the careful publicity with which it was promoted. Great Western propaganda reached its apogee in the post-Great War era, with a huge array of jigsaws, train-spotting books, postcards, and essay competitions for girls and boys. Locomotives were given carefully chosen, evocative names such as *Cornubia*, *Trelawney*, *Tre Pol and Pen*, *Trevithick*, *Chough*, *One and All* and *Cornishman*.

Central to this effort was the production of an impressive series of Great Western posters, much of which drew heavily on the visual images already produced by Stanhope Forbes and the Newlyn school of artists. Two classic early posters were those released in 1906. The first placed a map of Cornwall alongside that of Italy, separated by two young women in 'national costume'. The map of Cornwall was distorted somewhat to produce a mirror image of Italy (there was no mention of scale), helping to reinforce the paradoxical message 'See Your Own Country First'. As the poster explained ambiguously: 'There is a great similarity between Cornwall and Italy in shape, climate and natural beauties'. Here was the earlier imagining of Cornwall as essentially Mediterranean in quality—sensual, sybaritic, even languid. The second poster, however, picking up on the newly dominant Celtic theme, emphasized the physical and cultural similarities of Cornwall and Brittany, depicting Cornwall's St Michael's Mount alongside the very similar (but even more impressive) Mont St Michel in Brittany. The message was: 'Another striking similarity. Beautiful Britain. Beautiful Brittany.'[52]

A second period of vigorous poster production occurred in the 1920s and 1930s. 'The Cornish Riviera', produced in around 1925 by Louis Burleigh Bruhl, depicted Cornwall as 'the warmest place in Britain and also as a land of legend, superstition and romance, the home of the wild and imaginative'.[53] Ten years later came Ronald Lampitt's highly distinctive (and eventually very famous) 'mosaic' portrayal of Newlyn, part of a co-ordinated poster campaign to popularize Newlyn, Penzance, Newquay, Looe, Perranporth and St Ives as tourist resorts. Even more than posters, Great Western guide-books produced in the immediate post-Great War period served as vehicles for Cornwall as the land of 'difference'. *Legend Land*, for example, was 'a collection of some of the Old Tales told in those Western Parts of Britain', the foreword written by one 'Lyonesse', a pen name redolent of Arthurian myth.[54] There was the story of the Hurlers stone circle at St Cleer, men turned to granite for playing the Cornish game of hurling on the Sabbath, and St Piran who, although 'Cornwall can boast many saints ... has greater right than any to be called the patron of the Duchy'.[55] The piskies of St Allen, the giants of St Michael's Mount, the impossible tasks performed by the evil Tregeagle and, of course, the famous legend of the Mermaid of Zennor were all told in engaging Great Western style.

Alongside such light-hearted tales, *Legend Land* displayed a surprisingly insightful appreciation of Helston's 'Furry Dance', performed on 8 May each year, including an analysis of the associated words and music. It was explained that: 'There is one line of the song, "God bless Aunt Mary Moses", that most people will find incomprehensible. It refers to the Virgin Mary, "Aunt" being among the Cornish a term of great respect; "Moses" being a corruption of the old Cornish word "Mowes", a maid. "Mary Moses" means literally "Mary the Maid".'[56] Here were intimations of co-operation between the Cornish revivalists themselves, with their 'insider' knowledge of the Cornish language and folk traditions, and 'outsiders' intent on developing the tourist industry. Responding to the crisis in Cornish mining, in 1898 Quiller-Couch had encouraged debate in his *Cornish Magazine* on the economic future of Cornwall. Reluctantly, he agreed with contributors who thought that the future lay in tourism. As he put it, the 'suggestion is that Cornwall should turn her natural beauty to account, and by making it more widely known, at once benefit thousands and honestly enrich herself ... Well then, since we must cater for the stranger, let us do it well and honestly. Let us respect him and our native land as well'.[57]

Quiller-Couch had recognized the inexorable movement towards a post-industrial economy, ingeniously wedding this to what would become the complementary post-industrial cultural agenda of the Cornish revivalists.[58] Indeed, there was a high degree of collusion, sometimes overt, between the Cornish-Celtic revivalists and the image-makers of the Great Western Railway, in which a significant section of Cornish society participated in the creation of touristic images of Cornwall. In a situation strikingly reminiscent of Brittany, the revivalists had found themselves in active alliance with the new image-builders. S.P.B. Mais, one of the Great Western's most prolific authors, acknowledged this process, writing in the preface to the third edition of his *The Cornish Riviera* (not to be confused with the earlier Broadley volume of the same name) that 'owing to the kindness of the [London] Cornish Association, the Rev G.H. Doble, Vicar of Wendron, Mr Trelawny Roberts, and other correspondents I have been able to rectify a few inaccuracies. Such help is invaluable, and will, I hope, be continued.'[59]

As *Through the Window*, another of the Great Western volumes, explained: 'Cornwall is so distinct from the rest of England as to seem almost another country.' Indeed, the book continued, this 'holds true even if one judges only by such superficial characteristics as the names of railway stations and things seen from the carriage windows. Its truth is emphasised as one probes into history, legend, and folk-lore, into the dead Cornish language and stories of the Cornish saints. Here, indeed', the book insisted, 'is a part of Britain with a culture and character peculiarly its own.'[60] This theme was echoed in S.P.B. Mais's celebrated *The Cornish Riviera*, first published by the Great Western in 1924 and reprinted on several occasions thereafter. Mais insisted that Cornwall was 'a Duchy which is in every respect un-English ... the Cornish people are not English people'. Thus: 'You may go there [Cornwall] with the idea you are in for a normal English holiday, and find yourself in an atmosphere of warlocks and pixies, miracle-working saints and woe-working witches'.[61] No longer dirty, lazy or unsettling, the Cornish were instead attractive and intriguing, welcoming of visitors rather than threatening.

The Cornish Coast and Moors, for instance, published in 1912, mused on 'the remote region so surrounded by the warm water of the Gulf Stream, that it possesses many of the allurements of the Mediterranean Littoral. Its name, to those who love it, is the Delectable Duchy, and its geographical appellation is Cornwall.'[62] The book admitted that the region's 'inhabitants have much that is foreign about them, both in appearance and customs. That is, of course, largely racial, but the equability of the climate has something to do with it.' Thus the Cornish 'have much in common with the emotional nature of the Spaniard and the Italian'.[63] Cornwall was 'one of those unconquered countries',[64] proudly independent, the book continued, and 'this land of primeval solitudes and prehistoric monuments is not to be discovered in a few weeks of sight-seeing'.[65] Indeed, 'in order to really know Cornwall—and to know her is to love her—it is necessary to leave the beaten tracks ... and to make the acquaintance of their warm-hearted, quick-witted Celtic inhabitants'.[66]

'The shores of Bude and Old Tintagel'

The London and South Western Railway, whose North Cornwall mainline crossed the Tamar at Launceston and penetrated as far west as Padstow, embraced similar sentiments, language and images: the visitor was 'thrown back five thousand years in the British region where successive centuries have failed to efface all trace of legend and romance. There is rich music in the very place names'.[67] This was North Cornwall, Arthur's realm, and the London and South Western made the most of the connection. Before the Great War, the railway produced *By the Cornish Seas and Moors: Holidays in King Arthur's Land*, designed to lure visitors to the enchanting locality, and as if to cement its Arthurian credentials, in 1918 introduced a new 'King Arthur class' of locomotives to haul its Cornish expresses westwards from London Waterloo: *Merlin, Lyonesse, Excalibur, Iseult, Sir Cador of Cornwall*, as well as *Tintagel, Queen Guinevere* and, of course, *King Arthur*.[68] When, during its construction, the North Cornwall line reached Camelford in August 1893, one of the directors welcoming the railway observed that it 'was a curious fact that on the very spot that they were assembled a great battle was fought between King Arthur and his nephew Modred', the new railway now connecting the distant outside world to 'the shores of Bude and Old Tintagel and the everlasting hills of Rough Tor and Brown Willy'.[69]

Pre-dating the arrival of the London and South Western Railway was the visit of Thomas Hardy to North Cornwall in March 1870.[70] The locality became the 'Off Wessex' of Hardy's literary imagination, a western appendage of his Dorset-centric 'Wessex'. Far more significantly, however, it also became his 'Lyonnesse', Hardy co-opting the name from Arthurian mythology (the distinctive spelling taken from Swinburne's 'Tristram and Lyonnesse') to lend an atmosphere of mystery and romance. Hardy had journeyed from Dorchester in his native Dorset to remote St Juliot, a few miles inland from Boscastle on the North Cornish coast, to restore the ancient parish church which was in danger of imminent collapse. During this and subsequent visits, he stayed at the vicarage, where he met and fell in love with Emma Gifford, the vicar's sister-in-law. Emma is glimpsed as the heroine Elfride in Hardy's novel *A Pair of Blue Eyes*. But she is featured more powerfully, albeit obliquely and not named, in Hardy's poem 'When I Set Out for Lyonnesse', penned after that memorable first visit in 1870 but not published until the eve of the Great War in 1914.

The poem chronicles the seismic change in mood experienced by Hardy as a result of encountering Emma, his future wife. Initially, the tone is wistful, sighing, but by the final stanza there is an air of exhilaration, even triumph:

> When I set out for Lyonnesse,
> A hundred miles away,
> The rime was on the spray,
> And starlight lit my lonesomeness
> When I set out for Lyonnesse
> A hundred miles away.
>
> What should bechance at Lyonnesse
> While I should sojourn there
> No prophet durst declare,
> Not did the wisest wizard guess
> What would bechance at Lyonnesse
> While I should sojourn there.
>
> When I came back from Lyonnesse
> With magic in my eyes,
> All marked with mute surmise
> My radiance rare and fathomless
> When I came back from Lyonnesse
> With magic in my eyes![71]

For Hardy, the arresting landscape and seascape of North Cornwall fused with the extraordinary personality of Emma to precipitate his electrifying, life-changing experience. Emma, as Hardy discovered, was a keen horsewoman, riding fearlessly along the clifftops to majestic Beeny Cliff, or seeking out mysterious, hidden places such as the Valency Valley or the waterfall at St Nectan's Kieve. On the second day of Hardy's visit, Emma drove him through Boscastle and Tintagel to view the impressive slate quarry at Penpethy, their relationship already developing apace. During their subsequent courtship, they visited Tintagel castle (with its supposed Arthurian associations), the magnificent beach at Trebarwith Strand, and secret Valency Valley, where they picnicked alone.

Hardy and Emma married in 1874 but, alas, the marriage was not a happy one, the routine of everyday life never matching the high drama and unexpected excitement of their first meeting. When Emma died in November 1912, Hardy was full of remorse. In March of the following year, he ventured again to North Cornwall, revisiting the sites of their early courtship, composing a series of expiatory poems—'The Poems of 1912–13', as he called them—which first appeared in his collection *Satires of Circumstance*, published in 1914.[72] Loss and atonement were constant themes, as Hardy visited once more—in his imagination as much as in reality—the scenes of his emergent love affair all those years before.

'Woman much missed, how you call to me, call to me',[73] he lamented in his poem 'The Voice', explaining in 'I Found Her Out There', another poem, how:

> I found her out there
> On a slope few see,
> That falls westwardly
> To the salt-edged air,
>
> Where the ocean breaks
> On the purple strand,
> And the hurricane shakes
> The solid land.[74]

References in the poem to 'Dundagel's [Tintagel's] famed head' and 'the tale / Of sunk Lyonnesse' lent an Arthurian flavour and context, while in 'A Dream or No', Hardy asked:

> Why go to Saint-Juliot? What's Juliot to me?
>   Some strange necromancy
>   But charmed me to fancy
> That much of my life claims the spot as its key.[75]

And then there was 'Beeny Cliff, March 1870–March 1913', which seemed to sum up all of Hardy's longings:

> O the opal and the sapphire of that wandering western sea
> And the woman riding high above with bright hair
>   flapping free—
> The woman whom I loved so, and who loyally loved me.[76]

As Adrian Tait has observed, for 'Hardy, Cornwall would always be Lyonnesse',[77] a sequestered space where, to use Simon Tresize's phrase, 'the ruthless logic of the material world [was] kept at bay'.[78] This was not far removed from Lawrence's own reading of Cornwall in his search for Rananim, with his desire to escape the smothering embrace of industrial modernity. Lawrence had always acknowledged his literary kinship with Hardy, and regarded him as a major influence on his own work, embarking on *A Study of Thomas Hardy* (published posthumously in 1932–33) which soon broadened into a wider treatise on art and literature.

The publication of Thomas Hardy's *Satires of Circumstance* in 1914 would not have gone unnoticed by Lawrence, who would have recognized the range of North Cornwall allusions—Arthurian and topographical—as well as appreciating the elegiac quality of the poetry. The significance for Hardy of his imagined Lyonnesse would shortly be heightened by what he called 'the dark madness' of the Great War, providing a much-needed mental refuge from the cataclysmic conflict.[79] Lawrence would soon feel the same way about Cornwall, envisioning his own utopia and emphatically claiming common cause with Hardy. On 5 September 1914, with Hardy uppermost in his mind, Lawrence wrote in desperation to his agent, J.B. Pinker, exclaiming: 'What a colossal idiocy, this war. Out of sheer rage I have begun my book about *Thomas Hardy*.'[80]

Chapter 3

Rananim Found and Lost: Lawrence at Porthcothan

'Beresford has lent us his house near Padstow, on the sea in Cornwall. Some members of our Florida expedition are coming too—we begin the new life in Cornwall. It is real.'[1]

This was D.H. Lawrence's excited message to Lady Cynthia Asquith, penned on Christmas Eve 1915. Lawrence was not the first to find in Cornwall an 'otherness' that allowed him—as he imagined it—to escape the oppressions of everyday life, and to find renewal and a sense of freedom rekindled. Nor would he be the last. But, as we have seen, Lawrence had long been dreaming of Cornwall, from his contemplation of a teaching post there in 1910 to his enthusiastic embrace of Thomas Hardy's work in 1914. The chance offer in late 1915 of a Cornish sojourn unveiled for him the opportunity to try to wrest free from the war and all that oppressed him in metropolitan England—or so he thought.

'Here one is outside England ... it is better in Cornwall'

J.D. Beresford, the author (he specialized in science fiction and horror stories), had acquired a substantial house in a commanding position overlooking the sea at Porthcothan, a small settlement near St Merryn, a few miles west of Padstow and the Camel estuary. Positioned between Bedruthan Steps and Treyarnon Bay, with Trevose Head in the distance to the north-east, Porthcothan was situated spectacularly on North Cornwall's Atlantic coast. In 1912 Porthcothan Cove was described as 'a delightful place for bathing ... where a stream that drains a considerable valley reaches the sea'.[2] Built above this tranquil setting sometime in the eighteenth century, Beresford's house had a solidity and spaciousness that complemented its dramatic location. It seemed to match Lawrence's mood perfectly. As he wrote to Dollie Radford in December 1915: 'We came down here yesterday, and we love it. It is quite a big house looking down on a cove of the sea.' It was, he explained, 'an old farmhouse with space and largeness and a sort of immemorial peace ... It does one good.'[3] To Edith Eder, he wrote similarly that it was 'a fine large house with clear, large rooms, and such lovely silence, with a little wind and a faint sound of the sea: such peace, I could cry'.[4]

Years after, Ottoline Morrell mused on the trauma that had sent Lawrence to Cornwall in December 1915—and later to Italy, Ceylon, Australia, America, Mexico. 'The War shook him', she said, 'the War and a very anti-English wife made him turn away in despair. His reaction against England ... was the passionate reaction of hurt feelings. His whole attitude to England was that of someone who has loved and has been hurt, bruised and disappointed'.[5] Cornwall was not America but also, as Lawrence was quick to point out: 'It is not England'.[6]

Writing to his agent J.B. Pinker from Porthcothan on 1 January 1916, just a few days after his arrival, he mused on the psychological distance between Cornwall and the London he had now abandoned, and on the healing power of Cornwall itself. 'Already, here, in Cornwall, it is better', he wrote, 'the wind blows very hard, the sea all comes up the cliffs in smoke. Here one is outside England ... it is better in Cornwall.'[7] Two days before, the night he and Frieda had arrived, he had written to his friend Kot. 'My dear Kot', he explained, 'This is the first move to Florida. Here already one feels a good peace and a good silence, and a freedom to love and to create a new life.' But there was still urgency beneath this apparent serenity, a plea not to lose sight of the original Rananim goal: 'We must begin afresh—we must begin to create a life all together—unanimous. Then we shall be happy. We must be happy.'[8]

A few days later and Lawrence got around to writing to his new landlord, J.D. Beresford. 'We have been here a week', he said, 'so I must report myself to you'. He enthused: 'We *love* being here ... The house is always peaceful and a real delight.' He and Frieda had already begun to explore the locality. 'We have walked to Padstow', he explained, 'and to the next bay north—and to-day right up on the downs, looking upon the country, upon St Columb and beyond Wadebridge.'[9] This growing familiarity with the topography of the hinterland encouraged Lawrence's awakening sense that Cornwall itself might indeed be his Rananim. 'I do like Cornwall', he told Beresford:

Rananim Found and Lost: Lawrence at Porthcothan

It is still something like King Arthur and Tristan. It has never taken the Anglo-Saxon civilization, the Anglo-Saxon sort of Christianity. One can feel free here, for that reason—feel the world as it was in that flicker of pre-Christian Celtic civilization, when humanity was really young—like the *Mabinogion*—not like *Beowulf* and the ridiculous Malory.[10]

Lawrence wrote to Kot the very next day, expansive now in extolling the charms of Cornwall, suggesting in effect that it might be his utopia, his Rananim. 'I am willing to believe there isn't any Florida', he said, 'it is very nice down here in Cornwall'. He and Frieda would be there until March, he added, after which 'I shall just go where the wind blows me, the wind of my own world.' But for the moment there was redeeming Cornwall: 'I like being here. I like the rough seas and this bare country, King Arthur's country, of the flicker of pre-Christian civilisation. I like it very much'.[11] It was a theme he repeated to Katherine Mansfield in a letter composed on 7 January. 'I love being here in Cornwall—so peaceful, so far off from the world. But the world has disappeared for ever—there is no more world any more: only here, and a fine thin air which nobody and nothing pollutes.'[12] Likewise, in a letter to Ottoline Morrell penned on 9 January, though complaining of the onset of one of his heavy colds (prompting Ottoline to send him a yellow woollen jersey by return), Lawrence explained that although they had only 'been here a week … I like it exceedingly. The sea rages under the black rocks, and the western sky is iridescent at evening … I have been much happier here.'[13] Two days later and he repeated again to Catherine Carswell, the Scottish author and drama critic, what was close to becoming a mantra:

> I like Cornwall very much. It is not England. It is bare and dark and elemental, Tristan's land. I lie looking down at a cove where the waves come white under a low, black headland, which slopes up in bare green-brown, bare and sad under a level sky. It is old, Celtic, pre-Christian. Tristan and his boat, and his horn.[14]

Similarly, writing to the literary duo Katherine Mansfield and John Middleton Murry on 17 January, Lawrence rehearsed once more the now familiar theme:

> I still like Cornwall. The house is a big, low, grey, well-to-do farm-place, with all the windows looking over a round of grass, and between the

stone gate pillars down a little tamarisky lane, at a cove of the sea, where the waves are always coming in past jutty black rocks. It is a cove like Tristan sailed into, from Lyonesse—just the same. It belongs to 2000 years back—that pre-Arthurian Celtic flicker of being which disappeared so entirely ... All is desolate and forsaken, not linked up. But I like it.[15]

Likewise, he told Barbara Low that 'I like Cornwall *very* much: it is so uncivilised, unchristianised—in spite of the churches. It is always King Arthur and Tristan for me ... I am very fond of that pre-christian Celtic flicker of civilisation.'[16] To Bertrand Russell, he repeated the mantra: 'I like being here *very much*. Cornwall isn't England. It isn't really England, nor Christendom. It has another quality: of King Arthur's days, that flicker of Celtic consciousness before it was swamped under Norman and Teutonic waves.'[17] To Mark Gertler, he explained that 'I like Cornwall, it is a bare, forgotten country that doesn't belong to England: Celtic, pre-Christian.'[18]

There was also a sense of domestic contentment, comfort even, at Porthcothan, enhanced by the presence of Emma Pollard, Lawrence and Frieda's housekeeper, inherited from Beresford. As Lawrence told Ottoline, 'Emma is a good soul, the housekeeper, and a good cook ... Emma has two illegitimate children. One, the elder, lives at Trevorrid [Trevoyan] farm, with her parents, the younger lives here. It is a rosy cheeked child of six.' He added that Philip Heseltine 'says a woman with two illegitimate children must be good. Emma is really splendid.' Emma was about thirty-five, Lawrence thought. Behind her back, Frieda and Lawrence called her 'Cornish Pasty', more in fun and affection, despite the pejorative overtones, but as Lawrence emphasized: 'I like Emma. She is Cornish ... a real decent woman'.[19]

It was an assessment Lawrence repeated to Beresford himself, explaining that the 'house is always peaceful and a real delight ... Emma is excellent, I think. We have a fine time, with her cakes and bread and puddings.' His affection for Emma extended to the local population: 'And most of the people seem nice—really very nice. There is a rare quality of gentleness in some of them—a sort of natural, flowering gentleness which I love.'[20]

'Heseltine is here also'

Perhaps Cornwall was Rananim. Lawrence urged Ottoline to visit him in Cornwall, to experience what he now felt so strongly: 'the sea on the wild coast is like the dawn of the world. Oh, it is good, there are no more Englands, no nations, only the dark strong rocks and the strong sea washing up out of the dawn of the sky. It is the beginning, the beginning only.'[21]

Charmed and intrigued by Lawrence's vivid descriptions and his enthusiasm, Ottoline decided that she would accept his invitation to visit. But in the event she went down with an illness—as did Lawrence, whose bad cold proved to be the prelude to a full-blown bronchial attack which confined him to bed for much of his time at Porthcothan and frightened him (and Frieda) into thinking that he might be dying. His 'weak chest'—formally diagnosed as tuberculosis in 1925—was catching up with him. Plainly, the escape to Cornwall, whatever else it was, was not an escape from ill health, and there were limitations to what this Cornish Rananim—with its damp climate and chill winds—could offer. To be ill in such a beautiful, peaceful place was not just frustrating—it was infuriating.

However, although his illness contributed to a sense of impatience and borrowed time, spurring him on in his writing, Lawrence was not defeated by the experience—far from it. He continued to focus on his planned community of like-minded souls in Cornwall. Even as he lay on his sickbed he had enjoyed the company of Philip Heseltine, whom he still considered a prime candidate and ideal partner for the Rananim project, and whom he had persuaded to join him at Porthcothan. Shortly to become a significant composer and music critic, Heseltine was in 1916 at the cusp of a successful career. Much of his work would exhibit a 'Celtic' influence—notably his well-known *The Curlew*, a song cycle for tenor and chamber ensemble based on four poems by the Irish writer and Celtic revivalist William Butler Yeats. Heseltine's songs, written mostly for voice and piano, would become enormously popular in inter-war Britain, although, even more than Lawrence, he had a restless, contrary, self-destructive streak. He died as a result of a domestic gas leak when aged only thirty-six, although it was never established whether this was suicide or an accident.[22]

Cecil Gray, his close friend and fellow composer, thought Philip Heseltine 'impish', not yet the 'boisterous and ribald Peter Warlock' that he would eventually become, but one whose mood 'perpetually oscillated between the highest exaltation and the deepest depression'.[23] Although often melancholy, especially in his correspondence with friends, there were moments of exuberance and attention-seeking which could cause surprise, even consternation. According to Gray, when Heseltine lived in Gloucestershire before the war, he took to 'riding a motor-bicycle through the village streets at midnight at a speed of sixty miles an hour, stark naked', and entertained in his shared 'house attractive young persons of the opposite sex who could not, even on the most charitable assumption, be considered to be the lawful and wedded wives of any of the inmates'.[24]

In his more serious moments, Heseltine rated Lawrence as 'simply unrivalled, in depth of insight and beauty of language, by any other contemporary writer'. Lawrence's novels, he said, were 'quite magnificent. I know no modern prose style so perfect as Lawrence's. Every word is weighed, and its precise effect calculated to the minutest nicety. Every adjective hits the mark exactly'.[25] Heseltine's attitude to the war chimed exactly with Lawrence's too. In November 1915, Heseltine had written to Colin Taylor, complaining that 'I feel more and more out of sympathy with the general temper of the country. The agglomeration of horrors of all kinds that this war has brought makes me so sick and fills me with impotent rage against the barbarous conditions of human life in this twentieth century of the Christian era'.[26] He rejected patriotic concepts such as 'national honour' and was disgusted by 'the self-righteous hypocrisy of England that muzzles every plain-speaking truth-teller and is ready to sacrifice not only the lives of all its inhabitants but every conceivable tenet of morality higher than that of brute beasts'. As he added, one 'cannot even raise one's voice in protest … such is the temper of one's countrymen'.[27]

A few days before Christmas 1915, shortly before his departure for Porthcothan, Lawrence had written to Philip Heseltine, reiterating that 'I do want a few of us to make a good thing of life, a new start. And I think we might do it together.'[28] In his current mood, Heseltine needed little further encouragement, and made arrangements to join Lawrence and Frieda in Cornwall, writing to Frederick Delius from Porthcothan in January to explain that 'with 1915 I have put behind me for ever a great deal of foolish and harmful stock-in-trade with which my life was encumbered … At any rate this is the beginning of a new start'. In marked contrast to the 'hypocrisy of England', he said, he now found himself in tune with the 'Stimmung of Cornwall'.[29]

'Heseltine is here also', Lawrence wrote excitedly to Ottoline in his letter of 9 January. Philip Heseltine had not yet developed his potential as an individual, Lawrence thought—'I like him, but he seems empty, uncreated'—yet there was promise, and 'one always believes in the miracle, in something supernatural'.[30] Heseltine had already warmed to the notion of Rananim, and like Lawrence saw in Cornwall the 'Celtic other' which distanced it from degenerate England and made it an ideal location for their proposed utopian community.

Although he was born in London, Heseltine's home was Cefn Bryntalch in Abermule, Montgomeryshire, where had he developed a consuming interest in all things Welsh and in pan-Celticism. He was thirteen years old when his widowed mother remarried, and together they had moved to Cefn Bryntalch, family home of his stepfather, Walter Buckley Jones, from where Heseltine spent many happy hours bicycling through the border counties of Shropshire, Montgomery, Radnor (where his mother was born, at Knighton) and Hereford, 'loving', as Beryl Kington has put it, 'the country with his extraordinary sensibility for landscape'.[31] He also loved the Welsh language, which, to his surprise and regret, many of 'his aristocratic neighbours [in Montgomeryshire] had despised'.[32] Enthusiastically, he told Delius that George Borrow's 'glorious book *Wild Wales* ... is one of my most treasured possessions, which I always have with me, and read constantly, over and over again'. As Heseltine explained, 'it is wonderful how Borrow caught the spirit of that heavenly country ... I love Wales, and never tire of such a delicious picture of it!'.[33] George Borrow was Cornish on his father's side, as *Wild Wales* made plain, no doubt adding an agreeable pan-Celtic dimension to Heseltine's appreciation.

'Mrs Henry Jenner'

It seems likely that it was Heseltine who introduced Lawrence to the subtleties and complexities of the 'Celtic world', giving further content and meaning to Lawrence's existing conceptions of 'King Arthur's country' and a 'pre-Christian Celtic civilization'. Yet Lawrence had also done his own Celtic homework and, through his knowledge of the work of 'Mrs Henry Jenner', was certainly aware of the activities of the influential Henry Jenner, the distinguished Cornish language scholar who in 1904 had produced his all-important *A Handbook of the Cornish Language* and was hailed later as 'the father of the Cornish revival'.[34]

'Mrs Henry Jenner'—Kitty (Katharine) Lee Jenner (née Rawlings)—was born at Trelissick Downs in Hayle, Cornwall, in 1853. Her father, William Rawlings, had published minor works on the functions of Cornwall's Stannary courts, and took an informed interest in the Cornish dialect of English, with its many Cornish-language words. These were literary and Cornish enthusiasms that Kitty Lee inherited. She was educated at home (her father was reputed to have a fine library), followed by study at the National Art Training School (later the Royal College of Arts) in London and at the Slade School of Fine Art, Bloomsbury. She became a correspondent of Henry Jenner, following his visit to her father in 1873 (presumably to discuss Cornish-language matters), the couple discovering to their delight much in common, including a penchant for ritualistic Christianity and—as Alan M. Kent has described it—a 'shared interest in the academic sphere of Celtic Studies'.[35] Jenner encouraged Kitty Lee to learn Cornish, some of his letters to her reading (as he admitted) like 'a lecture on Celtic philology'.[36] For example:

> I hope the Cornish is progressing well. I recommend it as a good cure for neuralgia [from which Jenner suffered]. I look forward to the time when we shall be able to correspond and talk fluently in our own language. I shall work at Breton a good deal now that I have got books therein. It is much nearer to Cornish than Welsh is, especially the Vannes dialect though I believe the dialect of the Breton Cornouailles is curiously still nearer. Cornouailles is the southern half of what is now the Department of Finisterre.[37]

By September 1874, Jenner was addressing Kitty Lee as 'my darling', evidence that their relationship had become close.[38] Eventually, in 1877, at St Erth in Cornwall, the two were married. Soon 'Katharine Lee' (her nom de plume) was developing a successful literary career, and for a time she was much better known than her husband. Her first novel, published in 1882, was *A Western Wildflower*, followed by five more works of fiction, the last and perhaps best-known being *When Fortune Frowns: Being the Life and Adventures of Gilbert Coswarth—A Gentleman of Cornwall*, published in 1895, the story of a Cornish Jacobite who had fought for Bonnie Prince Charlie in the 'Forty-Five'. Jenner was himself a convinced Jacobite, with links to various shadowy 'Legitimist' causes in Britain and continental Europe, and he and Kitty Lee fashioned their own political-religious creed, combining elements of Jacobitism, Catholicism and Celticism.[39] In 1904, Kitty Lee was made a bard of the Welsh Gorsedd, taking the bardic name 'Morvoren', meaning 'mermaid' in the Cornish language.

Kitty Lee had also nurtured a parallel interest in Orientalism and 'the East', which in turn fed her growing preoccupation with Christian art. She published three important books on the subject, under her name as 'Mrs Henry Jenner', the final being *Christian Symbolism* in 1910. It was this volume that had caught Lawrence's attention. He was reading it avidly in December 1914, writing on the 20th of that month to the Irish barrister Gordon Campbell (later Lord Glenavy) to sing its praises and to recommend it as essential reading. Lawrence hoped that it would lift Campbell from his fixation with Ireland to a wider appreciation of 'the Celtic Vision' (as he called it), enabling him to 'understand the Celtic Symbolism in its entirety'.[40] In the same letter, he had also urged that this 'Celtic Symbolism' be considered alongside the religious cultures of 'the *East*: Christian, Mohammedan, Hindu, all'.[41] The influence of 'Mrs Henry Jenner' was unmistakeable here, as was Lawrence's emerging interest in pan-Celticism and its links with Eastern esotericism.

A month later, in January 1915, Kitty Lee's impact upon Lawrence was made even more plain in a letter to Kot. 'What about Rananim?', Lawrence enquired impatiently. 'Oh, we are going. We are going to found an Order of the Knights of Rananim.' Its badge, he explained, would be a 'phoenix argent, rising from a nest of scarlet, on a black background'.[42] To show Kot exactly what he meant, he sketched his idea of the phoenix resurgent—an almost identical copy of the illustration of a 'Phoenix Rising from the Flames' opposite page 150 in 'Mrs Henry Jenner's' *Christian Symbolism*.[43] Thereafter, Lawrence adopted the phoenix as his personal symbol, a lasting tribute to the influence of Kitty Lee Jenner and Celtic Cornwall. Intriguingly, Henry Jenner's *A Handbook of the Cornish Language* of 1904 was published, coincidentally or not, at the 'Sign of the Phoenix' (the publisher's mark), which Jenner thought a 'good omen' when considering whether 'anything will come of the Cornish part of the Celtic movement'.[44] It was a motif that Lawrence shared and understood, an early link with Cornwall and the work of the Jenners, Kitty Lee and Henry.

'The Cornish language should be revived'

Philip Heseltine was probably aware of much of this background. Indeed, while Heseltine was at Porthcothan, Lawrence was writing to Ottoline Morrell asking her to search out books for him 'on interesting Norse literature, or early Celtic, something about Druids ... or the Orphic Religions, or *Egypt*, or on anything really African', reflecting the eclectic study he had urged on Gordon Campbell a year before.[45] Heseltine, for his part, was bent on pursuing his own brand of Celticism. Although this came to full fruition after he had left Cornwall—following his stay at Porthcothan and later at

Zennor—and when he had fled to Ireland during 1917 to avoid conscription into the Army, it was surely in his discussions with Lawrence that his own ideas on the place of Cornwall in the Celtic world had first taken firm shape. Indeed, the relationship between Lawrence and Heseltine was at that moment critical for both men, and it is useful to pause briefly to consider the impact of Cornwall and the Celtic world upon Heseltine's own life and work, and thus Lawrence's too. Ian Copley has emphasized:

> the effect on his [Heseltine's] music of his absorption ... of the ideals of the Pan-Celtic movement—an interest which led him to dabble in comparative Celtic philology, to learn to speak Erse [Irish], to teach himself the old Cornish language, to set Yeats [to music], to contemplate the composition of an opera on a Celtic subject, to utilize themes from Gaelic folk tunes in instrumental works, and study with great perception the music of Breton composer Paul Ladmirault.[46]

As the Scottish composer Cecil Gray was to write, Heseltine had conducted:

> a comprehensive comparative study of all the various branches of the Celtic languages—Irish, Welsh, [Scots] Gaelic, Breton, Manx and Cornish ... he obtained as thorough a knowledge of Irish as any Englishman can hope to do, and ... This he acquired chiefly during a stay of two months either in Achill or in the Aran Islands ... during which time he did nothing else except study the language ... But the Celtic language which attracted him above all others was Cornish.[47]

As Heseltine himself intimated, writing to Cecil Gray, learning Cornish had been an act of faith in Lawrence's original conception of Rananim—the 'mystic centre of a new culture' and an 'anti-national ... protest against imperialism'.[48] As Heseltine put it:

> The Cornish language should be revived—nay, is being revived, for am I not myself reviving it? ... All neo-Celtic nationalism is in effect anti-national, in the sense in which we detest nationality; it becomes an individualizing moment—a separating one, at any rate. What more effective protest against imperialism (in art as in other matters) could

Rananim Found and Lost: Lawrence at Porthcothan

you or I make by adopting, as a pure ritual, a speech, a nationality, that no longer exists.[49]

Henry Jenner was initially hesitant about reviving Cornish as a spoken language, and, paradoxically, would have stoutly resisted Heseltine's contention that Cornish 'nationality' no longer existed. No matter; he and Heseltine embarked on a collaboration that would see several of Jenner's Cornish-language poems put to music by Heseltine. Heseltine was fast emerging as a composer of distinction. His earliest surviving orchestral work, 'An Old Song', was probably begun in Cornwall in 1916 and completed in Ireland a year later. It was intended originally as part of a *Celtic Triad*, together with a 'Dirge' and a 'Cornish Rhapsody' that unfortunately was later destroyed.[50] As Heseltine wrote to a friend in August 1917 from County Kerry: 'The tune is Gaelic but the piece for me is very much the Cornish moor where I have been living. The tune should emerge, as from afar, chiming in with one's thoughts while walking ... a mood half-contented and half-sad'.[51]

Next was 'A Cornish Christmas Carol', the music composed in 1918 but not published until 1924, the second of two carols on which Heseltine had been working. 'The music of these carols is inseparably associated with the actual Cornish words', he insisted, 'any translation would pervert the whole character of the works'.[52] As he explained to Cecil Gray, 'I am writing with great enthusiasm two Cornish hymns: it is probably the first time the old language has ever been musicked deliberately ... it is wonderful for singing purposes, containing many sounds almost unknown in English (except Cornish-English dialect) which have a real musical value of their own'.[53]

The 'Cornish Christmas Carol' created something of a sensation in the Celtic world, the Breton commentator Paul Ladmirault in 1927 eulogizing Heseltine as 'one of the greatest English composers of our time' and heaping praise on that 'peal of all the carols, a *Cornish Carol* for four voices, on a text in the old Cornish language, dead sister of Armorican [Breton]'.[54] As Ladmirault put it:

The very name Cornwall calls up a multitude of enchantments: the tragic love of Tristan and Isolde; the wooded dale; the picturesque remains of the legendary forest of Morois and of Tintagel, a name which is already music; and Dolly Pentreath, the last woman to speak Cornish, dead in 1768 [1777]. That country, which is a continuation of our Brittany in its appearance and its past history, is in itself enough to

D.H. Lawrence and Cornwall

arouse our complete sympathy and to make us expect a great deal from a *Cornish Christmas Carol* written by Peter Warlock [Philip Heseltine].

And we are not disappointed. A feeling of remarkable calmness dominates the 13 pages of this work, conceived in the mysterious tonality of A flat major, from which it rarely departs. There is an impressive all-pervading religious atmosphere; a dream music which brings us the syllables of a forgotten language, dear to our ancestors: 'Bedneth Nadelek genough re bo ...' (in Breton: 'Bennez Nedelek ganeoc'h ra vo ...' The Blessing of Christmas be upon you).[55]

The words to 'A Cornish Christmas Carol' had been written by Henry Jenner in 1901, and appeared in the pan-Celtic magazine *Celtia* in the following year, with an English translation by L.C. Duncombe-Jewell. The Cornish was in its Late or Modern form, Jenner explaining that it was: 'En Tavaz Kernuak an Sethdegvas Cans vledhan' ('in the Cornish Language of the Seventeenth century').[56] Heseltine was captivated by the euphonious words, with their similarity to Welsh and Breton:

> En pedn an vledhan, pan gwav o gwyn,
> Be genes Map Dew a Varya wyn,
>   Rag sawya dihort pehas an bys-ma,
> Ha bownans rag dry dh'an pople da.
>
> Rag kana an El dh'an bugely en gwel,
> Hedna on kan pur lawenek dho whel:
> 'Gorryons dho Dew e zen Nef braz,
> Cres war an tir dho deez vodh vaz!'.
>
> A vez an dhuyran war degl an Stul,
> A dheth teez fyr, o Maternow ul,
> Ha'n gy rig dos aberth an bow-gy,
> Hag ubba rig 'gorria 'gan Arluth ny.
>
> Ha ny vedn mos dho worria genzyns,
> Teez fyr, ha bugely ha chattel ul myns.
> En termen Offeren ny vedn e gwellas,
> Pan ef'ra dyskynnya rag dh'agan whellas.

Rananim Found and Lost: Lawrence at Porthcothan

Dew reffa sawya coth Gernow wheg,
Dhort Pedn an Wollas bys Tamar teg,
Ha gwitha y bisqueth en carenja ef,
Dho worria Map Dew ha Maternas Nef.

Bennath Nadelik gena why re bo
Dhort an Tas Dew ny, ha dhort e Hloh,
Ha dhort Dama Dew, an Vahteth 'lan
Hedna yw duath dho ul ow han.

[*At the end of the year, when the winter was white,*
Was born the Son of God of Mary Blessed,
For to save the world from sin,
And life to bring to good people.

The Angel did sing to the shepherds in the field,
That was a song very joyful to man:
'Glory to God in the heavens high,
Peace upon Earth to men of good will!'

From out of the East on the Epiphany,
Came the wise men—they were kings all—
And they did come into the stable,
And there did homage to our Lord.

And we will go for to worship with them,
The wise men, and the shepherds, and cattle all
At Mass-time Him shall we see,
When He shall descend to seek us.

God save old Cornwall dear,
From Land's End to Tamar fair,
And keep it ever in His love,
To the glory of God and the Queen of Heaven.

A Christmas blessing with you be
From God the Father, and from His Son,
And from the Mother of God. The Virgin pure
This is the end of all my song.][57]

D.H. Lawrence and Cornwall

The first of Heseltine's two *Kanow Kernow* (Songs of Cornwall) was not published until as late as 1973, being the music set to words written by 'Gwas Myhal' (the bardic name of Henry Jenner). Entitled 'Benneth Nadelik ha'n Bledhen Noweth' ('Christmas and the New Year Blessing'), the piece was simpler than the earlier carol but included a pronunciation glossary to help choirs unfamiliar with the Cornish language. It was, in its way, an unforeseen but lasting outcome of the Rananim quest, and of Heseltine's complex relationship with both Lawrence and Cornwall.

'Peter Warlock'

Together at Porthcothan, Lawrence and Philip Heseltine no doubt shared their knowledge of the Jenners—Kitty Lee and Henry—swapping notes on the Celtic revivalism that had become so apparent in Cornwall, and accommodating this vision within their own conception of Rananim. It is even possible that, during his later stay at Zennor, Lawrence may actually have met the Jenners, who lived nearby at Hayle, although there is no supporting documentary evidence to support the intriguing suggestion.[58]

A further dimension to Heseltine's Cornish-Celtic enthusiasms was his fascination with the occult. Reinventing himself as 'Peter Warlock', Heseltine had come under the spell of Aleister Crowley, famously dubbed 'the most wicked man in England'. Crowley was a member of the Hermetic Order of the Golden Dawn, a secret magical order which, in the late nineteenth and early twentieth centuries, had a deep impact upon Western occultism. It attracted several prominent Celtic revivalists to its ranks, including the Irish nationalist and 'Celtic Twilight' writer William Butler Yeats and the Welsh novelist Arthur Machen, author of *The Great God Pan* (1894) and *The Secret Glory* (1922), the latter a book which greatly influenced the young John Betjeman.[59]

Likewise, Aleister Crowley was an associate of L.C. Duncombe-Jewell, the Cornish-Celtic revivalist who in the early 1900s had been a leading luminary of the revivalist Cowethas Celto-Kernuak—the Cornish-Celtic Society—of which Henry Jenner was also a prominent member. Moreover, Crowley had found himself in tune with much of Jenner's philosophical thought, attracted as he was by 'what they called the Celtic Church' and 'the quest of the Holy Grail', and becoming 'a romantic Jacobite ... a bigoted legitimist'.[60] But increasingly Crowley leant towards paganism and supernatural magic, gaining his infamous reputation as 'the Beast 666'.[61] There were wild rumours

Rananim Found and Lost: Lawrence at Porthcothan

of his activities in Cornwall—of black masses on Bodmin Moor, on the Isles of Scilly and (even more improbably) in St Buryan church—and it was alleged that he (with his Devil-worship) was implicated in the strange and sudden death of Katherine Arnold-Forster at Zennor in May 1938.

It was probably Crowley who introduced Heseltine to drugs, especially hashish, and who urged him to find his real self or 'True Will' by seeking spiritual wisdom through the occult. By the time Heseltine arrived at Porthcothan to stay with Lawrence in early 1916, he was already something of a specialist in the occult, with an awareness of Crowley's links with Duncombe-Jewell, Jenner and the world of Cornish-Celtic revivalism. It is difficult to gauge the extent to which this particular enthusiasm affected Lawrence. But we know that Lawrence unhesitatingly described Cornwall as 'pagan' and 'pre-Christian', echoing Heseltine's conviction, a view that he was not afraid to repeat or to deploy in fictional writing.

As Lawrence's first real recruit to what he hoped would become his Cornish Rananim, Philip Heseltine had much to recommend him—he was artistic, musical, other-worldly, anti-war, a loather of the nation-state and empires, an escapee from oppressive England, and a budding Celticist with an interest in 'pagan' and 'pre-Christian' Cornwall and in contemporary Cornish revivalism. Yet despite their obvious intimacy and their shared goals and enthusiasms, it was soon apparent that all was not necessarily harmonious between Lawrence and Heseltine. It was the first intimation that the road to Rananim would be *always* tortuous and difficult, for close-quarter communities would surely breed their own disagreements, quarrels and jealousies. Indeed, Cecil Gray would later write that Heseltine's 'close contact with Lawrence was definitely harmful to him'.[62]

To begin with, Heseltine had not come to Cornwall alone. He had brought with him his already pregnant girlfriend 'Puma', Minnie Lucy Channing, sometimes also known as 'Bobby', one-time model of Augustus John. With a reputation for sexual promiscuity and a volatile temper, Puma was bound to set nerves jangling at Porthcothan. She was thought to be 'exotic' and 'exceptionally beautiful', and the artist Adrian Allinson, who had introduced Puma to Heseltine, described her as 'Italian-like, feline … fierce'. Heseltine had been captivated by her laugh, said Allinson: 'She was Philip's ideal woman—dark, with fur all over her'. And he added, 'a puma, of course, is a feline beast of prey'.[63]

At Porthcothan, there were already signs of tension between Heseltine and Puma. Lawrence confided to Ottoline Morrell in his letter penned on

13 January 1916 that Heseltine 'says he despises her [Puma] and can't stand her, that she's vicious and a prostitute'. But, wrote Lawrence, 'She's not so bad, really.' Indeed, he added, 'I'm not sure whether her touch of licentious profligacy in sex isn't better than his deep-seated conscious, mental licentiousness. Let them fight it out between them.'[64] Heseltine's love life, it turned out, was even more tangled than it had at first seemed, and Lawrence and Frieda observed with some amusement his vacillations between Puma, Dorothy Warren (Ottoline's niece, now a new recruit for Rananim) and the Swiss governess on Ottoline's staff at Garsington who had caught Heseltine's eye, Mlle Juliette Baillot. Lawrence reported these twists and turns in his correspondence with Ottoline. 'About Heseltine and Mlle', he wrote on 15 February, 'He wants Mlle for *companionship*, not for the blood connection, the dark, sensuous relation. With Puma he has this second, dark relation, but not the first.'[65]

When Heseltine found out that Lawrence had been speculating in letters to Ottoline about the intimate details of his private life, he was not pleased. Likewise, when it became apparent that Heseltine had himself written to Ottoline, attempting to intervene in a misunderstanding between Ottoline and Frieda, it was the Lawrences' turn to be upset. Things at Porthcothan were becoming somewhat strained. Another young recruit to the Rananim project had by now arrived in Cornwall, the Bulgarian writer Dikran Kouyoumdjian (Michael Arlen, as he would become), whom Lawrence thought was showing promise. But he soon decided that he did not like this loud and offensive foreigner. Nor did Heseltine. 'Heseltine is still here', Lawrence reported to Ottoline, 'But he and Kouyoumdjian are most antagonistic, so it's a bit trying'. In fact, Kouyoumdjian had 'brought the atmosphere of London', Lawrence complained, 'most disturbing', not at all what one expected from a Rananim recruit. 'How I loathed that London', Lawrence added, 'that England out there'.[66] He also wrote to John Middleton Murry and Katherine Mansfield, telling them about 'Kouyoumdjian, whom I don't care for really'. Significantly, Lawrence anticipated that 'he will go soon', an intimation that membership of Rananim could be conditional, that, despite the ostensible openness to all, one would be expelled or frozen out if one did not measure up to Lawrence's standards.[67]

The Bulgarian left but Heseltine persevered for a time, trying to put together a private publishing scheme that won Lawrence's admiration. But, as Lawrence explained to Ottoline on 25 February, Heseltine remained in a state of some agitation. He was 'in a great state of (unjustly) hating the Puma, and looking on Mlle as a white star', he wrote, and would 'oscillate violently' in his affections. 'He is really very good', Lawrence admitted, 'and I depend on him and believe in him. But he is exasperating'. However, as Lawrence acknowledged, part of Heseltine's anxiety was his fear of conscription into the British Army. '[C]onscription hangs over his head like the sword of Damocles', Lawrence explained to Ottoline, adding with an air of resignation that Heseltine would probably remain with them in Cornwall, but only 'if he escapes conscription'.[68] The looming conscription issue weighed heavily on Lawrence, not only because he feared for Heseltine's future, but because its hectoring presence in Cornwall now represented the unwarranted, obtrusive influence of the England he hated. For all Cornwall's non-English attributes, the dead hand of England still held ultimate sway.

'Cornish people still attract me. They have become detestable'

Not long after Christmas 1915, Lawrence had felt the creeping, insidious influence of England's war already making itself felt in Cornwall. Lawrence was saddened when the war intruded on Emma's simple life, the housekeeper's sister-in-law becoming involved in the preparation of military uniforms of those about to go to the front. 'There is some war here now', he reported bleakly to Barbara Low, 'the Derby scheme did it'.[69] The scheme, which required the registration of every eligible male aged eighteen to forty-one, was a prelude to the introduction of conscription to the armed forces in early 1916, making the locals 'very sad', as Lawrence told J.D. Beresford.[70]

Despite his admiration for the Cornish in their passive stoicism in the face of coercion, Lawrence bridled at their inability to react, to do anything about it. Like many of his time and education, he sat uncomfortably on the cusp of two alternative constructions of 'the Celt'. He had readily embraced the contemporary Edwardian view, the 'Celtic Twilight' picture of the Celtic peoples as dreamy, other-worldly, creative, artistic, poetic—an almost pre-Raphaelite, neo-Arthurian construction that saw the Celts as somehow ethically and culturally superior to the dull, hard-headed, unimaginative, utilitarian Anglo-Saxons, the English. In such a view, the Celts were an unsullied pre-modern people, like the 'Red Indians' of America (as Lawrence would have imagined it), pure and elemental and free from the destructive forces of modernity and industrialization. Such were the thoughts that had drawn Lawrence to Cornwall in the first place. Yet English prejudice was not yet free of the alternative construction, exacerbated by the Irish and Highland potato famines in the 1840s, according to which the Celts were fey, feckless, even subhuman, incapable of reasoned or measured behaviour and destined for ever to remain under England's guiding rule. In his darker moments, Lawrence turned to this view. He had nothing but contempt for the Irish rebels of Easter 1916, condemning them for pouring further miseries on an already troubled people, and he dismissed David Lloyd George as a 'Welsh *rat*'.[71]

When the war had intruded on Cornwall so soon after his arrival, Lawrence felt somehow betrayed, since the Cornish had failed to give the 'not of England' protection he had anticipated. It was a rude shock, and Lawrence blamed the Cornish for their lack of moral courage, as he saw it, for their infuriating self-satisfied, introverted complacency. They had turned in on themselves, he said, and were now only interested in pecuniary advantage. As he had complained to Bertrand Russell, there was already in his mind a contradiction between idealized imaginings of the Cornish Celts and the local people he had encountered thereabouts. He had somehow hoped that 'there really might be rock-hurling giants and odd pixies ... If only the Cornish hadn't become foully and uglily Wesleyan. Alas! Alas!'.[72] Yet, in the same breath, he was prepared to tell Russell:

> I like it [Cornwall] very much. I like the people also. They've got a curious softness and intimacy. I think they've lived from just the opposite principle to Christianity: self-fulfilment and social destruction, instead of social love and self-sacrifice. So here there's no social structure, hardly, and the people have hardly any social self: only the immediate intimate self. That's why they're generally disliked. And that's why they were wreckers and smugglers and anti-social things: And that's why the roads are too dodgy to be grasped. And that's why there is such a lovely, intimate softness in the women.[73]

There were similar inconsistencies and contradictions, including unsettling gender distinctions, expressed in a letter to Barbara Low:

> But at last I have found a place where some of the men and women really love each other with a fine softness and rareness that delights me. The women are so soft and so wise and so attractive—so soft, and unopposing, yet so true: a quality of winsomeness and rare, unconscious

Rananim Found and Lost: Lawrence at Porthcothan

Female soothingness and fertility of being. I would marry a Cornish woman. But some of the men are detestably small-eyed and mean—real cunning nosed peasants mean as imbeciles.[74]

In singling out Cornish men for such withering treatment, Lawrence probably had in mind one Hawken, a local landowner to whom he had taken an instant dislike. 'He came in—with his small eyes and his paunch', sneered Lawrence, 'talking about how he had turned the old woman out of this house, for he wouldn't have a tenant like her—and his property Truro way. But we have known the peasant type before—mean and stupidly cunning and base'.[75] A few weeks later, Lawrence reported in a rather amused tone his latest encounter with the irascible Hawken: 'Hawken was very cross because Heseltine, who is staying with me, chopped down a dead old tree in the garden. I said to him (Hawken), "I'm sorry, but don't trouble. It was so dead it soon would have fallen. And you may take the wood"'.[76]

Lawrence attempted to explain his contrary feelings about the Cornish to J.D. Beresford, writing on 1 February 1916:

The Cornish people still attract me. They have become detestable, I think, and yet they *aren't* detestable. They are, of course, strictly *anti-social* and un-Christian. But then, the aristocratic principle and the principle of magic, to which they belonged, these two have collapsed, and left only the most ugly, scaly, insect-like, unclean *selfishness*, so that each one of them is like an insect isolated within its own scaly, glassy envelope, and running seeking its own small end. And how foul that is! How they stink in their repulsiveness.[77]

And yet, despite this appalling fall from grace, Lawrence argued, there were still redeeming features, a hint of the old aristocratic, magical superiority that somehow still survived in the Cornish people:

Nevertheless, the old race is still revealed, a race which believed in the darkness, in magic, and in the magic transcendency of one man over another, which is fascinating. Also there is left some of the old sensuousness of the darkness, a sort of softness, a sort of flowing together in physical intimacy, something almost negroid, which is fascinating.

But curse them, they are mindless, and yet they are living purely for social advancement. They ought to be living in the darkness and warmth and passionateness of the blood, sudden, incalculable. Whereas they are like insects gone cold, living only for money, for *dirt*. They are foul in this. They ought all to die.[78]

The rant over, Lawrence added sheepishly: 'Not that I've seen very much of them—I've been laid up in bed. But going out, in the motor and so on, one sees them and knows what they are like'. Yet behind his anguish, as Lawrence well knew, was the war. 'The cursed war will go on for ever', he told Beresford, admitting the real source of his anger.[79]

It was a bubbling rage, liable to surface at any time. Three weeks later, Lawrence was again writing to Beresford, railing in even stronger terms against the Cornish:

> I don't like these people here. They have got the souls of insects. One feels, if they were squashed, they would be a whitey mess, like when a black-beetle is squashed. They are all *afraid*—that's why they are all so mean. But I don't really understand them. Only I know this, I have never in my life come across such innerly selfish people, neither French, German, Italian, Swiss, nor English. I have thought French peasants vile, like hedge-hogs, hedge-pigs. But these people haven't any *being* at all. They've got no inside.[80]

He had been down to Zennor, further west, to view a cottage he thought he might rent when the tenancy at Porthcothan expired, and was prepared to admit that the locals there could be better:

> There are very few at Zennor, and they seem decent. I like Emma [the housekeeper] still. But when we were nice to her, she only became more greedy: she never did anything for us in return. One has to keep them down. They are just like all the rest of people who have no real *being*, but only a static ego, they are a very bottomless pit, if one was to pour any kindness into them. The only thing to do is to use them strictly as servants, inferiors: for they have the souls of slaves, like Aesop.[81]

Beatrice Beresford, J.D.'s wife, seems to have been offended by Lawrence's outburst, and soon a somewhat chastened Lawrence was writing again, to recant and, in his way, to apologize:

You are quite right about the people ... I wrote in a fit of irritation at them, they all seemed so *greedy*. But it is true, there is in them, as I felt at first, a very beautiful softness and gentleness, quite missing in English people nowadays. And really, I am, we are all *very fond* of Emma ... I like her presence in the house: which is saying something. I like her very much, in fact.[82]

Rananim deferred

Meanwhile, Philip Heseltine was already having second thoughts about Lawrence and Rananim. Alongside the personality clashes that had become apparent at Porthcothan, the dread fear of conscription, and the alarming effect of war and illness on Lawrence's moods was a growing disaffection with the utopian project. Heseltine confided to Delius that 'I don't want to identify with him [Lawrence] in anything beyond his desire for an ampler and fuller life ... He is a very great artist, but hard and autocratic in his views and outlook, and his artistic canons I find utterly and entirely unsympathetic to my nature.' He conceded that Lawrence was 'an arresting figure, a great and attractive personality, and his passion for a new, clean, untrammelled life is very splendid'. Nonetheless, he 'seems to be too metaphysical, too anxious to be comprehensive in a detached way and to care too little for purely personal, analytical, and introspective art'.[83]

Cornwall, too, aroused mixed emotions, despite the initial impressions of affinity. 'It is a wild, open country of vast expanses', he told Delius; 'on the stormy coast the winds blow through and through one from mid-Atlantic, and the waves surge and thunder and break right over the cliffs, and the spray falls on one's face with a chill, cleansing moisture'.[84] Yet the 'Cornish coast is strange and sinister', he added, the topography singular and disorienting:

All the roads, for some curious reason, are cut very deep down in the rock, below the field level, and on the rock, at the level of the field, grows the high hedge of evergreen tamarisk, so that one is always overshadowed. On the uplands, there are scarcely any shrubs or trees; the hedges are replaced by stone walls built in an intricate and very beautiful herring-bone pattern. It is all stark and elemental, rather cheerless and repelling if one wanted to assimilate with it, identify oneself with it, but for a while invigorating, cleansing—essentially a country for deliberation at a turning-point rather than for settled work.[85]

'While this war lasts', he added, Cornwall was a bolthole: 'one feels that "sauve qui peut" is the only possible rule of life—if one does not want to throw one's life away'. But in the end Lawrence proved too much, and Heseltine went back to London, informing his friend Robert Nichols: 'I am not returning to Lawrence; he has no real sympathy. All he likes in one is the potential convert to his own reactionary creed. I believe firmly that he is a fine thinker and a consummate artist, but personal relationship with him is almost impossible.'[86] The first attempt at Rananim was already at an end.

Andrew Harrison has cast a critical, sceptical eye over Lawrence's short time at Porthcothan. For Harrison, Cornwall was only ever 'a makeshift America' in Lawrence's estimation, a first step on the road to Florida, while Lawrence's '"Cornwall" was a fantasy created out of mythology, nurtured through his selective reading of pre-Christian historical and literary sources, and indulged time and again in his letters.' Additionally, according to Harrison, Lawrence's letters indicated 'the fragility of his Cornish fantasy', not least in his wildly contradictory opinions of the Cornish people themselves.[87]

However, such a view pays scant attention to the wider impact on Lawrence of contemporary imaginings of Cornwall, including the Cornish-Celtic Revival, in which Lawrence was not alone in his 'fantasy' but drew upon a broad spectrum of ideas and beliefs current at the time. Moreover, Lawrence had been enamoured with Cornwall since at least 1910 (as Harrison acknowledges), when he first thought of moving there, and would remain so in the years ahead, a deep nostalgia that would find full expression in Australia in his novel *Kangaroo*.

Chapter 4

Rananim Regained? Lawrence at Zennor

Philip Heseltine's sudden departure from Porthcothan had brought Lawrence's utopian project to an at least temporary halt. Yet Lawrence and Frieda were already searching for a new home in Cornwall, somewhere to keep the project alive, now that their tenure at Porthcothan was coming to an end. Despite his earlier vacillations and inconsistencies, Lawrence wanted desperately to remain in Cornwall, or so he insisted to J.D. Beresford, to whom he wrote meekly on 1 February 1916. 'I should like to stay in Cornwall', he admitted, 'I like it so much. We might afford a cottage, I think ... [but] we are very badly off'.[1]

'When I looked down on Zennor, I knew it was the Promised Land'

As Lawrence cast around for somewhere new to live, and to revive his Rananim adventure afresh, the overwhelming temptation was to head still further west, towards the sun and the Atlantic and America, away from England and into the yet more remote Celtic fastness of the West Penwith peninsula. On 24 February, Lawrence wrote in upbeat mood to his friends John ('Jack') Middleton Murry and Katherine Mansfield (the 'Murrys') to say that he and Frieda had found somewhere: 'It is about 7 miles from St Ives, towards Land's End, very lonely, in the rocks on the sea, Zennor the nearest village: high pale hills, all moor-like and beautiful ... very wild'. It was a wonderful spot, he said: 'Primroses and violets are out, and the gorse is lovely. At Zennor one sees infinite Atlantic, all peacock-mingled colours, and the gorse is sunshine itself'.[2]

Here, indeed, was the prospect of Rananim regained. As Lawrence exclaimed, still in a state of wonder, 'when I looked down on Zennor, I knew it was the Promised Land, and that a new heaven and a new earth would take place ... I have a sense of a new spring coming very joyful from the unknown.'[3] It was a theme he repeated shortly after to Ottoline Morrell: 'When we came down over the shoulder of the wild hill, above the sea, to Zennor, I felt we were coming into the Promised Land. I know there will be a new heaven and a new earth ... we have triumphed. I feel like a Columbus who can see a shadowy America before him'. Zennor would be, he said, 'a new continent of the soul. We will be happy yet, doing a new, constructive work, sailing into a new epoch'.[4]

Such were the high hopes of Rananim renewed. Staying initially at the Tinners' Arms in Zennor, while their cottage at nearby Higher Tregerthen was made ready, Lawrence wrote enthusiastically to the Murrys, whom he hoped to recruit as the latest initiates for his utopian project, explaining on 5 March that 'We have been here nearly a week now. It is a most beautiful place: a tiny granite village nestling under high, shaggy moor-hills, and a big sweep of lovely sea beyond, such a lovely sea, lovelier even than the Mediterranean.' The countryside around Zennor 'is all gorse now, flickering with flower; and then it will be heather; and then, hundreds of fox gloves'. It was, he concluded, 'the best place I have been in, I think'.[5]

Zennor Churchtown, 'a tiny village nestling under high, shaggy moor hills'.

Rananim Regained? Lawrence at Zennor

These were vivid first impressions that never left Lawrence, and which he repeated in *Kangaroo*, his semi-autobiographical novel, penned in Australia in 1922, where he recalled how at Zennor 'the Cornish night would gradually come down upon the dark, shaggy moors, that were like the fur of some beast, and upon the pale-grey granite masses, so ancient and Druidical'.[6] And 'Cornish night' would be followed by a 'Cornish, magic morning', where walkers savouring the daybreak Zennor air 'passed the stony little huddle of the church-town, and on up the hill, where the great granite boulders shoved out the land, and the barrenness was ancient and inviolable'. Here they might 'see the gulls under the big cliffs beyond' or watch 'a buzzard circling over the marshy place below church-town'.[7]

It was a pristine, seemingly timeless landscape, where Lawrence felt close to the ancient Celtic civilization of his imagination. In *Kangaroo* he would evoke this sense of personal intimacy and the seductive atmosphere of Zennor and surrounding West Penwith. Here, at last, he thought, was the essence of Celtic Cornwall. In *Kangaroo*, he has Richard Lovat Somers, his alter ego, contemplate the

> twilight, awesome world of the previous Celts. The spirit of the ancient, pre-Christian world, which lingers still in the truly Celtic places ... The old Celtic countries never had our Latin Teutonic consciousness, never will have. They have never been Christian, in the blue-eyed, or even in the truly Roman, Latin sense of the world. But they have been overlaid by our consciousness and our civilization, smouldering underneath in a slow, eternal fire.[8]

And as Lawrence wrote in *Kangaroo*:

> Cornwall is a country that makes a man psychic. The longer he stayed, the more intensely it had that effect on Somers. It was if he were developing second sight, and second hearing. He would go out into the blackness of night and listen to the blackness, and call, call softly, for the spirits, the presences he felt coming downhill from the moors in the night. 'Tuatha Dé Danann!' he would call softly [invoking the pre-Christian Celtic gods of Irish mythology]. 'Tuatha Dé Danann! Be with me. Be with me'. And it was as if he felt them come.[9]

Here in this dramatic Celtic landscape, as Lawrence imagined it, were intimations of what he would call 'blood consciousness', something deeper and more intuitive than ordinary mental consciousness. He had mused on the possibilities of blood consciousness before coming to Cornwall but it was at Zennor that his ideas crystallized.[10] As Jane Costin has observed, it was here at Zennor that Lawrence decided that 'landscape ... has the power, concentrated in its rocks, to alter consciousness and to reawaken latent blood-consciousness', a realization that also affirmed for him the 'strong connection between blood-consciousness and the primitive'.[11] In *Kangaroo*, Lawrence explains how Somers, in awe of the Celtic landscape, had drifted 'into a sort of blood darkness', feeling 'in his blood the thrill and presences of the old moorland dusk', and taking up 'in his veins again the savage vibrations that still lingered round the secret rocks, the place of pre-christian human sacrifice ... he could feel his dark, blood-consciousness tingle to it again, the desire of it, the mystery of it'.[12]

'Here Beauty slumbers in the lap of Terror'

For all Lawrence's imaginings, fanciful or otherwise, Zennor, then as now, presented an arresting landscape and seascape, at once unique but at the same time exemplifying all the attributes that made Cornwall itself so distinctive. Concentrated into one relatively small area, Zennor possessed in abundance all the features that, in popular estimation, made Cornwall 'Cornish' and 'Celtic'. By the turn of the twentieth century, the Romantic movement had at last arrived in Cornwall, so what had been considered a bleak, dreary country, disfigured by mining, and with a fearsome, dangerous coastline, had been transformed into something infinitely alluring. And if this was so for Cornwall as a whole, then it was especially true for Zennor and West Penwith. John Hobson Matthews caught this changing mood in the preface to his *History of the Parishes of St Ives, Lelant, Towednack, and Zennor*, published in 1892, where he reproduced some 'Lines on "A Scene in West Cornwall"' by J.M. Tinney, only recently published in the *Cornishman* newspaper:

>No leafy crown may poor Cornwall wear,
>Wind-swept from sea to sea her cairns outstand: Stranger
>   away! No charm detaineth here—
>   Only brown heath, low wood, and level sand.
>
>But there between, unseen by passer-by,
>   May hidden nook and faery dell be found,

> Lovelier because unlooked for: gems, they lie
>   In summer beauty, consecrated ground.
>
> So human nature, often poorly shows
>   To level eyes, when from the height above
> Surveyed, may mirror beauty of its own,
>   Kind Heaven will deign to pity and to love.[13]

Not all shared in this Cornish reawakening. W.H. Hudson, for example, unstinting critic of the Cornish as he was (see pp. 28–30) and author of *The Land's End*, published in 1908, visited Zennor in the depth of winter, when, even as rainwater froze in pools, relentless winds fanned the brush fires that had broken out on the heights. 'I went out to Zennor Hill', he wrote, 'to see the sun set from the top and watch the big furze and heath fires which were burning far and wide on the moor'. At the summit, he said, as 'I tried to shelter myself from the fury of the wind among the large black masses of granite, the scene I looked upon was exceedingly desolate. The brown moor stretched away inland, lonely and dark, to the horizon.' But the heath fires had a certain fascination, 'yellow flames running before the wind and leaping a dozen to twenty yards high', while the 'sun seen through the vast clouds of dun smoke had the appearance of a globe of fiery red copper'. And as the sun set, 'the earth began to darken, the smoke took an intense orange colour from the flames, which seen against the pale blue sky gave a dreadful magnificence to the scene'.[14]

Perhaps, then, even waspish Hudson was not immune to the sublime majesty of Zennor. By the time A.G. Folliott-Stokes' *The Cornish Coast and Moors* appeared in 1912 (a book dedicated 'To all who feel the Witchery of the West'), such awe had become de rigueur for those visitors to the far west come to sample its 'unique aesthetic value'. But even Folliott-Stokes admitted that 'Here Beauty slumbers in the lap of Terror', visitors encountering an agreeable frisson of faux danger which many found arousing as well as attractive.[15] To this was added that 'England may be said to terminate on the shores of the Tamar', the Cornish themselves being, he said, 'a race still in many ways as distinct from the English as the Bretons are from the French'.[16] Folliott-Stokes lived at St Ives, close to Zennor, and considered that the 'Penwith highlands are the most arresting of Cornwall's uplands … Nowhere else in the "Delectable Duchy" will you find a grander coastline, a wilder more picturesque moorland, or such a wealth of pre-historic villages, cromlechs and stone circles. This is the *sanctum sanctorum* of the Cornish Celts'.[17]

In purple prose that might be said to have anticipated Lawrence's own effusive musings in *Kangaroo*, Folliott-Stokes wrote of West Penwith:

> Here you will find him [the Cornish Celt] still clinging to his granite hills, still listening to the song of the sea and the moan of the moorland wind. The same dreaming, mystic creatures as his forefathers who reared these mighty cromlechs, whose massive outlines still so impressively cut the sky-line of the hills, and beside which our oldest cathedrals are but of yesterday. Nor can one wonder if his heart is still somewhat tinged with phantasy.[18]

Alongside such flights of fancy, Folliott-Stokes offered an illuminating pen-picture of Zennor parish, sketching its topography and capturing its defining features. Thus, at Zennor Head:

> we suddenly see beneath us Pendour Cove, a spot so wild and beautiful, and presenting such vivid contrasts of colour, that we shall not be likely to forget it for many a long day. Three hundred feet below, between huge buttresses of rock, the Atlantic comes stealing like a smelted sapphire; and as it shallows the sapphire changes into emerald-green of crystal purity. Before descending we will make our way, through the heath and dwarf furze, to the boulders on the summit of the head, and look around.[19]

To the south, Folliott-Stokes explained, was the rock-strewn summit of Zennor Hill, and then 'the long ridge of Trewey Hill', and in the distance 'the jagged silhouette of Carn Galva, the finest of all these moorland heights'. To the west, he continued, 'couchant upon the sea like some mythical monster asleep in the path of the sun, is the Gurnard's Head; while nearer to us, across the cove, rises the shapely Carnellow cliff. To the north stretches the Atlantic dotted with passing ships. It is a picture conceived in noble lines, and painted with some of Nature's strongest colours.'[20] In Zennor village itself, the 'church tower rises across the road; the Vicarage, school, and a couple more houses on our right. These constitute "Churchtown"'.[21]

The 'Crankan Rhyme'

This, then, was the prospect that had awaited Lawrence and Frieda as they travelled westwards to Zennor in early 1916, just a few years after Folliott-Stokes had crafted his fulsome account. To this astonishing physical environment, deemed the ultimate milieu of the 'Cornish Celt', a reading echoed before long by Lawrence himself in *Kangaroo*, was added tantalizing evidence of the recent survival of the Cornish language in the locality. Zennor place names, overwhelmingly, were in Cornish, especially in its Late or Modern form, as it was last spoken as a vernacular in Cornwall: Bosporthennis, for example, meaning 'the dwelling at the island cove', or Cartreve, 'the fortified farm', or Chykembro, 'the Welshman's house'.[22] So too field names: Broaz ('large'), Hallangear ('moor of the fort'), Park Cludgie ('lazar-house field').[23] For the sensitive or inquisitive observer, such as Lawrence, the historical proximity of the Cornish language and its visibility in the landscape enhanced the already heightened 'Celticity' and 'otherness' of West Penwith.

Dolly Pentreath, the Mousehole fishwife who died in 1777, was reckoned to be the last fluent native speaker of Cornish, although she was survived by others with a knowledge of the language, notably William Bodinar (died 1789), who had learnt the tongue going to sea with elderly fishermen. Edward Lhuyd, the Celtic philologist, published his *Archaeologia Britannica* in 1707, and listed the parishes in which the Cornish language was still spoken, clustered as they were in the West Penwith peninsula and along the coast from Land's End to St Keverne on the Lizard. This heartland, if it can be called such, included Zennor and the neighbouring parishes of Morvah, Madron and Towednack.[24]

Henry Jenner in his *A Handbook of the Cornish Language*, published in 1904, traced the subsequent retreat of Cornish and its apparent confinement to Mount's Bay, around Newlyn, Paul and Dolly Pentreath's Mousehole. However, Jenner also noted that John Hobson Matthews had included 'an interesting chapter on Cornish' in his *History of the Parishes of St Ives, Lelant, Towednack, and Zennor*, in which he had given 'reasons for supposing that the language survived in St Ives, Zennor, and Towednack even longer than in Mount's Bay'.[25] Matthews, indeed, had argued that 'the wild uplands of Towednack and Zennor were no doubt very late in exchanging the Celtic speech of their inhabitants for the all-conquering idiom of the Saxon'. In particular, he singled out the families of Stevens and Trewhella, 'among the last to keep up the Cornish language in the parish of Towednack'.[26] Both families were also well represented in neighbouring Zennor and its environs, including in Lawrence's time.

Intriguingly, Matthews had also observed that in 'the year 1890 there was still living at Boswednack, in Zennor, an old man named John Davy [or Davey], who had some hereditary knowledge of Cornish. He knew the meanings of the place-names round about, and could converse on a few simple topics in the ancient language'.[27] Jenner repeated the claim in his own book but, despite his desire to track down and celebrate every last remnant of Cornish, he was somewhat sceptical. Unless Matthews, 'whose judgement one would trust in such a matter', had actually heard Davey speaking Cornish, the 'statement is not easy to believe', he opined.[28] Jenner's reluctance was all the more remarkable given that he and Matthews had much in common and were clearly well acquainted with one another. Although Matthews was born in Croydon, near London, his father hailed from St Ives. Matthews was proud of his Cornish credentials, and learnt Cornish and Welsh, becoming a bard of the Welsh Gorsedd (as Jenner did), taking the bardic name Mab Cernyw, 'Son of Cornwall'. He was also a Catholic, which would have commended him to Jenner. Unfortunately, Davey died in 1891, before Matthews' volume was published, so Jenner was in no position to verify personally the veracity or otherwise of the book's assertions.

Jenner's doubts were amplified by John Westlake, a native of Lostwithiel in East Cornwall, who had a summer home at Eagle's Nest in Zennor. Westlake was Professor of International Law at Cambridge, and took an informed interest in all things Cornish. In his notebook, he recorded that Davey had provided him with many unusual dialect words still extant in the parish, and had taught him to count from one to twenty in Cornish, allegedly from traditional knowledge. But, Westlake concluded, there was no wider evidence that Davey could converse in Cornish or had an extensive knowledge of the language.[29]

It may also be significant that John Davey had in his possession a copy of William Pryce's *Archaeologia Cornu-Britannica*, published in 1790, which Davey had inherited from his father. Pryce's work included a Cornish vocabulary and grammar, so it possible that Davey had memorized parts of the book. In other words, his knowledge of the language, such as it was, may have been learnt rather than traditional. Even so, Davey's keen interest in the language—and in the Cornish dialect of English in Zennor, with its

Rananim Regained? Lawrence at Zennor

many unusual words—was in itself compelling evidence of the historical closeness of Cornish, of a folk memory of the language being spoken in the parish in recent times by local families. As Henry Jenner put it, 'the memory of it lingers on' and 'even if the spoken Cornish be dead, its ghost still haunts its old dwelling'.[30]

Perhaps the most authentic illustration of this folk memory came from Davey himself. Alongside his ability to count in Cornish, and to utter a few phrases in the language (even if lifted from Pryce) was his 'Crankan Rhyme', which he had learnt from his father. Despite his own knowledge of Cornish and his proficiency in the language, John Hobson Matthews could make nothing of the rhyme and dismissed it as 'a mere jumble of placenames':

> A grankan, a grankan,
> A mean a gowaz o vean;
> Ondez parc an venton,
> Dub trelowa vean.
> Far Penzans a Maragow
> Githack mackwee,
> A githack macrow,
> A mac trelowza varrack.[31]

Robert Morton Nance, however, recognized Cornish content and idiom in the rhyme that went beyond the obvious place names, and offered his own conjectural reconstruction in Unified Cornish, his revived version of medieval Cornish. According to Nance, Davey's rhyme, suitably unscrambled, could be rendered as:

> A Grankan, A Grankan,
> War'n men ny-gefough saw byghan
> Hons es Park an Fenten
> A-dhek try lows a ven
> Forth Pensans ha Marghas-Yow,
> Hag uthek moy cryf
> Hag uthek moy cro,
> A-vak try lows a varghak.

This, in turn, could be translated into English:

> O Crankan, O Crankan,
> On the rock you will find but little
> Further than the Well Field
> That bears three shoots for each stone.
> The Penzance and Market Jew [Marazion] Road
> Both vastly more green
> And vastly more fresh,
> Rears three shoots for each horseman.[32]

The rhyme, it seems, is a weak joke, comparing the barren nature of the rocky fields at Crankan, a nearby farm, with the relative fertility of the road to Penzance and Marazion. What is significant, however, is not the mild humour but rather that the rhyme itself is surely evidence of traditional knowledge of the Cornish language. The 'Crankan Rhyme' does not appear in Pryce, nor in any other Cornish document, and is thus original rather than derivative. Even if John Davey did not fully understand its content or meaning, the rhyme was nonetheless on his lips at Zennor in the closing decade of the nineteenth century, a fragment of traditionally acquired Cornish.

John Hobson Matthews' suggestion that Davey could 'converse on a few simple topics' prompts the question, with whom? Rod Lyon's recent forensic examination of those individuals in the locality who may have had at least a smattering of Cornish throws up some intriguing possibilities. John Mann, for instance, interviewed aged eighty at his home in St Just-in-Penwith in 1914 by one John Hall, insisted that when he was young he and other children always talked in Cornish as they played at Boswednack, Zennor, where Davey had lived and died.[33] The evidence is circumstantial rather than documentary, and worthy of further research, but it supports Matthews' contention that Zennor and surrounding parishes *were* perhaps the last home of spoken Cornish.

How much of this Lawrence knew is also conjecture. But, as we have seen (p. 47), he had admitted his own 'Celtic vision', and had sought books on Celtic literature and history. He had also acknowledged the influence of Katharine Lee Jenner (née Rawlings), wife of Henry Jenner, the Cornish-language enthusiast, adopting *her* symbol of the phoenix resurgent as the defining emblem for his own Rananim. Equally significantly, Henry Jenner's *A Handbook of the Cornish Language* had been published at the 'Sign of the Phoenix', which he took optimistically as a metaphor for the rise of the

Cornish-Celtic movement. It seems more than likely that Lawrence was familiar with the *Handbook*, from which Philip Heseltine had presumably learnt his Cornish, and he was aware too that Heseltine was putting Henry Jenner's compositions to music. For Heseltine, the revival of the Cornish language had been integral to the Rananim project, as Lawrence understood and appreciated.

'Mermaid of Zennor'

Lawrence relished this new milieu, writing excitedly to Catherine Carswell that, at Zennor, 'in this queer outlandish *Celtic* country, I feel fundamentally happy and free'.[34] Distance from England's reach, as he saw it, underscored this sense of freedom. But immersion in the alternative culture of Celtic Cornwall was an antidote to his own anxieties as well as to England's ills. His long-standing interest in 'Celtic symbolism' also extended to folkloric motifs, which in Zennor were aplenty.

Lawrence was fascinated, for example, by stories of the Phoenicians in Cornwall, part pre-history and part legend, which in his own mind fused 'Celtic symbolism' with the cultures of 'the East', reflecting his own enthusiasms and those of Kitty Lee Jenner whose writings on the subject he had absorbed (see pp. 46–7). It was a fascination that would lead, as Jane Costin has observed, to Lawrence's preoccupation with the ancient pathway that led directly from his cottage at Higher Tregerthen to Zennor Churchtown, the quickest way of walking to the village, which he used frequently during his stay. The path was part of a much longer track that ran from the mining country around Pendeen to the harbour at St Ives, which Lawrence imagined was connected to the Phoenicians and their presumed tin-trading presence in Cornwall.

This track was first constructed by prehistoric farmers, crossing their small fields and passing through gaps in the stone-walled Cornish hedges. Later, from the ninth century, the way was marked by wheel-headed Cornish crosses (of which today only a few survive in situ) and possibly menhirs (standing stones). The erection of granite crosses marked the Christianization of the way but, according to Jane Costin, it was its older significance that 'convinced [Lawrence] of the spiritual importance of this place'.[35] Here again were intimations of 'blood consciousness', of the entwinement of the landscape and the primitive, and of something ancient, mysterious and

Higher Tregerthen, Lawrence and Frieda's cottage at Zennor.

perhaps sinister. As Jane Costin has mused, Lawrence seemed alive to the folkloric connotations of the track:

> Local folklore identifies this as a path used by a shape-changing witch but there is now [in 2012] a strong resistance to the idea that previous generations may have considered it a route for evil spirits. However, this denial raised many questions. Why has an ancient farmhouse that straddles the pathway been known for centuries as Wicca? Why is the adjoining hamlet, where Lawrence lived, called Tregerthen, the Cornish word for rowan tree? Previous generations considered rowan trees a powerful antidote to witches but they are rarely found in this gale-swept landscape. And why, in 1833, did a group of Bible Christians, a movement noted for confronting the devil in all its forms, choose to build a chapel in this remote location between Wicca and Tregerthen—across the pathway—forcing it to deviate?[36]

There were also intriguing local stories of giants, like Holiburn, who 'loved to dwell amongst the rocks of Carn Galva', and tales of the 'small people', such as the fairy child visited upon a poor unsuspecting woman at

Rananim Regained? Lawrence at Zennor

Zennor Hill, and 'old Mary Colineck of Zennor' who discovered that a girl missing from the village had been abducted by the fairies. Similar was the story of 'Cherry of Zennor', who was likewise enticed away by the small people. Witches abounded, it being said that to become a witch one must climb 'on the Giant's Rock at Zennor Church-town' without moving it, no mean feat as it was a logan stone, which would rock at the slightest touch. Zennor was also the place 'where at Midsummer all the witches of the west met'. Numbered among them was the witch of Treva, 'a hamlet in Zennor, a wonderful old lady skilled in necromancy ... [whose] charms, spells, and dark incantations made her the terror of the neighbourhood'. All these stories and more were recorded by the antiquarian Robert Hunt, his collection first published in 1865 and republished periodically thereafter, including in 1908, the edition extant when Lawrence was in Zennor.[37]

The most powerful of these folkloric motifs was the Zennor mermaid. According to Ronald M. James, the folklorist, the '"Mermaid of Zennor" stands alone when compared to folklore from Ireland, Scandinavia and other parts of Britain', its peculiar attributes reinforcing 'the idea that it is possible to define a unique ecotype for the larger body of Cornish oral tradition that is linked to but nevertheless distinct within the realm of northern European folklore'.[38] Here again, the salience of Zennor in Cornish tradition is clear.

The story of the 'Mermaid of Zennor' was 'well-known',[39] as Ronald M. James acknowledged, and by the early twentieth century had been popularized in tourist literature, not least by the Great Western Railway in its publicity booklet *Legend Land*. 'Carved on one of the pews in the church of Zennor in West Cornwall', the booklet explained, 'is a strange figure of a mermaid. Depicted with flowing hair, a mirror in one hand and a comb in the other, the Zennor folk tell a strange story about her.'[40] The Zennor Church guide offers one such telling, where it is explained:

> In the side chapel is the famous Mermaid Chair. Two bench ends preserved from the restoration of 1890 form the sides of the chair. The legend tells how a beautiful woman in a long dress used to sit at the back of the church listening to the singing of the chorister, Matthew Trewhella. One evening she succeeded in luring him to the little stream which runs through the village. Together they went down the stream and into the sea at Pendour Cove, now known as the Mermaid's Cove. It is said that if you listen carefully on a warm summer's night you can hear the pair of lovers singing together.[41]

Perhaps significantly, H.G. Wells had in 1902 published his novel *The Sea Lady*. In a plot that mirrors the Mermaid of Zennor, a beautiful mermaid comes ashore and succeeds in seducing young Harry Chatteris, who is on the verge of a successful career in politics. Like Matthew Trewhella, Harry Chatteris disappears beneath the waves with his mermaid, leaving behind his fiancée, family and career ambitions. Desire triumphs over duty, as does adventure in the face of society's staid norms and expectations. It is a resolution of which Wells, as author, heartily approves.[42] And, as Elise Ruthenbeck has pointed out, Harry Chatteris's decision, echoing as it does the Cornish legend and the lure of the sea, anticipates Lawrence's own bold search for Rananim in Cornwall.[43] *The Sea Lady* had been serialized in *Pearson's Magazine* in July–December 1901, where the youthful D.H. Lawrence may well have seen it.

Later, when exploring Zennor parish, Lawrence would have entered the church—unlocked, then as now—and found the mermaid bench-end. The story of Matthew ('Mathey') Trewhella was common knowledge in Zennor, and perhaps reminded Lawrence of H.G. Wells's mermaid novel. Certainly, Lawrence was sufficiently enthused by the Mermaid of Zennor to deploy the surname Trewhella in his novel *Kangaroo* in the character Jaz Trewhella, a Cornish immigrant in Australia, one drawn 'down under' rather than 'down under the waves'.

William James Trewhella, to give Jaz his formal name in *Kangaroo*, has been in Australia since the age of fifteen, having emigrated from Cornwall with his brother. Subsequently, his brother died and Jaz has married his widow, taking responsibility for his brother's daughter but also inheriting his property, St Columb (a resoundingly Cornish name). Contrasting his lot with the destitution of his early life in Cornwall, Jaz considers that he has done well in Australia, where he is now comfortably off. Richard Lovat Somers, however, takes issue with Jaz's materialistic view of the world, insinuating that he has abandoned his Celtic heritage. 'You know Cornwall, do you?', responds Jaz accusingly, 'the Cornish singsong still evident in his Australian speech'.[44] Somers (for which, of course, read Lawrence) explains that he had lived there for a time, and together Jaz and Somers 'talked for a while of the bleak northern coast of Cornwall, the huge black cliffs, with the gulls flying away below, and the sea boiling, and the wind blowing in huge volleys: and the black Cornish nights, with nothing but the violent weather outside'.[45]

For Jaz, it is not a pleasant memory. 'Oh, I remember it, I remember it', he says, 'Though I was a half-starved youngster on a bit of a farm out there, for everlasting chasing half a dozen heifers from the cliffs, where the beggars wanted to fall over and kill themselves, and hunting for a dozen sheep among the gorse-bushes, and wading up to my knees in mud'.[46] Somers interjects: 'But there was a great fascination for me, in Cornwall.'[47] 'Fascination!', retorts Jaz: 'And where do you find fascination? In a little Wesleyan chapel of a Sunday night, and a girl with her father waiting for her with a strap if she's not home by nine o'clock? Fascination, did you say?'[48] But Somers is adamant: 'It had a great fascination for me—a magic—a magic in the atmosphere.'[49] And so the conversation continues:

'All the fairy tales they'll tell you ... Why ye didn't go and believe them, did ye?'
'More or less. I could more easily have believed them there than anywhere else I've been.'
'Ay, no doubt. And that shows what sort of a place it be. Lot of damn silly nonsense.'[50]

However, for all his distancing from Cornwall and embrace of Australia, Jaz Trewhella, as David Game has observed, 'is fundamentally an outsider in Australian society'. He betrays an 'underlying Celtic sensibility', as Game puts it.[51] In the typical Cousin Jack way, Jaz fosters links with other migrants from Cornwall, cultivating a clannishness in which the Cornish look out for one another. As Jack, another character in *Kangaroo*, explains: 'He's got one or two Cornish pals down town, you see—they tip one another the wink. They're like the Irish in many ways.'[52] Jaz will never really be at home in demotic Australia, it seems, and the narrator in *Kangaroo* senses that the 'Celt needs the mystic glow of real kingliness. Hence his [Jaz Trewhella's] loneliness in the democratic world of industry, and his social perversity.'[53] Additionally, despite (or even because of) his exile in distant Australia, Jaz personifies the inherent contradiction Lawrence had detected in the Cornish—heirs of a majestic Celtic tradition but immersed now in a hidebound and narrowing Nonconformist utilitarianism.

Jaz Trewhella deplored the Cornish 'fairy tales' that Somers (and Lawrence) professed to more than half-believe, but his experience in Australia mirrors that of his namesake, 'Mathey' Trewhella, in the 'Mermaid of Zennor' story. In the latter, the listener or reader is asked to accept that Matthew and his mermaid lover are content in their underwater world, singing harmoniously together on summer evenings, but there is the lingering, unsettling knowledge that Matthew has been snatched irrevocably from his natural habitat and his grieving family. Is he really happy? Likewise, Jaz Trewhella, despite his protestations that he is a success in Australia, has been unceremoniously uprooted from his native Cornwall where, *Kangaroo*'s narrator contends, his spirit really belongs.

'The advocate of every oppressed nationality'

For all his immersion in the Celtic mythos of Zennor and West Penwith, Lawrence was not the only one attracted to the locality by this intense sense of place and 'otherness'. As Alison Symons put it in her memoir *Tremedda Days: A View of Zennor, 1900–1944*, there was a 'fraternity of artistic-minded folk who were drawn to Zennor like moths to a candle, trying to capture some of the wild grandeur in words, music or paint'.[54] Or, as the Cornish put it, Cornwall was shaped like a Christmas stocking, 'and all the nuts go to the toe'.[55] A periodic visitor before the Great War, for example, was Alfred Munnings, one of Britain's finest painters of horses. A member of the Newlyn School of artists from 1912 until 1914, Munnings would bring his horse over to Zennor to paint it amidst the wild landscape, paying local boys two pence a time to hold the animal while he worked at his easel.[56] Such visits were cut short by the suicide in July 1914 of his wife, Florence Carter-Wood, another artist and equine enthusiast, after which Munnings changed direction and became a distinguished war artist. Like Lawrence (pp. 110–11), Munnings had been medically examined 'in the dreary barracks at Bodmin' (as he termed it) but, being blind in one eye, was declared exempt from military service.[57] Undeterred, he put his name forward and was duly selected as official artist to the Canadian Cavalry Brigade, painting Canadian soldiers and their mounts in the battlefields of France.

Years later, Munnings, reflecting on his time in Cornwall, wrote that 'Cornish people were used to artists. It was the home of artists, and everybody understood their ways.'[58] On occasion, travelling over from Lamorna, he would sojourn at Zennor, lodging with Mrs Griggs and being loaned a stable by Mr Berryman, a 'hefty, six-foot Cornish farmer'.[59] He also remembered the landscapes that formed the backdrop of his paintings: 'a wild, almost treeless, stone-walled country, with dairy cows grazing everywhere', a 'chess-board of fields and walls rising to a group of farms where a narrow lane wound its way through labyrinths of irregular, rough-built stone walls enclosing tiny grass fields'.[60] In the midst of this Cornish countryside, Munnings cut an eccentric figure, with his artist's paraphernalia and formal attire, a source of good-natured amusement for local people.

More intriguing still was the novelist Ranger Gull, who wrote under the nom de plume Guy Thorne. When staying at Zennor, Gull was reputed to drink a bottle of whisky a day, following which he 'wrote until one or two in the morning. The next day he was "very bad" until he started on the bottle again'.[61] As the Great War approached, Gull became increasingly interested in the possibilities of submarine warfare, a fascination given full vent in his novel *The Secret Service Submarine: A Story of the Present War*, published in 1915.[62] His foresight was uncannily prescient, as we shall see in Chapter 5. Edward 'Eddy' Sackville-West, the novelist and music critic, a member of Ottoline Morrell's Garsington circle (and therefore possibly known to Lawrence), was another Zennor habitué, as was Maisie Gay, the popular Edwardian comic actress and singer. And so it went on.

Such sojourners were 'foreigners', as the Cornish deemed them, but John Westlake was both 'insider' and 'outsider', born at Lostwithiel in 1828 and later a senior Cambridge academic and briefly a Liberal politician. He was Cornish by both birth and inclination but was also integral to the metropolitan elite, an unusual combination. From 1900 to 1906, for example, Westlake was the United Kingdom representative on the International Court of Arbitration at The Hague, following its foundation in 1900. Among his principal publications were *International Law Part 1: Peace* (1904) and *International Law Part 2: War* (1913), key deliberations in the deteriorating international climate that led to the outbreak of the Great War in 1914. He also enjoyed something of a left-wing reputation. As well as being a progressive Liberal, he was sympathetic to the Christian Socialist movement, and married Alice Hare, the artist and women's suffrage campaigner.[63]

Westlake was especially supportive of the Balkan peoples and their aspirations for self-government, not least during the bloody Balkan wars, serving on the Liberal-supported Balkan Committee from 1905 until his death in 1913. He considered that the Ottoman Empire's behaviour in the region had placed it beyond the normal bounds of civilization, and opined that the 'Sultan ... has lost all claim to be regarded as a ruler to whom international law should apply'.[64] As Norman Bentwich was to observe, Westlake's championship of Balkan independence extended to his wider sympathy for the rights of small nations. Westlake, according to Bentwich, was 'the advocate of every oppressed nationality'.[65]

It seems unlikely that Westlake considered the Cornish an 'oppressed nationality'. However, as we have seen, he was a Cornish enthusiast, with a great interest in the Cornish language (he befriended John Davey of Boswednack), and did much to focus attention on Zennor parish, his adopted home. In 1873 he purchased Eagle's Nest, a small house high on the slopes of Zennor Hill, soon extending the property and rechristening it Tregerthen Cottage, a recognizably Cornish name and one that reflected its topographical situation. Marian Andrews, Westlake's sister-in-law (and author of *A Loyal Heart: A Tale of the Cornish Coast*), recalled his role in establishing Zennor as a magnet for creative people:

> During the changes and chances of forty years, hither have come one generation after another of friends and kinsfolk, from far and near. Men of distinction in every branch of science and literature, artists and scholars—young people full of life and eager delight in the free, wild country—the lonely and the sad-hearted—all alike have found a hospitable welcome from the kindly host and hostess of that summer paradise on the slope of Zennor Hill.[66]

Likewise, as Gertrude Phillpotts wrote shortly after Westlake's death in 1913:

> Nearly forty summers and autumns found Mr Westlake in his much-loved Cornish home. It was indeed home to him, for he knew every stone from St Ives to the Land's End, and he greeted as a friend the outline of every tor, cliff, and hill ... landscape beauty was a passion with him, and he revelled in the contemplation of earth, sea, and sky as seen from these breezy moorland heights.[67]

At Tregerthen Cottage, Phillpotts continued, the 'key-notes of the place were liberty and activity' and Westlake 'took a genial interest in every one's choice of pursuit'. Some of the house guests, she added, 'were sure to be inclined for a walk under Mr Westlake's guidance, to one of the tors or to some of the many interesting antiquities of the neighbourhood, and with them he would start upwards on the Moors'.[68] From the heights:

> If the walkers ... looked towards the west, the village of Zennor and the ancient tower of the church soon came into sight. The Vicar, Mr Borlase, was an intimate friend of Mr Westlake, and they had

many tastes in common. Mr Borlase in his long life had been an acute observer of Cornish character and peculiarities, and he never tired of talking of the villagers of Zennor, and telling stories of their ways and views of life.[69]

Westlake's interest in Zennor Church extended to practical and financial support for its restoration in 1890. According to Phillpotts, Westlake and his wife Alice 'gave most careful thought and study to every portion of the work, allowing nothing to be done that would in any way interfere with the characteristic simplicity and beauty of the building'. They visited the church almost daily to view progress and consult the architect, and among their achievements was the preservation of the 'Mermaid of Zennor' bench-end, which they took great pride in showing to their house guests. These visitors 'were all honoured by the introduction to the Mermaid with tail and looking-glass and comb carved on one bench-end, and recalling the legendary beliefs of that rocky shore'.[70]

Although John Westlake died before the outbreak of the Great War, his stature in international law, his reputation as a defender of small nations, and his criticism of the Ottoman Empire ensured that Zennor remained distinctly visible within the body politic of the United Kingdom. It was a political visibility that lingered after Westlake's death, and may even have affected Lawrence's own experiences at Zennor during the war, when, eventually, he came under the full glare of the Establishment's spotlight. But yet more interesting is that Westlake had created a community of like-minded intellectuals at Zennor years before Lawrence had alighted upon the locality as a suitable candidate for his Rananim renewed. Westlake may not have sought an alternative utopian lifestyle for himself and his 'guests', their leisured bourgeois activities ranging from outdoor sketching and 'bathing and exploring parties' to hockey and tennis, with dances or charades in the evening.[71] But, with his progressive and sometimes unconventional views, Westlake was an almost subversive Establishment figure, his circle of invited guests and their interests not far removed from those of Ottoline Morrell's salon, of which Lawrence was a member. Westlake and Lawrence were perhaps not as far apart as we might imagine, and both had chosen Zennor for their social experiments.

Be that as it may, Lawrence was certainly selective about whom to invite to join his community. He met Alice, Westlake's widow, in July 1916 but by then she was quite elderly and very frail, hardly a potential recruit for Rananim. Nonetheless, she visited Lawrence and Frieda at Higher Tregerthen, exhibiting a dutiful but reluctant neighbourliness. As Lawrence wrote: 'The Westlakes have come: the old Mrs Westlake, a doctor and his wife, and a Madame Mott, a sort of companion. For these four people they have brought four servants'. This sounded like upper-middle-class indulgence, but Lawrence was quick to point out that the 'old woman is invalid', and that she and her companions now lived a quiet life up the hill at Tregerthen Cottage: 'We never see anything of them: I have only heard the voices of the maid servants'.[72]

'Such a lovely place ... our Rananim'

Superficially, more to Lawrence's taste were the occultist and writer Meredith Starr (author of a book on yoga) and his wife, 'Lady Mary Stamford'. They had been introduced by Philip Heseltine, and, as Paul Newman has put it, 'ostensibly a friendship was struck'.[73] But Starr's garrulous and forceful opinionated style began to grate on Lawrence, who no doubt resented this potential threat to his leadership of Rananim. Lawrence had sought a utopia of alternative lifestyles, but the Starrs were just too much. As he complained to Lady Cynthia Asquith in September 1917, the Starrs were:

> a pair of herb-eating occultists: they fast, they eat nettles: they descend naked into old mine-shafts, and there meditate for hours and hours, upon transcendent infinitude: they descend on us like a swarm of locusts, and devour all the food on shelf or board: they even gave a concert, and made most dreadful fools of themselves, in St Ives: violent correspondence in the *St Ives Times*.[74]

The concert, or rather play, entitled *East and West*, was staged in support of the Red Cross—seen universally as a good cause during the Great War—but the performance sorely tried the audience's patience. It lasted a good two hours, and, among other things, featured singing by the self-styled talented couple. A.G. Folliott-Stokes, author of *The Cornish Coast and Moors*, joined the chorus of disapproval in the *St Ives Times*, provoking an ill-judged response from Meredith Starr in which he attributed to Lawrence the assertion that ninety per cent of British art was 'buffoonery' or worse.[75] Any claim to Rananim allegiance was thus expunged.

Rananim Regained? Lawrence at Zennor

In any case, Lawrence had already indicated his preferred candidates for Rananim membership, looking beyond mere eccentricity to identify real literary or artistic merit, together with visions of the future that complemented his own. John Middleton Murry and Katherine Mansfield were the ideals, the model types, and Lawrence's appeal to them was immediate and direct. 'I feel we ought to live here', he explained to the Murrys, 'pitch our camp and unite forces, and become an active power here, together.'[76] Although not married until 1918, the 'Murrys' (as they were known) were already a couple, and were recognized as such by friends and literary acquaintances. John (or Jack) was an author, editor and literary critic, and had worked on the staff of the *Westminster Gazette* and *Times Literary Supplement*. Katherine, a New Zealander by birth, was already a literary figure of some standing, renowned for her short stories. In July 1914 she and John had been witnesses at the Lawrence's wedding but by early 1916 were living in the south of France. They enjoyed the countryside and the weather but Katherine had been greatly shocked by the death in October 1914 of her brother, Leslie, another victim of the Great War, and was still grieving.

Lawrence had set out almost at once to entice the Murrys to Zennor and to plan his utopian project in detail. He drew a little sketch-map to show the Murrys what Higher Tregerthen was like: 'One block has three cottages that have been knocked into one, and the end room upstairs made into a tower-room ... Katherine would have the tower-room with big windows and panelled walls ... rent will be very low and all is *perfectly lovely*'.[77] The adjoining block, where Lawrence and Frieda would live, consisted of two cottages. Lawrence hoped that Philip Heseltine might also be persuaded to rejoin them, and that Emma could be encouraged to come from Porthcothan as housekeeper. It sounded idyllic: they would be 'like a little monastery ... we will eat together in the dining-room of your house ... [and] share expenses ... It would be *so splendid* if it could but come off: *such* a lovely place: our Rananim.'[78]

The moral pressure on the Murrys was now relentless. Three days later Lawrence wrote to the couple again. He and Frieda had taken their cottage at Higher Tregerthen for five pounds a year, and 'Really, you must have the other place. I keep looking at it. I call it already, Katherine's house, Katherine's tower.' There would be no 'quarrels and quibbles', he insisted, and there would be a binding '*Blutbrüderschaft* between us all'.[79] Here Lawrence was proposing a yet deeper spiritual dimension to his search for Rananim, the stipulation that they should all become 'blood-brothers'.

D.H. Lawrence and Cornwall

'Katherine's tower', the 'Murry's' cottage at Higher Tregerthen.

He had seen in the Zennor landscape suggestions of 'blood sacrifice', as he put it, part of the 'pregnant malevolency of Cornwall' and its 'blood-consciousness' which he found strangely and powerfully compelling.[80] He had been attracted, as he admitted in *Kangaroo*, to 'the savage vibrations that still lingered round the secret rocks ... old awful presences round the black moor-edge ... the blood-sacrificial pre-world, and the sun-mystery, and the moon-power, and the mistletoe on the tree'.[81] 'I am *Bludbruder*', Lawrence declared to the Murrys in almost menacing tones.[82] But if the idea had alarmed Jack and Katherine, it did not prevent them from being seduced by Lawrence's purple prose and his passionate advocacy of the delights of Zennor. As Lawrence wrote to Katherine, 'we count you two as our only two *tried* friends, real and permanent and truly blood kin. I know we shall be happy this summer; so happy.'[83]

Jack and Katherine arrived in early April 1916. 'The Murrys have come', Lawrence wrote eagerly to Ottoline Morrell on the 7th, 'and we are busy getting their cottage ready: colouring the walls and painting and working furiously ... we all enjoy ourselves'.[84] As Frieda recalled, they envisaged 'a wonderful place where we were all going to live in complete bliss; Rananim it was called ... By the hour we could talk Rananim.'[85] She continued, 'in Cornwall I can remember days of complete harmony between us', including the balmy day they all ventured out on the sea in a boat 'in bright sunshine', singing:

> Row, row, row your boat
> Gently down the stream,
> Merrily, merrily, merrily, merrily,
> Life is but a dream.[86]

'From the beginning the experiment was a failure'

But the truth was that the Murrys were shocked by what they found. Although Jack avowedly enjoyed his long walks across the moors with Lawrence, he and Katherine found Lawrence a changed man—ill (the encroaching tuberculosis, as it turned out), and often angry and frustrated and ranting. And although Katherine wrote approvingly to her friend Virginia Woolf, explaining how she walked across the fields to collect bread from Katie Berryman, returning along the coastal footpath beside the bewitching Atlantic, she did not really take to the harsh, grey beauty of Zennor and West Penwith. It was too bleak, and she complained that in damp weather the walls of her cottage ran with wet. This was not at all the romantic 'Katherine's tower' that Lawrence had led her to expect. As she wrote in a letter in May 1916, describing her miserable sense of isolation at Zennor:

> To-day I can't see a yard, thick mist and rain and a tearing wind with it. Everything is faintly damp. The floor of the tower is studded with Cornish pitchers catching the drops. Except for my little Cornish maid [Hilda] ... I am alone, for Murry and Lawrence have plunged off to St Ives with rucksacks on their backs and Frieda is in her cottage. It's very quiet in the house except for the wind and the rain and the fire that roars very hoarse and fierce.[87]

As John Middleton Murry put it in his *Reminiscences of D.H. Lawrence* in 1933, it had been 'a cold, slatey-grey day in early April when we arrived at St Ives. Lawrence was on the platform. The white gulls wheeled about, crying desolately, and our hearts sank. We tried to be gay, not to disappoint Lawrence, as we drove out to the Tinners' Arms at Zennor; but we felt like weeping. Our fairy-tale was over.'[88] The renewed quest for Rananim appeared to be finished almost before it had begun. 'From the beginning the experiment was a failure', confessed Murry: 'There were wonderful moments of happiness, but they were seldom. We fell back into a depression from which it was impossible to escape'. In particular, 'Katherine conceived a hatred of Cornwall that lasted for the rest of her life'.[89] Moreover, 'Lawrence, at times, was positively terrifying: a paroxysm of black rage would sweep down on him, and leave us trembling and aghast.' At such moments, Murry feared, 'he hated me to the point of frenzy. One night it became a kind of delirium, and I heard him crying out from his bedroom next door "Jack is killing me"'.[90]

'I was bewildered and terrified', continued Murry, 'more bewildered, and really more terrified, when the next day Lawrence would be kinder and more affectionate than ever towards me. Life began to be an awful phantasmagoria'. Murry and Katherine tried to behave as though nothing untoward was occurring but knew that at length they could not go on pretending. 'Katherine and I would talk things over', Murry recalled, 'and wonder what was happening. Was Lawrence really going mad? It added to the hopelessness of the situation that neither of us dared to ask him point-blank what *was* the matter?'[91]

Especially traumatic were the fights between Lawrence and Frieda. Katherine had decided she did not much like Frieda—she was a 'huge German pudding'—but nonetheless was appalled when it became apparent that Lawrence was beating her. 'Let me tell you what happened on Friday', Katherine wrote to a friend, 'I went across to them for tea. Frieda said Shelleys Ode to a Skylark was false.' Lawrence had lost his temper at this remark, and he and Frieda began to quarrel. 'Out of my house—you little God Almighty you', she cried, and Lawrence threatened that he would 'give you a dab on the cheek to quiet you, you dirty hussy'.[92] At that point Katherine diplomatically slipped out to return to her own cottage. Later in the evening, Frieda turned up to report that it was finally all over between her and Lawrence, and that she had left him for good. Then Lawrence himself appeared at the door. As Katherine continued:

Suddenly Lawrence appeared and made a kind of horrible blind rush at her and they began to scream and scuffle. He beat her—beat her to death—her head and face and breast and pulled out her hair. All the while she screamed for Murry to help her. Finally they dashed

> into the kitchen and round and round the table. I shall never forget how L[awrence] looked. He was so white—almost green and he just hit—thumped the big soft woman. Then he fell into one chair and she into another. No one said a word. A silence fell except for Frieda's sobs and sniffs ... L. sat staring at the floor, biting his nails.[93]

After fifteen minutes or so, astonishingly, Lawrence looked up and asked Jack a question about French literature. Slowly the atmosphere changed, and before long Lawrence and Frieda were swapping notes on the making of macaroni cheese! Next morning, a thoroughly chastened Lawrence could not do enough for Frieda. As Katherine observed, 'he was running about taking her up breakfast to her bed and trimming her hat'.[94]

To these unsettling episodes was added Lawrence's renewed approaches to Jack about *Blutbrüderschaft*, the suggestion now being not so much an understanding between them all, the 'Lawrences' and 'Murrys' together, but—as Jack feared—perhaps some kind of secret, darker 'pre-Christian blood rite' to be performed out on the moors. As Murry recalled:

> He wanted me to swear to be his 'blood-brother', and there was to be some sort of sacrament between us. I said, perhaps rather childishly but with perfect sincerity, that I thought I was his 'blood-brother', and I did not see the need of any kind of sacrament. 'If I love you, and you know that I love you, isn't that enough?' No, it was not enough: there ought to be some mingling of our blood, so that neither of us *could* go back on it. For some cause or other, I was half-frightened, half-repelled, and I suppose my shrinking away was manifest. He suddenly turned on me with a fury: 'I hate your love, I *hate* it. You're an obscene bug, sucking my life away'. The vindictiveness with which he said it made me almost physically sick. But the words were burnt into my brain.[95]

Altogether, the Murrys endured life with Lawrence for about six weeks, then moved to Mylor on the softer south coast of Cornwall, near Falmouth. Lawrence reported blandly to Ottoline Morrell, drawing a veil over the drama, explaining that 'Unfortunately the Murrys do not like the country— it is too rocky and bleak for them. They should have a soft valley, with leaves and the ring-dove cooing'.[96] As he added to another friend, Barbara Low, writing on 30 May, 'the Murrys are going away in a fortnight. They have taken a house near Falmouth. The walls of their cottage are rather damp'.[97]

'Only the *people* were wrong'

Lawrence found it difficult to understand why he had repelled the Murrys, and he and Frieda later visited them at Mylor to ensure there were no hard feelings. Outwardly, relations were restored (although, alas, it seems at least possible that Katherine Mansfield had caught from Lawrence the tuberculosis that was shortly to kill her). But inwardly Lawrence was in turmoil. 'I have done with the Murries [sic], both, for ever', he wrote to Kot on 7 November 1916, 'so God help me'. He continued: 'I tell you my Rananim, my Florida idea, was the true one. Only the *people* were wrong.'[98]

Murry put it slightly differently. The 'bad time at Higher Tregerthen seemed then like a bad dream', he said, but Mylor 'was a good time'. When Lawrence and Frieda came to visit, 'once more we were happy'. However, 'from this time forward we were conscious of a certain hostility. It was not a personal hostility: as persons we were very fond of each other still. But I was now vaguely aware that we represented different principles and were bound to go different paths, and I think Lawrence was acutely aware of this'.[99]

As Lawrence half-admitted, his Cornish Rananim was again stalled. After the initial difficulties at Porthcothan, especially with Philip Heseltine, here was a further debacle at Higher Tregerthen, this time with the Murrys. But he was in no mood to admit defeat, and he invited a string of other guests—including Catherine Carswell and Barbara Low—to stay in the cottage vacated by the Murrys and to experience something of his Cornish vision. In marked contrast to the upheavals of the Murrys' sojourn, Catherine Carswell recalled that 'My visit to Cornwall was all happiness—one of the quietest kind.'[100] She and Lawrence talked a great deal, especially about Dostoievsky, the Russian author, about whom Murry had written a book, on the main thesis of which Lawrence (predictably) disagreed. They enjoyed doing ordinary tasks together, such as the washing-up, and went for walks despite the inclement weather.

But it was not quite Rananim. 'Nothing particular happened', recalled Carswell, painting a perhaps surprising picture of contentment and harmony. Yet there was a telling insight which revealed much about Lawrence's current state of mind, perhaps providing answers to the questions that had puzzled the Murrys. One day Carswell had remarked how unproductive a writer she was compared to Lawrence. To her surprise, Lawrence replied: 'Ah, but you will have much longer than I to do things in'. She knew that he was 'delicate' but was shocked by 'his own certainty that time for him might not be lost'.[101] Here, maybe, was an explanation for Lawrence's restlessness and his mood swings. His conviction that time was not on his side reflected his sharp awareness of his illness and own mortality, made more acute by the unsettling feeling that his days in Cornwall might be numbered.

And despite the calm Catherine Carswell had experienced at Higher Tregerthen, there was a further insight into the turbulence that often bubbled below the surface. Although there were no violent outbursts during her stay, when she first arrived in Zennor both Lawrence and Frieda told her about a recent quarrel. Thinking the argument over, Lawrence had retreated to the scullery to do the washing-up, singing quietly to himself, his apparent insouciance further infuriating Frieda. She crept up on him (he was slightly deaf) with a stone dinner-plate, hitting him hard over the head. As Carswell observed, it 'hurt him very much and might, of course, have injured him seriously'.[102] Yet Lawrence appeared to take it in his stride, adding to Carswell's conviction that any 'miserable account' of Lawrence at Zennor would be a 'misleading account'. As she concluded: 'He had far too magnificent a talent for enjoyment, far too fine a capacity for work, to be miserable in the true sense of misery, which is dreariness, regret, sterility and doubt.'[103]

The contrast between Catherine Carswell's placid, almost dreamy account and the violent drama of the Murrys' recollections has led to suspicion that both were deliberately overstating their respective cases, seeking, as Jonathan Long has put it, 'to establish their own versions of him [Lawrence] for posterity'.[104] Jack Middleton Murry's account has been treated with particular scepticism but Catherine Carswell's memoir exhibits bias too. As Long observes: 'Murry was not always wrong and Carswell right.'[105] Indeed, the very complexity of Lawrence's personality, and the often sharply contrasting nature of his friendships, makes any attempt at generalization unreliable or oversimplified. Different people saw different things in Lawrence, especially as his opinions and behaviour vacillated. 'As Carswell and Murry remind us', Long concludes, 'Lawrence was a product of his own conflicted times and relationships'.[106]

At Zennor, despite recent reverses and the flight of the Murrys, Lawrence had striven to keep the prospect of Rananim alive. During 1917 his dreams received a boost when Cecil Gray, the Scottish composer and close friend of Philip Heseltine, took a cottage at Bosigran, about three miles west of Higher Tregerthen. Significantly, Heseltine was by now also on the scene, apparently having rekindled his friendship with Lawrence, although even

D.H. Lawrence and Cornwall

as they patched things up Lawrence was busy depicting Heseltine and his erstwhile girlfriend Puma as the unsavoury characters 'Halliday' and 'Possum' in his new novel *Women in Love*.

'This wild end of England which isn't England at all'

Heseltine had arrived at Zennor in April 1917, staying initially at the Tinners' Arms, where he wrote to his friend Robert Nichols, war poet and playwright, enthusing over the locality and encouraging Nichols to join him. 'This is an excellent inn', he wrote, 'and there is a furnished cottage to let for about a pound a month right out on the open moor'. It was a tantalizing invitation: 'Come—one can work here as nowhere else. Miles and miles of moor, two seas, and a forty-mile horizon, right away to the Scillies! ... Let us have done with the past, once and for all. Oh, this spring! My head is dancing all day long'.[107]

Heseltine wrote in similar vein to another acquaintance:

> And what space and freedom there is, and what distances one sees! All the coast along to Trevose Head, nearly forty miles off, and the Scillies the other way, that always look so impossible—one can never believe they exist like ordinary islands and are inhabited by ordinary human beings. They are like a mysterious gateway leading to a mysterious, unknown fairyland of impossible dreams come true—like [the mythical island of] Hy-Brasil the old Celts used to see shining far out in the western sea at sunset.[108]

To emphasize his point, Heseltine appended a newly written verse, penned in high spirits and eulogizing the idea of Hy-Brasil:

> 'You'll never come to Hy-Brasil',
>   A piskie whispers through your hair,
> 'By bending to another's will.
>   For picks and packs you may not bear
> Across the sea to Hy-Brasil.
>   And you may sweat and you may swear
> And swink and think until you're ill
>   And die before you're 'ere aware
> There's such a place as Hy-Brasil.

Rananim Regained? Lawrence at Zennor

> So have a care, so have a care …
> From Trewey Down and Zennor Hill
> You'd ride a puffin through the air
> And circle over Hy-Brasil.[109]

Hy-Brasil was cognate with Atlantis, the fabled lost land beyond Cornwall, with its own mythical connections with the drowned landscape of the Scillies. Here was Heseltine's tendency to strike pan-Celtic poses (see pp. 45–8), drawing upon Irish lore (the story of Hy-Brasil) and placing it in a Cornish context. It was a sophisticated appreciation of the Celtic world, such as he also showed in his fascination with the Cornish language, which he had taken the trouble to learn alongside his acquisition of the other Celtic tongues. As Cecil Gray wrote, Cornish had become critical to Heseltine's sense of being, 'the internationally minded pacifist with his private Cornish language against the bellicose and insular Englishman, the cultured and exquisitely refined aesthete against the beer-swilling pub-crawler'.[110] Indeed, as Heseltine himself declared, he had experienced a new beginning in Cornwall, 'in this wonderful country—this wild end of England which is not England at all'.[111]

Given this level of empathy and sensitivity, Heseltine's startling aside in another fulsome letter to Robert Nichols comes as a profound shock:

> There is an extraordinary fascination about this little remote end of Cornwall … We ought to re-people this wonderful neighbourhood, for the indigenous man is vile. It is very well to wax romantic about the Celt in the abstract (though I suspect most of the Zennor stock of being pre-Celtic Iberians), but your average Cornishman is a veritable savage—ignorant, suspicious and quite hysterically ill-tempered.[112]

Heseltine was often dangerously disruptive, as we have seen, capable of holding contrary views at the same time, a Jekyll and Hyde personality that ultimately found expression in his Philip Heseltine/Peter Warlock dichotomy. As an exasperated Cecil Gray put it on another occasion, in 'all this, as in so much else, it may perhaps seem difficult to decide whether Philip was serious, or simply deliberately playing the fool … this half-mocking, half-serious, ironical attitude of mind which was so characteristic of him'.[113] But the advocacy of ethnic cleansing, even if meant as a joke, was deeply offensive, although its dismissive attitude to the indigenous Cornish was reminiscent of Lawrence's own estimation, expressed earlier at Porthcothan and no doubt communicated to Heseltine there. Additionally, Heseltine would not be the first (or last) to express disappointment that, put alongside the popular romantic constructions of 'the Celt in the abstract', the inhabitants of the Celtic lands when met at last turned out to be just ordinary people living ordinary lives. Moreover, Heseltine would not be the only one to suggest that the singular environment of Cornwall ought really to be the preserve of a metropolitan elite, equipped by superior education, enhanced aesthetic appreciation and comfortably adequate resources, to fully develop its potential.

In Heseltine's defence, it might also be protested that he was often more at home with the natural world than with humans. He wrote to Robert Nichols from Trewey, for example, explaining that 'I am now living in a little wooden house on the highest point of the moor that separates the two seas, north and south—between Zennor and Penzance. All round, on all sides, nothing but open moorland and rock-strewn hills'.[114] On the lower slopes,

> the hills are covered with a dazzling profusion of gorse and blackthorn—I have never seen such blazing masses of gorse. Tiny lizards dart about among the violets of the sunny banks and splendid gold-and-black adders often cross one's path on the moors. The other day, looking down from the cliffs into a clear, green sea-pool, I caught sight of a lovely young seal, gambolling about under the water. Up here on the moor all the birds and beasts come near to one, not suspecting any human presence. Foxes lollop leisurely along the road, bunnies hardly take the trouble to hop out of the way when one walks by. A chorus of larks makes the air ring all day long, and there are cuckoos innumerable, piping from near and far with delightful variations of pitch and interval.[115]

This too was a utopian imagining, a solitary life among the wondrous abundance of nature's gifts, almost Yeatsian in its 'Lake Isle of Innisfree' atmosphere. Indeed, Heseltine was insistent that the Celtic vision remained integral to the new life in Cornwall, and that he continued to pursue his Cornish enthusiasms, including his study of the language. More than thirty years later, the Cornish writer J.C. Trewin and the Bodmin journalist H.J. Willmott mused on the puzzling contradictions of Philip Heseltine. Willmott emphasized 'how Cornish Heseltine' had become in his interests and affiliations, in those happier days before 'the Warlock got the better of him, led him too far, split his personality'.[116]

For Heseltine, the arrival of Cecil Gray at Zennor was, he hoped, a portent of things to come. 'Gray has taken a big, lonely house about three miles away in a very wild spot', he reported excitedly to Delius, 'almost on the cliffs. He is going to live here permanently and is moving all his belongings from London'.[117] Suitably enthused, Heseltine urged Gray 'to make your dwelling the centre of Celtic rebirth', and looked forward to a projected trip to Brittany together, 'a pilgrimage with me to Carnac, where to speak French were a blasphemy'.[118] (In fact, Heseltine settled briefly at Camaret, near Finistere, in 1921, 'staying here', as he put it, 'on the Breton—and quasi-Cornish—coast', still intent on visiting 'Carnac, the mystical centre of the Celtic World'.)[119] Gray understood and tolerated Heseltine's exuberances but, as he later admitted, 'I hardly saw myself in the role of the creator of "the mystic centre of a new culture", "the centre of a Celtic re-birth"'. As he concluded, 'I have imagined many strange things in my time: never quite that'.[120]

No matter; for a short time, Bosigran became the twin pole, along with Higher Tregerthen, of what was to prove the last real attempt to found Rananim in Cornwall. During those months Lawrence and Gray met almost daily, Lawrence even helping Gray with domestic chores at the cottage at Bosigran. Frieda took a special shine to Gray, who had something of a reputation as a 'lady's man', to use the terminology of the day, and in the summer of 1917 she began to walk across to Bosigran alone—for the purpose, it is said, of frequent love-making with the handsome young Scot. It was not surprising that Gray would later recall that summer as 'halcyon days without intermission'.[121] Perhaps not surprising either was that this experience should have affected his estimation of Lawrence, the cuckolded husband, a view made more jaundiced as their relationship deteriorated over time. Lawrence 'was definitely not attractive to women in himself', Gray opined, 'as apart from the seductive magic of his pen. His physical personality was puny and insignificant, his vitality low, and his sexual potentialities exclusively cerebral.'[122]

As Gray also explained, Philip Heseltine had planned to stay in Cornwall for some time, if not permanently. However, in the summer of 1917, as manpower shortages on the Western Front became acute, there was a rigorous review by the authorities of existing exemptions from military service. Heseltine was duly called forward for re-examination. His 'nervous disorder' and 'unimpeachable medical certificate', as Gray described them, made further exemption a certainty. But Heseltine panicked: 'foolishly, though very characteristically, he simply decided to ignore the summons altogether, and left Cornwall for Ireland'.[123] Ireland was excluded from the conscription applied elsewhere in the United Kingdom, and, unmolested, Heseltine was able to devote himself to musical composition and to his comparative study of the Celtic languages, as well as meeting W.B. Yeats, poet and doyen of the 'Celtic Twilight' movement. Virtuous as this was, it meant nonetheless that Heseltine had once again summarily abandoned Rananim, leaving Lawrence and Gray to pursue their utopian visions alone.

'Something manly and independent about him— and something truly *Celtic*'

By this time, however, Lawrence had made another important friendship, with a local farmer, thirty-three-year-old William Henry Hocking, one of two brothers down at Lower Tregerthen. Initially, Lawrence lent a hand on the Hockings' farm, in the late summer of 1916 helping to bring in the harvest. As he explained to his friend Dollie Radford on 5 September, 'We have had outrageous seas, and of a dark, wine-blue colour. The bracken is withering, the sunsets are tremendous, almost terrible, the autumn is coming in'. But the harvest was not yet gathered. 'The corn stands in "mews"—small ricks, in the field—not carried yet. Of course, William Henry is behind. He has got half his cut yet. It must all be cut by scythe'.[124] Lawrence liked helping out, enjoying the physical labour and being outdoors, and feeling that he was making himself useful. It also gave him his first real opportunity to get to know the Cornish on their own terms, as equals. They were still 'different', but now in a sensuous, seductive way that contrasted with his earlier depiction of the Cornish as 'insects gone cold' (p. 58). William Henry, Lawrence told Dollie Radford on 11 October, had 'something manly and independent about him—and something truly *Celtic*—something non-christian, non-European, but strangely beautiful and fair in spirit, unselfish'.[125]

Here was an estimation of the Cornish that had eluded Lawrence at Porthcothan, and which was radically at variance with Heseltine's more recent denunciation of the indigenous inhabitants at Zennor. At Zennor, Lawrence had had the opportunity to get to know local families and their place in the community. There was the Stevens family, for instance, their recent forebears supposedly among the last speakers of the Cornish language.

William Henry Hocking, Lawrence's intimate Cornish friend.

James Stevens, who died in April 1918, shortly after Lawrence had left Zennor, had been born in 1847, and spent his entire life in the locality as miller, miner and then farmer, in 1884 moving to Foage farm, about a mile from the churchtown. As he prospered, James Stevens moved his allegiance from the Methodists to the Anglicans, and was churchwarden during the restoration of the parish church, the cost of which was partly met by John Westlake. He kept a diary from 1877 to 1912, its entries dominated by the calendar events of the farming year. His favourite saying was: 'Farm as though you were going to live forever and live as though you were going to die tonight.'[126] It was a maxim that Lawrence would have discovered was commonplace among the Zennor folk, a window into their motivations and daily lives.

The Zennor people were also sharp, with their wry Cornish sense of humour, as Alison Symons recounted in her *Tremedda Days*:

Will's Will and Anne Berryman, brother and sister, lived in the Row in the village and farmed the Glebe, milking eight or nine cows. They were aunt and uncle to Sidney Berryman from the Post Office. Will's Will was a great character and loved a drop of drink and a good coose [talk], and had a quick wit. The story goes that a rather superior visitor, intending to take a rise from the simple country fellow, asked if he had seen a cart load of monkeys pass by. Will's quick reply was, 'No, dropped off, did 'ee'.[127]

The post office, as Lawrence discovered, was a hub of village life, run by Tom and Katie Berryman, Sidney's parents. As well as the usual post office activities—stamps, postal orders, pensions, and the like—it sold a wide variety of provisions, from bacon, cheese and salt to pinafores and aprons, as well as animal feed. Katie also baked bread in her open chimney. Frieda remembered fondly that her 'standby and friend was Katie Berryman. Her saffron cake and baked stuffed rabbits were our modest luxuries'.[128] Another local 'character' was Mr Pascoe, a stonecutter who quarried at Tremedda Hill before moving to Treen, where his wife managed a small shop. He was 'all bent up' from using a 'jumper' (an iron bar, about five feet long, used in quarrying), occupational disabilities not being unusual in early twentieth-century Cornwall. There was also Mr Nankervis, who kept the Tinners' Arms. Asked about the legal requirements for opening times, Nankervis would reply: 'What time? My time's up there', pointing to the sundial on the adjoining church. He also 'wasn't particular', and would feed 'the beer droppings to a sow which would come day every day from Trewey for its pint'.[129]

There was Charlie Jelbert, known for 'his prowess as a wrecker', salvaging goods washed up in local coves, who possessed a powerful bass voice, singing Cornish carols in the pub at Christmas. Jimmy Limpots from St Ives (see p. 113) was another familiar figure, often seen picking mushrooms in the early morning at Zennor, and turning up at threshing time to earn a little money on the farms and to participate in the 'gargantuan feasts' that were laid on for the labourers in the fields.[130] The farmers were the mainstay of this community, the Hockings at Lower Tregerthen prominent among them, and Lawrence was proud to work alongside them. These had become his people, at least for now.

Lawrence was welcome as a labourer on the farm. Sometimes he would stay all day, according to Stanley Hocking, one of the family at Lower Tregerthen, 'providing the weather was suitable ... if it was pouring with

Rananim Regained? Lawrence at Zennor

rain, you wouldn't see him for a week'. But, said Hocking: 'He wasn't very strong. He would do the little—what shall I say?—the insignificant jobs in the fields and on the ricks. He could get on the rick and hand the hay from the pitcher to William Henry [Hocking] who was building the rick— he loved that.' Harder work, however, was beyond Lawrence, especially 'pitching a load'. As Stanley Hocking put it: 'It's no joke pitching a load of hay from a wagon: that's hard work. But as soon as hay is taken from a wagon and placed on a rick, the hay is loose. Lawrence could hand loose hay or sheaves to the builder. A boy of eleven could do that.'[131]

Lawrence was also unversed in Cornish ways. Not only could he not 'handle the fork in the orthodox way that we stout country farmers did', said Stanley Hocking, but he 'would bind sheaves in the Midlands way. He had a different method of making the knot.' In the winter the sheaves would be pulled from the rick and brought through to the barn to feed the cows. Sometimes the sheaves would come apart, and the Cornish farmers would exclaim: 'Oh, this is one of Lawrence's sheaves here.' But Lawrence was an integral part of the team. He especially enjoyed harvesting, because, Stanley Hocking said, 'it was always done in beautiful weather. The sun was shining and it was warm and comfortable. Frieda would sometimes come down … Lawrence and Frieda were delighted when my sisters bought out croust [a substantial snack] in the afternoon.'[132]

By 1917 Lawrence and William Henry Hocking had become close, and Lawrence may even have considered him a potential recruit for Rananim. Subsequently, Lawrence's several biographers have argued about the precise nature of the relationship between Lawrence and William Henry Hocking. The consensus appears to be, as Brenda Maddox has put it, that 'in the fine summer of 1917, lying in the bracken and talking about sex, Lawrence and Hocking consummated their love'.[133] William Henry's younger brother, Stanley Hocking, always strenuously denied that Lawrence had any homosexual tendencies. But Frieda was not so sure, and was inclined to believe the stories about Lawrence and William Henry. Years later she affected not to care, but at the time the rumours had made her unhappy.

Arthur Eddy, one of the Hocking family circle, was more forthcoming. 'I don't know if I ought to tell you this', Eddy told his interviewer (C.J. Stevens), 'but William Henry told me one day that Lawrence was [homosexual]. Yes, that's what William Henry told me. He told me that Lawrence used to come down to the farm and talk to him about it a lot.'[134] Even Stanley Hocking admitted: 'Oh yes, Lawrence and William Henry used to talk together for hours after I had gone to bed. Lawrence was no clock watcher, and neither was William Henry. If Lawrence had been in the field helping with the harvest, he would come to supper at the farm and stay with William Henry until half past ten or midnight.'[135]

Significantly, William Henry appears to have been Lawrence's model for the 'strange Cornish type of man' with 'dark, fine, rather stiff hair and full, heavy, softly-strong limbs' sketched in a prologue written (but never published) for *Women in Love*, the novel he penned at Higher Tregerthen, a 'type of man' to whom Rupert Birkin, the book's main male character, was intensely attracted.[136] Likewise, in *Kangaroo*, Lawrence's alter ego, Richard Lovat Somers, lies in the Cornish countryside with a handsome young farmer, talking of 'the mysterious change in man with the change of season, and the mysterious effects of sex on a man'.[137] Tellingly, in the novel William Henry's character is given the name John Thomas. As Lawrence was clearly aware, Thomas was a common patronymic in West Cornwall, and thus an authentic choice. But he must also have realized that it was a suggestive clue, and not, as Richard Aldington later averred, an unfortunate Freudian slip.[138]

'The Cornish farmers are filled with the sense of inevitable disaster'

Whatever the precise details of the relationship, D.H. Lawrence's intimate friendship with William Henry Hocking opened for him a new window onto Cornish life. The Cornish were no longer people to be observed from 'a motor', as they had been at Porthcothan, but now could be work colleagues and friends. He began to understand the interests and anxieties of the Zennor community, from following the seasonal rhythm of the farming year to sharing in local events. On 5 May 1917, for example, he wrote to Murry to report a local tragedy that had unsettled him. 'Annie Thomas, the washerwoman, had a son of sixteen years, illegitimate son of Willie Berryman. This selfsame son went and fell off the cliffs on Sunday, getting gulls' eggs, and is quite lost.' Somehow, Lawrence thought, this calamity was emblematic of a wider dread he now sensed in Cornwall. 'All the Cornish farmers are filled with the sense of inevitable disaster', he told Murry, and 'talk freely of the end of the world.'[139]

It was a prescient fear, and the war that Lawrence had sought to escape, thinking Cornwall his refuge, at last caught up with him, leading to his

Rananim Regained? Lawrence at Zennor

expulsion from Zennor in September 1917. Ironically, Cecil Gray had played an important, albeit unwitting, part in the events that led to the eviction of Lawrence and Frieda from Cornwall, as we shall see in Chapter 5. Ironic too, was that Gray was able to remain at Zennor after Lawrence's sudden departure. The extended stay was not without consequences, however. Despite his tendency to discount Heseltine's mystical imaginings, including his dabbling in the occult, Gray sometimes succumbed to the loneliness of his Cornish eyrie, a large former count-house (administrative building) of a long-abandoned tin mine at Bosigran Castle, a wild and remote spot. Gray was troubled by knocking noises, seemingly from the depths of the old mine below, and in moments of vulnerability wondered whether this might be the hammering of the 'knockers', the underground sprites of Cornish folklore.[140]

In Cornwall, he felt, 'the boundary between the subjective and the objective' had become 'vague and indecisive'.[141] To this anxiety was added the growing suspicion of the locals, who wondered why Gray had settled in such an unlikely place, and speculated that he might be part of an enemy spy ring. Indeed, Gray, increasingly nervous, imagined that on one occasion a mob 'armed with scythes and pitchforks' came to attack him but took fright at the last minute, as 'the malevolence of the Cornish was only exceeded by their cowardice'.[142] Stanley Hocking, when asked much later about the alleged incident, replied: 'I think this is all nonsense … and I would never believe it'.[143]

A further complexity was the arrival at Bosigran of 'H.D.'—Hilda Doolittle, the American poet—wife of Richard Aldington, the writer. H.D. had developed an almost obsessive interest in Lawrence, imagining him to be in love with her, and the two had engaged in an extensive correspondence, all of which was later destroyed by Aldington. In March 1918, H.D. turned up in Zennor. Although Lawrence had departed some months before, H.D.'s arrival was nonetheless an intimate expression of their curious relationship. It was, however, complicated emotionally by her cohabiting with Cecil Gray at Bosigran, by whom she became pregnant, giving birth to a daughter, Perdita. Aldington was equally unconventional in matters marital, but H.D.'s liaison with Gray no doubt prompted the rueful observation in his noted anti-war novel, *Death of a Hero*, that it was 'in the nature of things, that those men who have most contempt for women are generally the most successful with them'.[144]

At any rate, by the time Perdita was born, H.D.'s relationship with Gray had already soured, and he had returned to London. Any thought that together at Bosigran, even without Lawrence's presence, they might have perpetuated something like the Rananim vision had come to nothing. Yet H.D.'s time at Zennor had been an act of homage, a pilgrimage in the footsteps (sometimes almost literally) of D.H. Lawrence. As Ella Westland has put it, H.D. at Zennor was 'deep under Lawrence's charismatic spell'.[145] She often walked the ancient pathway trod so recently by Lawrence, and in her semi-autobiographical novel, *Bid Me to Live,* mused on the historical and spiritual significance of the path, echoing Lawrence's belief that it had been forged by 'Phoenician donkeys taking tin from the mines to the ships', and imagining that the Phoenicians had endowed the track with 'more than the imprint of countless sandals'.[146]

Like Lawrence, H.D. was adamant in her estimation of Cornwall. 'It is not England', she declared, 'it is out of the world, a country of rock and steep cliff and sea-gulls'.[147] At Porthcothan, Lawrence had given full vent to his belief in North Cornwall as King Arthur's land, as Tristan's land, but this was an imagining that had faded as he had shifted further west to Zennor, the realm of the Tuatha Dé Danann and the Phoenicians. No doubt, in the lost correspondence with H.D., Lawrence had written often from Porthcothan, his letters full of Arthurian allusions, images that H.D. brought with her to Bosigran. Although Porthcothan, along with Tintagel, King Arthur's castle of popular fancy, lay many miles to the north-east, H.D. rather touchingly fused—or confused—the two locations, Porthcothan and Zennor, in that section of *Bid Me to Live* directed at Lawrence personally. 'I felt when I came here that the Phoenicians on the track from the mine to the sea, that you wrote me about, had left an imprint', she said, 'not only the track past the Druid stones on the hill. The Druids left the same track or traces as Arthur did, Tintagel and his Druid round-table. The round-table or Arthur's Druid circle wasn't all warriors. There was Merlin.'[148]

H.D. walked up to Higher Tregerthen, now tenantless, and peeped through the windows, voyeur-like, observing Lawrence's bookshelves and his orange and blue cushions. Lawrence had been like Merlin, leaving traces of his magic, but, alas, things had changed already. Rananim at Zennor was not to be. 'I have not seen Hilda [H.D.] for some time', Lawrence wrote nonchalantly in June 1918, 'but believe she is happy in Cornwall—as far as it is possible to be happy, with the world as it is.'[149]

Chapter 5

War in Cornwall: 'The Nightmare'

'The War is just hell for me', D.H. Lawrence wrote to his friend Eddie Marsh in August 1914, 'I can't get away from it for a minute: I live in a sort of coma, like one of those nightmares when you can't move. I hate it—everything.'[1] Rananim might hold the solution, perhaps even salvation, he thought, but, as we have seen in earlier chapters, the war had dashed the dream of going to Florida to establish his utopian community. Confined now to Britain, Lawrence had sought Rananim instead in Cornwall, first at Porthcothan on the north coast and then further west at Zennor. As Paul Delany has explained, 'Cornish people', according to Lawrence, 'were racially and morally separate from the English, and uncontaminated by the spirit of war'.[2] It was a belief to which Lawrence clung frantically over the next few years in sometimes desperate hope, until at last 'contamination' arrived. Yet the initial response of Cornwall to the outbreak of hostilities had appeared to confirm his deep-felt opinions, as Lawrence himself recognized.

'On the evil of war'

One day, in the autumn of 1914, a visitor fishing in the upper Delank river in remotest Bodmin Moor, the heart of Cornwall, came across a local farmer 'who was quite unaware that we had been at war with Germany for over two months'.[3] Isolation and a lonely existence devoid of human contact accounted, no doubt, for the farmer's ignorance. But his seeming indifference mirrored a wider mood in Cornwall in the early months of the Great War. Newspapers, of course, had brought reports of the outbreak of hostilities. The *Cornishman*, published in Penzance, announced 'Europe at War: Dreadful and Incredible Nightmare is a Reality', a headline that reflected the uncertainty and foreboding felt by many in Cornwall.[4] The Tory *Royal*

Cornwall Gazette struck a more defiant note when it exclaimed: 'A Continent in Arms. Great Britain Accepts Germany's Challenge. A Fight for Honour, Truth and Justice.'[5] Yet there was little of the war enthusiasm that had apparently greeted the outbreak of hostilities in other parts of Britain, or indeed across Europe. As historian Stuart Dalley has remarked, such exuberant responses 'did not extend to Cornwall'.[6] And as the *West Briton* newspaper put it in August 1914, capturing the bemused mood prevalent in Cornwall, 'the supreme surprise [here] is the enthusiasm with which a proportion of the population of every country receives the news that war has been declared'.[7] Such 'enthusiasm', it was clear, made no sense in Cornwall.

Indeed, Stuart Dalley has argued that what 'is most striking about the response in Cornwall to the outbreak of war is the difficulty in finding evidence to suggest that news of the war was popularly received'.[8] Melanie James, in her own examination of the outbreak of the Great War in Cornwall, agrees, and notes that as early as September 1914 the Cornish were already being chastised for their 'poor response to the call for arms'.[9] There were occasions, she adds, when 'Cornwall, particularly its rural areas, was deemed unpatriotic'.[10] For many, like the uninformed farmer on Bodmin Moor, the war had simply come as a complete surprise. At Penryn, an incredulous Elsie Stephens admitted in her diary entry for 9 August 1914 that 'everything has come onto us like a sudden thunderstorm'.[11] A general air of dismay and disbelief had everywhere greeted news of war, casting a sombre gloom over daily life. The *Cornish Guardian*, for instance, detected a distinct 'absence of gaiety' at normally fun-loving seaside Newquay, with August Bank Holiday activities attracting fewer attendees than usual because 'people did not feel like amusement'.[12]

For many in Cornwall, the continental geopolitics that had led to war seemed remote, even irrelevant, unlike the earlier Boer War with its immediacy and high stakes, Cornish socio-economic well-being at the turn of the century having been so dependent on the efforts of its emigrant miners in South Africa.[13] As mining declined in Cornwall, so remittances sent home from South Africa were vital to the Cornish economy and its social fabric. As Gary Magee and Andrew Thompson have argued, 'South Africa's constant flow of money orders back to the UK provided a lifeline for Cornwall until at least the 1920s'.[14] When the Boer War threatened to disrupt this arrangement, there had been widespread alarm. People in Cornwall had understood the Boer War and its significance; this new war with Germany was mystifying.

War in Cornwall: 'The Nightmare'

Bernard Walke, vicar of St Hilary in West Cornwall, captured this sense of distance and disinterest in his memoir *Twenty Years at St Hilary*. 'We were far away at St Hilary from all that was happening in France', he explained: 'There were no troop trains or convoys of wounded passing through the county; so that, apart from the mustering at Goldsithney of horses from the farms of the district, the first contact with the war was the march of a detachment of the Cornish Regiment through the county to gain recruits'.[15] Nonetheless, early in the war, there *had* been Cornish casualties at 'the front'. As Walke returned to his vicarage, the new recruits having passed by with an officer on horseback at their head, he encountered an elderly man whose grandson had been killed recently in France. 'The old man turned on me viciously', Walke recounted, 'and brandishing his stick shouted, "He is a butcher, that officer on his horse. A butcher, who has taken away the prime bullocks to the slaughter-house, and has come back to drive in the lean".'[16] It was a retort worthy of Lawrence himself. In their initial estimation of the war, the Cornish and Lawrence were at one.

Initially, there was little enmity towards Germany, although, as Walke noted, there was small sympathy either: increasingly the war was seen as 'a crude but terribly revealing indictment of our Christian civilization, where in Germany human life had become so much "cannon fodder"'.[17] Pacifism there certainly was, especially in the Society of Friends, the Quakers, a religious community of particular long standing in Cornwall. At Falmouth, where a number of German ships had been arrested and their crews detained, Mrs George Henry, 'a committed Quaker', warned the local Liberal Association against 'excessive bitterness towards Germans'.[18] The prominent Fox family, based in Falmouth, were leading Quakers, and in the first week of war held a prayer meeting for peace at their imposing house at nearby Glendurgan. There was similar concern in other denominations. Walke, a High Church Anglican, spoke 'on the evil of war … in my sermons at St Hilary', and later 'found myself launched on a campaign of peace that went on to the end of the war'.[19] At St Hilary he discovered an ally in a 'Wesleyan Minister named Luckman', and at Helston the local Wesleyan superintendent confessed himself horrified by the outbreak of hostilities.[20] At St Austell the Revd G.A. Bennetts implored his congregation to do 'all they could to conquer the war spirit'.[21] At Falmouth Wesley Church each member of the congregation signed a letter to the government expressing their 'horror [at] the terrible outrage to humanity and the menacing challenge to Christianity involved in a European war'.[22]

Tin miners at Troon, south of Camborne in the politically radical 'Mining Division', shouted abuse at the Duke of Cornwall's Light Infantry recruiting march as it made its way around Cornwall in the spring of 1915, as did young men at nearby Illogan, and in the clay district near St Austell, only recently the scene of a bitter strike broken by police brought in from outside, there was similar hostility.[23] Reginald Clemo, father of Jack Clemo, later an acclaimed poet, had participated in the clayworkers' strike in 1913. Like his colleagues, Reginald Clemo knew that 'he could not kill Germans in cold blood', admitting his 'lack of personal hatred for the enemy'.[24] He too refused to volunteer but was conscripted in 1916, killed in action in the following year just before Christmas when his ship, HMS *Tornado*, was mined.

China-clay export markets, principally German and Russian, dried up during the war, while the tin mines which survived the initial shock of the closure of the London Metal Market were systematically stripped of their ore without any development work for the future. As historian John Rowe put it, 'through the war ... Cornish tin mines had been exploited', the British government having set an artificially low price for tin, the needs of wartime production prioritized over the industry's long-term well-being.[25] As it was, nine mines had been abandoned by September 1914, at the outset of war; St Ives Consolidated was closed in April 1915 with debts of £14,000. Moreover, the outbreak of war in 1914 had coincided with the harvest, and agricultural labourers were actively discouraged from enlisting by their employers, an attitude that persisted throughout the conflict.[26] There was also a sense, widespread in Cornwall, that to enlist as a soldier was somehow to take a step down the social scale, that soldiering was not a proper occupation for a Cornishman.[27]

'A matter for the Navy'

However, behind this general reluctance, there was one exception in Cornwall which maybe somehow proved the rule. This was a general conviction that if there was to be a war, then it ought to be a Royal Navy affair, that warfare was 'a matter for the Navy'.[28] The *West Briton* detected places 'where calls for the army are unheeded by youths ... who are really anxious to join the navy', and Cornish contributions to the Royal Navy were said locally to surpass those 'of any other county in the United Kingdom in proportion to its population'.[29] One observer insisted that 'the Duchy provides a larger share of the Navy's personnel than any other similar portion of His Majesty's

Dominions'.[30] It was even suggested that recruits from Cornwall and Devon together made up two-thirds of the Royal Navy's total manpower.[31]

Insofar that there were any displays of 'war enthusiasm' in Cornwall in the opening days of conflict, it was in the maritime communities when thousands of fishermen and other mariners in the Royal Naval Reserve and Royal Naval Volunteer Reserve received their mobilization papers. At St Ives, it was said, 2,000 cheering people lined the streets as the Reservists set off to join the fleet at Devonport.[32] Yet even in coastal Cornwall there were doubts and ambiguities, and, as Alan M. Kent has noted, these are played out in Arthur Quiller-Couch's novel *Nicky-Nan, Reservist*, first published in 1915.[33] Nicky-Nan (the nickname of Nicholas Nanjivell) is an inhabitant of fictional Polpier (for which read Polperro). He has served in the Royal Navy and on discharge has transferred to the Reserve, as have many others in the locality: 'For Polpier lives by the fishery, and of the fishermen a large number—some scores—had passed through the Navy and now belonged to the Reserve.'[34] They were ready to do their duty but, like others in Cornwall, had only the faintest idea of what had led to war:

> The good fellows had the haziest notion of what newspapers meant by the Balance of Power in Europe, nor perhaps could any of them have explained why, when Austria declared war on Servia [Serbia], Germany should be taking a hand. But they had learnt enough on the lower deck to forebode that, when Germany took a hand, the British Navy would soon be clearing for action. Consequently all through the last week of July [1914], when the word 'Germany' began to be printed in large type in Press headlines, the drifters putting out nightly on the watch for the pilchard harvest carried each a copy of *The Western Morning News* or *The Western Daily Mercury* to be read aloud, discussed, expounded, under the cuddy lamp in the long hours between shooting the nets and hauling them.[35]

Nicky-Nan, like the other Naval Reservists in Polpier, receives his call-up papers. But he has developed epithelioma of the leg, an abnormal tumorous growth, which has increasingly incapacitated him and now prevents him from joining up. He is left behind as the other Reservists depart for the fleet:

> The whole town had assembled by this time, a group about each hero. It was a scene that those who witnessed it remembered through

many trying days to come. They knew not at all why their country should be at war ... Not a soul present had harboured one malevolent thought against a single German. Yet the thing had happened: and here, punctually summoned, the men were climbing aboard the brakes, laughing, rallying their friends left behind.[36]

Nicky-Nan is left to ponder the men's incomprehension, and how dutifully they went off to war without knowing why, especially when they had been taught in chapel that war was wicked. Nicky-Nan himself remains ambivalent about the war, not least as he sees others departing to join the colours, leaving Polpier to survive as best it can in straitened circumstances, especially as there are no longer any fishermen to catch the seasonal pilchard shoals that now swarm unmolested in Cornish coastal waters. For many in Cornwall, the war remained a puzzle. As A.L. Rowse wrote approvingly in his biography *Quiller Couch: A Portrait of Q*, the novel *Nicky-Nan, Reservist* is 'a faithful record of how that war took West Country people—mostly by surprise and wonderment'.[37]

This was the Cornwall—remote, peripheral, apart, different, still beyond England's reach, as he imagined it—that Lawrence had envisaged, a suitable location for his cherished Rananim but also the site of resistance to England's 'war spirit'.[38] Cornwall had not been swept up in the tide of war enthusiasm, instead remaining immune, even aloof. But times changed. Eventually, not even Cornwall could avoid the embrace of total war, and the introduction of conscription to the armed forces after January 1916 brought the war into almost every household, as it did elsewhere in Britain. Moreover, paradoxically, although far removed from the metropolitan seat of government in London, Cornwall was also in the strategic front line of the war, just as it had been in so many previous conflicts.[39] Here again the maritime dimension was prominent, not only in the presence of the Royal Navy, especially at Falmouth, but in the emergence of Cornish coastal waters as a major and unrelenting battleground, a dramatic theatre of death and destruction.

'Two German officers landed from a submarine'

In early 1915, Germany had announced its policy of unrestricted submarine warfare, declaring the seas around Britain a war zone, and warning that all shipping—including that of neutral countries—within the proscribed area would be liable to attack. On a single day in March 1915, for example, the

War in Cornwall: 'The Nightmare'

German submarine U-29 sank four vessels off the Isles of Scilly.[40] However, the sinking of the liner *Lusitania* in May 1915 provoked international condemnation, not least from America, leading to a temporary curtailment of Germany's policy. But unrestricted submarine warfare was back with a vengeance in February 1917, as the Germans sought desperately to win advantage in the war of attrition. Local shipping suffered heavily. Edward Hain & Son of St Ives, which operated cargo vessels of between 3,000 and 4,000 tons, lost no fewer than sixteen ships to U-boat action during the course of the war. R.B. Chellew of Truro lost a further five ships.[41] The *Olivia*, 110 tons, from Portreath, another Cornish ship, was bound for South Wales in February 1917, soon after unrestricted sinkings were resumed, when it was apprehended by a patrolling U-boat. According to one newspaper report, the *Olivia* was systematically looted by the 'pirates' (as the German submariners were described) before explosives were detonated in the ship's hold. The crew was then set adrift in an open boat, later picked up by a friendly vessel and placed in the care of the Shipwrecked Mariners' Society at Fishguard in south-west Wales.[42]

But sinkings were not confined to Cornish vessels. On the afternoon of 22 February 1917, just weeks after the reintroduction of unrestricted submarine warfare, U-21 sank six neutral Dutch ships off the Isles of Scilly, near Bishop Rock. It was said that, having previously put into Falmouth, the Dutchmen had been assured of safe passage by the German authorities, the vessels' subsequent destruction interpreted as evidence of German duplicity and malice. Little by little the mood in Cornwall was changing. Less than two months later, the Australian troopship *Ballarat* was torpedoed off Wolf Rock lighthouse, just within sight of Land's End, by U-32. She was taken in tow but later sank off the Lizard, thankfully with no loss of life.[43] One memorable episode in this period was the destruction of the *Kintuck*, an Admiralty transport, which was mined or torpedoed some six miles north-west of St Ives, on the afternoon of 2 December 1917. The ship went down by the stern, the fifty-four crewmen taking to the boats. All but one survived, the majority rescued by the St Ives lifeboat. The huge explosion when the *Kintuck* was struck was heard as far away as Treveal, neighbouring farm to Tregerthen in Zennor parish, home until very recently of D.H. Lawrence.[44]

By 1917, some U-boats were spending the greater part of their operational lives in Cornish waters. U-86, commissioned in November 1917, for example, was one of the many German submarines that had brought the war to Cornwall's doorstep. During its short career, under the command of one Hans Trenk, U-86 sank four merchant steamers, three off the coast of North Cornwall. The *Gregynog* was torpedoed in April 1918, and then on 17 August the submarine despatched both the *Denbola* (off Gurnard's Head, on the cliffs at Zennor) and the Danish ship *Helene*, off St Ives. The *Denbola* had been armed with a 19-pounder gun but was given no opportunity to defend herself, being struck by two torpedoes on the evening of the 17th and sinking almost at once. Most of the crew was rescued by a Royal Navy patrol boat and landed at St Ives, although two lives were lost. The *Helene*, meanwhile, had been sailing in ballast from Rouen to Swansea when it was fatally intercepted off the Cornish coast.[45]

U-112, commissioned in April 1918, had a similar run of luck under its captain, Wilhelm Rhein. The *Atlantico*, a Portuguese sailing ship, was stopped and sunk by gunfire off the Isles of Scilly in September 1918, and on 1 October U-112 accounted for both the *Aldbaran*, a Swedish steamer sunk near Wolf Rock, and the *Gjertrud*, a Norwegian ship sunk two miles west of the Lizard. The next day it was the turn of the *Bamse*, a British merchantman, torpedoed off the Lizard, the survivors being picked up and landed at Falmouth. On the same day U-112 sank the *Polijames*, another British ship, travelling from Newport to St Malo with a cargo of coal, again off the Lizard. The following day, 3 October 1918, the Norwegian steamer *Atlantis* was sunk six miles south-east of the Lizard, as was the *Westwood*. On 4 October 1918 the *Nanna* was sunk in the same vicinity by U-112.[46] And so it went on, until the end of the war in November.

The indiscriminate nature of U-boat warfare, and the seeming impunity with which the German submarines appeared to operate off the Cornish coast, gave rise to numerous improbable rumours which soon passed into local lore. A.L. Rowse, the Cornish historian, had been a teenager during the latter Great War years, and as a young man toured Cornwall, recording snippets of folklore. Thus, according to one story he collected, 'two German officers landed from a submarine, made their way to Penzance, dined at the Queen's hotel and left a note to say so. Returned to sub concealed in remote cove'.[47] Although patently absurd, the tale seemed plausible enough to some at the height of the U-boat campaign, the supposed insolence of the two German officers further inflaming the passions of impotent rage. Bernard Walke recalled an occasion when he was in Penzance, and he:

> passed by the dock where a ship torpedoed by a German submarine had been brought alongside. At the moment of our passing, the mutilated

War in Cornwall: 'The Nightmare'

body of a boy was being carried ashore through a crowd of women who were calling down curses, and shouting threats on the men who had broken the law of the sea in attacking merchant vessels and killing boys. I was shaken at the sight of the mutilated body and the cries of the women.[48]

Such events served to incite local opinion, as Walke found when he attended a peace meeting, again in Penzance. 'A Quaker lady was speaking from the platform', he recalled, 'when I heard the tramp of men marching up the narrow street. I knew what it meant'.[49] He continued:

A girl, who was present, had told me she had been at a dance given by the Naval Reserve, when an officer had warned her to keep clear of any meetings in the cause of peace, as they were determined to end such meetings … The doors were pushed open and the body of men, whose steps I had heard marching up the street, about a hundred and fifty of them, dressed in mufti [civilian clothes] with an officer at their head, crowded into the room. For over an hour I struggled with this howling mob … these men in their hate had for the time ceased to be human.[50]

As the U-boat war had become ever more intense during 1917, so British countermeasures became increasingly apparent along the Cornish coast. In May 1917 Rear-Admiral John Luard was appointed Rear-Admiral Falmouth, his senior rank and operational title an indication of the strategic importance of the port and neighbouring waters.[51] Falmouth became the base for decoy vessels, known as Q-ships, which would lure U-boats to surface in their expectation of sinking a small vessel by gunfire (rather than an expensive torpedo, used on larger ships), only to find at the last minute that the Q-ship had hoisted the Royal Navy's White Ensign and revealed its own armament. Some Q-ships successfully engaged German submarines but their main value was as a psychological deterrent, U-boat commanders never quite sure whether their intended quarry was actually a warship in disguise.[52] Anti-submarine motor launches, based at Penzance, St Mary's on the Isles of Scilly, and Padstow, also played an important role in U-boat hunting, as did airships, first introduced in 1916, which operated from Mullion on the Lizard and Bude on the north coast. In early 1917, an airship bombed what appeared to be the wake of a U-boat off the Lizard. A few days later, a damaged U-boat (presumably the same submarine), trailing oil and bubbles, was spotted off Cape Cornwall, and was successfully attacked by the airship and armed trawlers using bombs and depth-charges.[53]

The violent life-and-death struggles now enacted almost routinely around the Cornish coast were often heard, and sometimes seen, by the local population. William Golding, the novelist, as a small child spent holidays with his grandmother in Newquay, her house 'Karenza' (ironically meaning 'love', in Cornish) providing a grandstand view of the harbour. Golding's older brother Jose, some five years his senior, was sometimes allowed to go down to the quay to watch survivors of U-boat attacks being brought ashore. William was thought too young for such grisly spectacles but one day, he recalled years later, he was watching from the bow window at 'Karenza' when three Royal Navy anti-submarine motor launches appeared round Trevose Head, apparently in hot pursuit of a U-boat. The launches dropped depth-charges close to Newquay harbour mouth, and, as William Golding remembered it: 'Vast columns of spray shot up, and then an oil slick spread across the surface with black bobbles and specks floating in it.'[54]

'The spirit of the war ... It came in advancing waves'

Now that the submarine war had hardened opinions, Cornwall became less equivocal in its support of the war effort. The Methodists, in particular, with their strong religious influence on Cornish attitudes, moved away from their earlier stance—that war was inherently un-Christian—to embrace a more combative position, that of the 'just war'. The Cornish novelist Joseph Hocking, for example, earlier ordained as a Methodist minister, through his popular fiction now depicted Germany as a quintessentially evil opponent. As Alan M. Kent has observed, Hocking's 'status as a preacher and novelist, made him a minor celebrity who travelled to various Cornish towns and villages to encourage young men to join up. Hocking was not always successful in his endeavour, but he was persistent'.[55] In the end, such persistence paid off. Young men were persuaded that to volunteer was more noble than to wait until conscripted. Shortly after the war the official history of *Cornwall's Royal Engineers* could insist proudly that 'the voluntary principle is very strong in Cornwall, and whatever role they may be called upon to perform, the engineers and seafaring men of Cornwall will give of their best'.[56] Once convinced of the righteousness of the cause, it was suggested, the Cornish were willing enough to lend a hand, as indeed they were.

War in Cornwall: 'The Nightmare'

The changing attitude to the war in Cornwall dawned on Lawrence but slowly. As Lawrence remembered it in *Kangaroo*, the book that for ever ties him to Cornwall, the 'spirit of the war—the spirit of collapse and human ignominy, had not travelled so far yet. It came in advancing waves.'[57] Even when the threat of conscription intruded, initially in the guise of the Derby Scheme, where all eligible males between eighteen and forty-one had to register, he was impressed by the subdued dignity of Emma Pollard's sister-in-law at Porthcothan. Quietly, she sewed a khaki armlet on her husband's sleeve, preparing his military uniform for whatever trials lay ahead. As Lawrence explained to J.D. Beresford, owner of the house at Porthcothan, 'the war has come. Derby's scheme has wrung their withers.'[58] He admired how Emma's sister-in-law had reacted with calm stoicism to the arrival of war in her community:

> 'It's come now' she said: 'We've never had it till now, but it's come now. I'm sure, when I look at these buttons, I think "We've got the Kaiser to thank for these". Every stitch I put in goes through my heart'.
> Which I think is rather beautiful [wrote Lawrence], showing sincere gentleness and a power of love. The English women stitch armlets on freely enough: they have lost the power to love. But it does linger here.[59]

'The young men are being called up around here', Lawrence told Beresford: 'They are miserable. There are loud lamentations on every hand. The only cry is, that they may not be sent to France to fight. They quite shamelessly don't want to *see* a gun. I sympathise perfectly with this'.[60] A prelude to conscription proper, the Derby Scheme was intended to coerce young men into making a commitment to join the armed forces, requiring an eligible male to make a public declaration as to whether he would enlist immediately or defer his joining to a later date, to be determined by the authorities. Undertaken during November and December 1915, the Derby Scheme exerted huge moral pressure on individuals. Canvassers were appointed to visit the homes of each eligible male to persuade them to volunteer for war service. A letter from Lord Derby, Director-General of Recruiting, handed to each man, explained the scheme, reminding waverers that Britain was fighting for 'its very existence'.[61] Such bullying had the desired effect, but not swiftly enough to prevent the passing of the Military Service Act on 27 January 1916, which introduced compulsory conscription.

Later, when he had moved further west to Zennor, Lawrence discovered a similar attitude to coercion, the young men locally dreading the arrival of the postman, cycling across from St Ives with his postbag brimming with OHMS call-up papers. As he wrote to Catherine Carswell: 'These Cornish are most unwarlike, soft, peaceable, ancient. No men suffer more than they, at being conscripted ... This is the most terrible madness.'[62]

The overriding emotion was still bewilderment and detachment from the war, Lawrence thought: 'Right and wrong was not fixed for them as for the English. There was still a mystery for them ... Only one thing was wrong—any sort of *physical* compulsion or hurt.'[63] Stanley Hocking, Lawrence's neighbour at Zennor, later explained in his interview with C.J. Stevens: 'Compulsion is never appealing to the Cornish. I don't think anybody wanted to go. The war was so far away, and as soon as anyone left the farm the whole way of life was disrupted.' As he put it, on 'a farm there are certain jobs to be done. If you have cattle, sheep, horses and pigs, they must be fed and looked after every day. And when one person from the family is missing, who is going to do his work?'[64]

Yet the Cornish seemed passive in the face of compulsion, and Lawrence was increasingly unsettled by the sense of resignation he began to detect in Cornwall. As he had explained to Cynthia Asquith: 'Over Cornwall, last Wednesday and Thursday, went a terrible wave of depression. In Penzance market, farmers went about with wonder-struck faces'. 'We're beaten', they had told Lawrence, 'I'm afraid we're beaten. These Germans are a wonderful nation ... more than a match for us'. As Lawrence concluded: 'That is Cornwall at the present time.'[65]

Lawrence was himself overtaken by compulsion, even resignation, when he was called for a medical examination to determine his fitness for military conscription. Meekly, he obeyed, despite every instinct in his body. As he wrote to Dollie Radford on 29 June 1916:

> I have just come back from Bodmin. Yesterday I had to go and 'join the colours' in Penzance. They conveyed me to Bodmin—a distance of fifty or sixty miles. We were kept—thirty poor devils—in the barracks all night, and treated as incipient soldiers. Luckily I got a total exemption—and am home again. But it was a great shock that barracks experience—that being escorted by train, lined up on station platforms, marched like a criminal through the streets to a barracks. The ignominy is horrible, the humiliation ... what a degradation and

War in Cornwall: 'The Nightmare'

a prison, oh intolerable. I could not *bear* it—I should die in a week if they made me a soldier. Thirty men in their shirts, being weighed like sheep, one after the other—God! ... I beg all my stars that I may never see Bodmin again. I hate it so much.[66]

This was an episode that Lawrence wove into *Kangaroo*, when Richard Lovat Somers, his alter ego in the novel, is also forced to make the same journey to Bodmin. Like Lawrence, he seemed 'pale, silent, isolated; a queer figure, a young man with a beard'—but not young enough to prevent other would-be recruits calling him 'Dad'.[67]

Like Lawrence, Somers 'never forgot that journey up to Bodmin, with other men who were called up. They were all bitterly, desperately miserable'. On the train to Bodmin, they had yelled tunelessly the words of 'I'll be your sweetheart, if you will be mine'. Now, Somers imagined, 'those ghastly melancholy notes' were 'Wailing down the lost corridors of hell'.[68] And like his alter ego, Lawrence felt as much for the other conscripts as he did for himself. After all, he had got his exemption—the presiding doctor immediately recognized his medical condition—but the others were already on their hellish journey to the trenches. 'I liked the men', he wrote to Catherine Carswell on 9 July 1916: 'They all seemed so *decent* ... It was the underlying sense of disaster that overwhelmed me. They are all so brave, to suffer ... so noble, to accept sorrow and hurt'. Lawrence was amazed at their resignation: 'they accepted it, as one of them said to me, with a wonderful purity of spirit—I could howl my eyes out over him—because "they believed first of all in their duty to their fellow man"'.[69] On 1 September he was still expressing his irrepressible anger, writing to Lady Cynthia Asquith: 'My blood cribbles with fury to think of it ... The whole of militarism is so disgusting'.[70]

In March 1917 Lawrence heard that, with the rules changed, he might be liable for call-up once more. Again he was summoned to Bodmin, and once more he had his exemption, but 1917 was already turning out to be a nightmare year. Stanley Hocking, in his interview with C.J. Stevens, admitted that things at Zennor 'were getting very difficult by 1917'. Earlier, he recalled, 'one scarcely knew that a war was going on—we were far away from it all'. But Hocking 'became scared' in 1917, he said, terrified by the sudden and random intensity of the naval battles fought out so close to home.[71] Once, when Lawrence was helping the Hockings in the harvest field on their farm at Tregerthen, 'there was a game going on at sea', as

Stanley put it. A few days before, Stanley explained, several ships had been torpedoed in the vicinity, and now a U-boat was being hunted 'by a grand circle' of destroyers, airships and patrol boats a mile or so out to sea, in full view of Lawrence and the Hockings.[72] Another time, Lawrence recorded, 'two ships were submarined [sic] just off here [Zennor]: luckily we [Lawrence and Frieda] didn't see them: but Stanley watched one go down, and the coastwatchers saw the crew of the other struggling in the water after the ship had gone: all drowned: Norwegians, I believe.'[73]

'And her name is "Sudden Death"'

Such close-quarters action unnerved local people, said Stanley Hocking, and, in an uncanny echo of A.L. Rowse's story, he explained that many had begun to imagine that the Germans would invade by stealth, doing 'it very quietly and secretly by submarine on our Cornish beaches. Probably send little raiding bands ashore, just to knock the wind out of us and terrify us'. Hocking continued, warming to his theme, adding that 'people began thinking: What's to stop those fellows on a quiet night from running ashore in one of our nice little coves? They could come up to our farms and cut our throats. It was possible'.[74]

In *Kangaroo*, Lawrence's alter ego, Richard Lovat Somers, tells a tale even more remarkably like that recorded by Rowse, a story that no doubt Lawrence had heard on several occasions and in its various forms, probably from the Hockings and their neighbours.

> The town was buzzing ... Two German submarine officers had come into the town, dressed in clothes they had taken from an English ship they had sunk. They had stayed a night at the Mounts Bay Hotel. And two days later they had told the story to two fishermen whose fishing boat they had stopped. They had shown the incredulous fishermen the hotel bill. Then they sunk the fishing boat, sending the three fishermen ashore in the row-boat.[75]

There were other rumours. The arrival of Lawrence and Frieda at Higher Tregerthen was thought by some to have heralded the upsurge of U-boat activity in the vicinity. As noted above, submarine attacks would not diminish after the Lawrences had left Cornwall in October 1917. Rather, they would increase. But for the suspicious-minded, there was circumstantial evidence sufficient to implicate Lawrence and his wife in the burgeoning submarine campaign. For example, there was a telltale smell of petrol emanating from nearby cliffs. Stanley Hocking later explained that this was from leaking drums washed ashore from torpedoed merchant ships, debris brought in by the tide along with other common items such as candle grease and bales of hay, but there were those locally who imagined that there was a secret fuel dump managed furtively by Lawrence to resupply German submarines. Similarly, when Lawrence retarred the cottage chimney at Higher Tregerthen, this was deemed to have special significance for U-boats lurking nearby, evidence that he was indeed a spy, in the pay of the enemy. As Stanley Hocking put it: 'What aroused suspicion was that Lawrence moved into Higher Tregerthen, and gradually the submarines began sinking our ships'.[76]

As early as February 1915, the Admiralty had sought the assistance of 'Coast Watchers and Civilians on Shore', offering rewards to 'persons on shore for information concerning hostile Submarines, Minelayers, and other War Vessels, and for reports of Mines washed up'.[77] Finding a mine on a beach brought £1 recompense; information leading to the apprehension of a U-boat or German minelayer attracted the not inconsiderable sum of £100. Coast-watching was not only doing one's duty but could also be a lucrative form of employment, or so some thought. As Bernard Walke mused, somewhat pejoratively, such activity had always had a ready appeal in Cornwall, long before the outbreak of war:

> Cornwall has always had its watchers—watching is in the Cornishman's blood. It is all that is left for old men who have spent their lives at sea—to go out to the end of the pier or up on the cliffs where they can watch the sea … There are others who are on the lookout for driftwood or for wreckage to come ashore. Jimmy Limpots, a man whom I knew at St Ives, was always searching for bodies; he and his two dogs would haunt the coast from Zennor to Carbis Bay … prying into caves and between boulders in the search for a corpse for which he would receive the reward of one pound.[78]

Some watchers, Walke averred, did not limit their attentions to such activities. 'Courting couples', he said, 'have a special interest for them', while others 'watch by doorways and peer into uncurtained windows, if only to discover what their neighbours are going to have for supper'.[79] Moreover:

The war gave added zest to these watchings. And nothing was too impossible to be believed: the ringing of bells from the church tower was held by some to be a method of signalling to the Germans; to be seen often on the cliffs was taken as proof of being engaged in supplying petrol to enemy submarines. For two years I was suspected by neighbours of preparing for a landing on Marazion beach ... 'You call yourself a parson, but you are nothing but a German spy. Half your pay do come from the Pope and the other half from the Kaiser'.[80]

Unwittingly or not, Gull Ranger's book *The Secret Service Submarine: A Story of the Present War*, published in 1915 under his pen name Guy Thorne, also added to the general air of unease and suspicion. Ranger was well known in Zennor, where his eccentric manners and alcoholic writing methods had been the subject of local gossip during his sojourns in the pre-war years (see p. 77). Now his latest novel appeared to be a warning, and, with its intimations of privileged insider knowledge, a sign that Ranger was actually to be taken very seriously indeed. Coincidently, Ranger had arranged for Higher Tregerthen to be renovated some years earlier, before Lawrence moved in, although he had never lived there himself. He did, however, appreciate its potentially strategic position, in full view of the Atlantic.

Making his theme crystal clear, Ranger had chosen as his preface for *The Secret Service Submarine* the verse 'The Story of the Submarine', penned in 1914 during the early months of the war by one William Booth, a grim forecast (and foretaste) of what maritime conflict would be like:

> This is the song of the submarine
>   Afloat in the waters wide.
>   Like a sleeping whale
>   In the starlight pale,
>   Just flush with the swirling tide
> The salt sea ripples her plates
>   The salt wind is her breath.
>   Like spear of fate
>   She lies in wait
> And her name is 'Sudden Death'.[81]

It is unlikely that Gull had Zennor specifically in mind, despite his intimate knowledge of maritime Cornwall, and he could not have anticipated the

War in Cornwall: 'The Nightmare'

catastrophe that would shortly overtake Lawrence, including the dramatic expulsion that would happen even as *The Secret Service Submarine* was being eagerly snapped up in bookshops. Yet the coincidence is striking. In Gull's novel, the protagonist John Carey and his brother Bernard, a Royal Navy officer, are from a family of 'west-country people, and all sons of Devon and Cornwall'.[82] Bernard becomes a 'Lieutenant-Commander of Submarines', and is privy to an urgent memorandum from Admiral Noyes, Chief of Naval Intelligence, which reveals that 'it seems recently there has been a tremendous leakage of information to the enemy'.[83] Bernard adds knowingly: 'We have our people on the look-out, and there is no doubt whatever that, during the last two months, over and over again the German ships have got information about our movements.'[84]

The novel played on contemporary fears about the sinister nature of submarine warfare, U-boats operating silently and unobserved within striking distance of the British coast, their terrible destructive power unleashed on the unwary when least expected. The story also exposed the existence of a treacherous fifth column of spies and enemy sympathizers, especially in coastal areas, traitors ever ready to betray Naval secrets vital to national security. Patriotic citizens were urged to be 'on the look-out', to identify and report strange behaviour or unusual events.

Frieda, in her memoir *Not I, but the Wind*, described this gradually encroaching atmosphere of suspicion, with its intrusive voyeurism. 'In the first year of the war Cornwall was still not quite engulfed by it; but slowly, like an octopus, with slow but deadsure tentacles, the war spirit crept up and all around us. Suspicion and fear surrounded us.' She remembered 'once sitting on the rocks with Lawrence, by the sea, near our cottage at Tregerthen. I was intoxicated by the air and sun. I had to jump and run, and my white scarf blew in the wind. "Stop it, stop it, you fool, you fool!", Lawrence cried. "Can't you see they'll think you are signalling to the enemy"!'.[85] Lawrence (or rather, Somers) had already been cautioned. 'You want to be careful', warned one of his Cornish friends. 'I've heard that the coast-watchers have got orders to keep a very strict watch on you.' 'Let them, they'll see nothing', he responded with bravado, but inwardly he was anxious.[86]

Like his alter ego Richard Lovat Somers in *Kangaroo*, Lawrence had felt uneasy ever since conscription had intruded in Cornwall and he had been forced to undergo his examination at Bodmin, a premonition that his days in Cornwall might be numbered, that he and Frieda would have to move on sooner rather than later:

> He loved the place so much. Ever since the conscription suspense he had said to himself, when he walked up the wild, little road from his cottage to the moor: shall I see the foxgloves come out? If only I can stay till the foxgloves come. And he had seen the foxgloves come. Then it was the heather—would he see the heather? And then the primroses in the hollow down to the sea: the tufts and tufts of primroses, where the fox stood and looked at him.[87]

Yet in some ways Lawrence seemed past caring. He told all who might listen how pointless was the war and how he would not fight just because Germany had invaded Belgium. To those whose sons, fathers, brothers had dutifully gone off to war—and perhaps to their deaths—this was deeply offensive as well as self-indulgent. The locals, not all of whom had warmed to Frieda's aristocratic manner, remembered that she was German—and a relation of the feared 'Red Baron', the German air ace. They knew that the Lawrences had German newspapers sent to Higher Tregerthen (they came from Frieda's sisters, sent via Switzerland). Some may have wondered whether the unintelligible Hebridean folk-songs sung so lustily when the Lawrences visited Cecil Gray at Bosigran were German patriotic compositions.

Indeed, when in one of his dark moods, Lawrence *did* sing German folk-songs at Bosigran; loudly, defiantly and aggressively, and likely to be heard by any passing listener. Making matters worse, Gray had been careless in observing the blackout, showing an unobscured light which, if not actually signalling to enemy submarines (as some suspected), could be conceivably a useful navigational aid for any marauding U-boat. The police called on Gray, and subsequently, in early October 1917, he was fined £20 for his misdemeanour—a substantial sum.[88] Gray was not inclined to take the blame, and accused the overzealous prying of the coast-watchers of causing his misfortune. 'One of the less engaging aspects of the Cornish character', he complained, 'consists in a mania for spying and listening at keyholes or windows'.[89]

Lawrence was implicated in the rumours that grew around the Gray incident and other supposedly suspicious activities. Individuals had their own pet theories. P.O. Eddy, brother-in-law of William Henry Hocking (on whom suspicion also fell, for being 'jolly good friends'[90] with Lawrence), reported that he had 'heard people say they used to see a little lamp flashing at the Lawrences".[91] Alison Symons remembered that,

War in Cornwall: 'The Nightmare'

During their stay at Zennor, a coal boat, the *Emanual Espana* was wrecked on Tremedda rocks. The foursome [Lawrence, Frieda, Murry, Mansfield] went down the cliff to look at the wreck and described it to Hilda [their maid] on their return. Fortunately no lives were lost. The locals thought D.H. Lawrence and his wife were spies and that they signalled to German submarines at sea. My mother's explanation was that Lawrence was asthmatic and in order to get enough air into his lungs, he opened the sea-facing window and the black-out curtains, thus showing a forbidden light, a strict blackout being in force at the time. After a few months people came snooping around, and a detective interviewed Hilda, asking her many personal questions and embarrassing her greatly.[92]

Quite what these 'personal questions' were is not clear, but presumably they revolved around habits, routines, opinions, behaviours, including anything odd, perverse or subversive. Despite the controversy that had surrounded the banning of *The Rainbow* in 1915, Lawrence's move to Cornwall did not initially arouse official suspicion. Prohibited areas had been established under the Defence of the Realm Act 1914, as Bertrand Russell discovered when he was barred from entering coastal areas in 1916 as a result of speeches he had made to munitions workers in South Wales. By 1917 restrictions had been tightened still further, with civilian entry into 'special military areas' around the coast subject to careful scrutiny. Although not yet affected personally, Lawrence was clearly aware of the potential difficulties when he advised his friend Kot (a Ukrainian Jew) not to visit him in Zennor: 'I shrink from asking you down here to the coast—they make such an absurd fuss about foreigners. Oh what fools people are'.[93]

The eager examination of the wreck of the *Emanual Espana* by Lawrence and the others was not as unusual or potentially incriminating as it might have seemed to any outside observers, for clambering down the cliffs to almost inaccessible coves to view ships that had come to grief was not an uncommon activity in Cornwall. This was 'wrecking', not in the mythical sense of deliberately luring ships onto rocks, but rather plundering materials from stricken vessels, especially those items that had been washed ashore. 'This was mainly wood', Alison Symons recalled, 'which was used for innumerable things: repairs, the making of chicken coops, doors, stools, gates, shelves, and of course firewood'. The whole community might be involved: 'No one was allowed to walk up the cliff empty-handed, even down to the smallest child who might be given a piece of firewood, a chopping board or a string of corks to carry'.[94] If especially valuable items had been washed up, then the customs officials might take an interest. But for the most part, 'wrecking' was seen as a harmless and indeed traditional activity, unlikely to draw the attention of the authorities.

Few, at least in officialdom, would have imagined that Lawrence had gone down to the sea to gloat or view the results of his nefarious handiwork. Yet it was an episode that played on Lawrence's mind, and which again he captured in *Kangaroo*:

> Day followed day in this tension of suspense. Submarines were off the coast; Harriet [aka Frieda] saw a ship sunk, away to sea. Horrible excitement ... Increasing rigour of coast-watching, and *no* light must be shown. Yet along the high road on the hillside above, plainer than any house-light, danced the lights of a cart, moving, or slowly sped the light of a motor-cycle, on the blackness. Then a Spanish coal-vessel, three thousand tons, ran on the rocks in a fog, straight under the cottage. Somers watched the waves break over her. Her coal washed ashore, and the farmers carried it up the cliffs in sacks.[95]

Professor John Westlake's presence at Tregerthen Cottage (Eagle's Nest) had endowed the locality with a certain political sensitivity before the war, given his strong views on international affairs—including his hostility to the Ottoman Empire, Germany's ally—and his entertainment at Zennor of prominent individuals perhaps had security implications. Westlake had died in 1913 but an aura of heightened alert remained during the Great War years, especially given the status of coastal areas under the Defence of the Realm Act. The submarine menace had created local anxiety about Lawrence and Frieda's motives, exacerbated by the hostility of the local vicar towards the unconventional couple, and the Bosigran incident, when Cecil Gray was fined for showing a light, had alerted officialdom to the rumours and suspicions.

'Now comes another nasty blow'

However, as Louise Wright has argued, it may have been the visit to Zennor of Robert Mountsier, an American journalist, that made Lawrence and Frieda real suspects in the eyes of the authorities.[96] Robert Mountsier visited

War in Cornwall: 'The Nightmare'

Cornwall in early November 1916, accompanied by another American journalist, Esther Andrews. They returned at Christmas, staying with the Lawrences; on 31 December Mountsier and Andrews were arrested in London. As Wright has noted, this was the period when Scotland Yard was cracking down on journalists they suspected were being deployed as German spies. A neutral power at this stage, the United States was easily penetrated by German agents for the purpose of recruitment, while American citizens could travel freely to any of the belligerent countries. A plan to flood Britain and Ireland with journalists sympathetic to the German cause was duly uncovered and countermeasures taken.

Lawrence was led to believe that Mountsier had come to Britain with the intention of interviewing prominent literary figures for leading American newspapers. In fact, Mountsier concentrated on the war, especially the home front. He sought out pacifists, and took an interest in Britain's war economy. Under his direction, Esther Andrews planned an article on Woolwich, the site of the Royal Arsenal and the manufacture of munitions. Mountsier compared the cost of living in Britain with that of America, opining in an article in the *New York Times* that 'I have been told by economists and shipping men that England is well provided with food for a long time ahead, so that the [German] submarine campaign must become far more effective than it has been to make a great impression'. Indeed, he added, 'I have very good authority for saying that England has imported vast quantities of foodstuffs and for a long period has been storing it against the possibility that the German submarine campaign might cut deeply into shipping'.[97] Perhaps coincidentally, only two days earlier the *New York Times* had reported that journalist spies recruited in America were being sent to Britain to seek information which could be useful to Germany in waging 'ruthless submarine warfare'.[98]

Mountsier had also taken an interest in the Irish question (1916 was the year of the Easter Rising), visiting Dublin immediately before calling on Lawrence in Christmas 1916. It was, Wright suggests, the Irish journey that led to Mountsier's arrest, one American newspaper noting that his 'Irish adventures ... were not looked upon favourably by the English'.[99] Intriguingly, Lawrence mentioned to Stanley Hocking (William Henry's brother) that on Christmas Eve a police sergeant had called at Higher Tregerthen, wanting to know all about Mountsier.[100] Here was the British—or English, as Lawrence would have imagined it—state intruding directly in Lawrence's life. So much for escaping England's reach.

Robert Mountsier was released after his arrest but remained under surveillance, returning shortly after to America. Lawrence was aware that Mountsier was a suspect, even writing to tell him that 'I think Wm H [William Henry Hocking] was scared when you were kicked out of Zennor and you were a "Spy"'.[101] But Lawrence seemed oblivious to the wider implications. To the gossip and innuendo of anxious locals, frightened by the encroaching war in Cornish waters, was added now the direct interest of the British state, which considered Lawrence a threat to national security. Remarkably, Lawrence and Mountsier remained close, Mountsier becoming his American literary agent.

Lawrence and Frieda had been the subject of low-level harassment, such as the occasion when Frieda was carrying home a bag of groceries from the shop in Zennor. She and Lawrence were accosted by two officious coast-watchers who demanded to know what she had in her bag, suspecting that it was a camera. According to Stanley Hocking: 'One wasn't allowed to take photographs in those days. In fact, I didn't get my camera until several years after the war—just to be safe'. Frieda showed the contents of her bag to the men: 'It was a loaf of bread. She said they looked mighty crestfallen.'[102] It was an incident that found its way into *Kangaroo*. In this version, Harriet (for Frieda) and Somers had been out shopping together, and on the way back to their cottage were stopped by men in military uniform, who tore open a parcel in Harriet's bag and found to their dismay that it contained a block of salt, not a camera.

Far worse was to come. On 11 October 1917, while Lawrence was in Penzance with William Henry and Frieda was over with Gray at Bosigran, the police raided Higher Tregerthen. They had gone through Lawrence's correspondence and disturbed Frieda's work-basket. The very next day the raid was followed up by a visit from an army major, together with a police sergeant and two plain-clothes policemen. Lawrence was presented with a military order, signed by Major-General W. Western of Southern Command, Salisbury, informing him that he and Frieda had three days to quit Cornwall. It seemed a draconian measure, even to the men who had had to deliver it. Stanley Hocking, who had been cutting weeds on the roadside nearby, heard them talking as they came away from Lawrence's cottage. 'Well, that's a job I would rather not have had to do', said one.[103]

Bewildered, Lawrence sat down to write to Cynthia Asquith. 'Now comes another nasty blow', he announced: 'The police have suddenly descended on the house, searched it, and delivered us a notice to leave the area of

Cornwall'. He could not understand why, he protested, perhaps a little disingenuously. 'This bolt from the blue has fallen this morning', he wrote, 'why, I know not ... We are as innocent even of pacifist activities, let alone spying of any sort as the rabbits in the field outside.'[104] In the face of the mighty power of the state, which had caught up with and crushed the last vestiges of his Rananim, Lawrence was impotent. He had little choice but to obey the order, and he and Frieda began to pack their belongings. Lawrence also made a great bonfire of many of his papers, in the process probably destroying some important work. Richard Aldington speculated that 'in this fire perished his copy of "The Goat and Compasses", the lost chapters of *The Reality of Peace*, and possibly some poems'.[105] As Frieda remembered it, the shock of the expulsion order 'changed something in Lawrence for ever'.[106]

Once more, it was an experience that Lawrence described in *Kangaroo*, in a chapter entitled 'The Nightmare'. Like Lawrence, Richard Lovat Somers has fallen under the spell of Cornwall but at a stroke all has been undone by the further encroachment of England's war: 'The war-wave had broken right over England, now: right over Cornwall. Probably throughout the ages Cornwall had not been finally swept, submerged by any English spirit. Now it happened—the accursed later war spirit.'[107] But the Cornish were tenacious and subversive, like all Celts, like David Lloyd George: 'A little Welsh lawyer, not an Englishman at all.'[108] Somers (and Lawrence) both hated and yet somehow secretly approved of their duplicity: 'Somers gradually came to believe that all Jews, and all Celts, even whilst they espoused the cause of England, subtly lived to bring about the last humiliation of the great old England ... Let the Celts work out their subtlety.'[109]

Like Lawrence, Somers and his wife Harriet (for Frieda) are given the summary order to get out of Cornwall forthwith:

> Somers, white and very still, spoke no word, but waited. Then the police-sergeant, in rather stumbling fashion, began to read an order from the military authorities that Richard Lovat Somers and Harriet Emma Marianna Johanna Somers, of Trevethan Cottage, etc, should leave the county of Cornwall within the space of three days. And further, within the space of twenty-four hours of their arrival in any place they must report themselves at the police station of the said place, giving their address. And they were forbidden to enter any part of the area of Cornwall, etc, etc, etc.
>
> 'But why?' cried Harriet. 'Why? What have we done?'.

'I can't say what you have done', said the young officer in a cold tone, 'but it must be something sufficiently serious. They don't send out these orders for nothing'.[110]

When Lawrence and Frieda left Cornwall, like the fictional Somers and Harriet, they made for London. William Henry Hocking drove them in his cart to the branch-line station at St Ives. An abrupt entry in his diary for 15 October 1917 was his only lasting commentary on his encounter with the great man: 'To St Ives—Lawrence'.[111]

William Henry was also a casualty of the expulsion, at least as far as Lawrence was concerned; he never answered the letters Lawrence wrote to him. Sadly, Lawrence decided that William Henry was not a candidate for Rananim, whenever and wherever that utopia might be achieved. Stanley Hocking acknowledged that Lawrence 'wrote William Henry several letters. But', he added perfunctorily, 'my brother would never answer a letter. He was no correspondent.'[112] Asked whether Lawrence had really considered William Henry for Rananim, Stanley Hocking replied: 'I did hear about that.' Elaborating, he explained that 'Lawrence had an imaginary place which he was calling Rananim ... Lawrence talked a lot about this ... I think William Henry was thinking that the whole thing was nonsense, and he wasn't having anything to do with it.'[113] The expulsion had spelt the end of Rananim in Cornwall, including Lawrence's relationship with William Henry Hocking and the high hopes he had harboured for his Cornish friend.

Asked if he thought that it was the Cornish who had finally driven Lawrence and Frieda out of Cornwall, Stanley Hocking was indignant. 'The coast guards were definitely not Cornish', he insisted: 'Neither were the military. I'm doubtful if some of the police were even Cornish.'[114] He was clear; it was the state that had expelled the Lawrences. From this perspective, Frances Wilson's recent suggestion that 'the couple were chased out of Cornwall by a pitchfork-wielding mob' seems very wide of the mark.[115]

'Time for us to go'

In London, Lawrence tried to put a brave face on things, continuing to insist that it was all a mistake and misunderstanding, making enquiries as to how to reverse the expulsion decision. 'I very much want to be allowed to go back to Cornwall', he wrote to an official on 29 October: 'We have got the house there, and are rooted there.'[116] He was quietly confident, as

War in Cornwall: 'The Nightmare'

he told Cecil Gray: 'These govt. people are the devil, with their importance and their "expediency" and their tyranny. But I believe we shall get back to Zennor next month.'[117] Deep down, however, he found it hard to suppress his feelings. In *Kangaroo*, he has Somers express his longing:

> he pined for his cottage, the granite-strewn, gorse-grown slope from the moors to the sea ... In his eyes, he saw the farm below—grey, naked, with the big, pale-roofed new barn—and the network of dark green fields with the pale-grey walls—and the gorse and the sea ... He craved to be back, his soul was there.[118]

Alas, it was not to be. In fact, for some time now Lawrence had known inwardly that he needed to get out of Britain altogether, to escape England's encroaching snare. As long ago as December 1916 he had told Catherine Carswell: 'I believe that England ... is capable of seeing only badness in me, for ever and ever. I believe America is my virgin soil: truly.'[119] Likewise, in January 1917, he had explained to Cynthia Asquith that he wanted 'to go far west, to California or the South Seas, and live apart, away from the world. It is really my old Florida idea—but one must go further west.'[120] It was, as he said to Catherine Carswell, prophetically:

> Time for us to go,
> Time for us to go ...[121]

To his constant friend Kot, Lawrence wrote on 9 February 1917: 'We shall all come to our Rananim before many years are out—only believe me—an Isle of the Blest, here on earth. But the first thing is to cut clear of the old world—burn one's boats: if only one could.'[122] In fact, he had tried to burn his boats, armed with his exemption from military service, and had applied for a passport to allow his once-and-for-all escape to America. But the authorities, with the intention of keeping a close eye on him, had rejected the request. For the duration of the war, he was grounded in the United Kingdom. Thereafter, let off the leash, as it were, Lawrence resumed his wandering, bringing him shortly to Australia, the principal setting for *Kangaroo*, first published in 1923.

During his relatively short spell in Cornwall, Lawrence's opinion of the Cornish had altered considerably. He had come to Cornwall armed with an array of English assumptions about 'the Celts'—some favourable, some not—and it is these colonialist prejudices that are often remembered today, especially in Cornwall itself. When Cornwall proved to be more susceptible to England's intrusion than he had anticipated, with the Cornish acquiescent in the face of coercion, Lawrence became angry. But he began to empathize with the Cornish, participating in their community activities, and even started to see the Celtic peoples as his allies, quietly subversive and duplicitous in their veiled attempts to erode England's sway.

Today, there is no one alive at Zennor who remembers D.H. Lawrence and his search for Rananim during the bleak years of the Great War. But when C.J. Stevens, an American writer of Cornish descent, visited Cornwall during the winter of 1967–68 to trace his Zennor ancestors, he found that Stanley Hocking—younger brother of William Henry—was living in retirement at nearby St Ives. Stevens soon won the confidence of the elderly Hocking, and was able to record a remarkable series of reminiscences about Lawrence, Frieda and their Zennor days. Towards the end of one interview session, Stanley Hocking suddenly asked his wife to go upstairs to fetch 'a metal box filled with yellowing newspaper clippings and what appeared to be a glass-framed picture'. It was an astonishing moment. As Stevens explained, 'Hocking rose stiffly from his chair. "This is a little keepsake that Lawrence gave us Hockings", he said. It was a tapestry of the phoenix on its nest of flames. "Lawrence made this".'[123]

The phoenix symbolized the spirit of Rananim, and it was fitting as well as significant that Lawrence should leave in Cornwall the tapestry he himself had crafted, in the hands of the Hocking family. Jane Costin is surely right when she argues that 'biographies of Lawrence have all failed to notice the enduring impact on him of his expulsion from Cornwall in October 1917'. As she has concluded, the 'expulsion from Cornwall was a deeply traumatic event that had a profound and lasting effect on his subsequent life and work, a disruption that is an important, but often overlooked, legacy of his time there'.[124]

Chapter 6

'So on to Australia!'

'There was no place for him in that rather sinister, post-war world. Either he must escape from it or it would crush him. He had to go into the wilderness or perish, cease to be the unique thing he was.'[1]

This was Richard Aldington's insightful assessment, a summing up which truthfully represented D.H. Lawrence's predicament in the aftermath of his summary expulsion from Cornwall. There was nowhere for Lawrence to go in England, and he and Frieda must look elsewhere. The war was over in November 1918 but that was little consolation, except in the knowledge that one must make the best of things and start again. As Lawrence wrote in the opening passage of his novel *Lady Chatterley's Lover* (first published privately in 1928), set in post-Great War England:

> Ours is essentially a tragic age, so we refuse to take it tragically. The cataclysm has happened, and we are among the ruins, we start to build up new little habitats, to have new little hopes. It is rather hard work: there is now no smooth road into the future: but we shall go round, or scramble over the obstacles. We've got to live, no matter how many skies have fallen … The war has brought the roof down … one must live and learn.[2]

As Jane Costin has observed in her important discussion, Lawrence's literary responses to the places he visited between 1919, the year he quit England, and 1922, when he produced *Kangaroo* (first published in 1923), 'can be seen as a cathartic experience that finally allowed Lawrence to shed his "sickness" over his expulsion and to move on beyond his yearning for Cornwall'.[3] As Costin also notes, Lawrence's biographers have tended to see his time in Cornwall as detrimental to his mental and physical health (perhaps taking their cue from Middleton Murry's caustic comments [see pp. 83–5]), yet Lawrence revelled in his outdoor life there—long walks on the cliffs and moor, helping out on the farm—and constantly expressed his desire to return to what he saw as a positive and energetic way of living. Cornwall was never far from his mind in the years after his departure. In August 1928, for example, he wrote to his old friend Kot, presumably just returned from a visit west of the Tamar, asking 'did Cornwall seem very spoiled? I've been thinking so much about it lately—I loved Cornwall'.[4]

Initially, Lawrence fought to return to Cornwall: 'It is foul—I hate London—God knows how it will all work out. But I am going to try hard to get back to Cornwall.'[5] It was not until the end of 1918, well over a year since his expulsion from Cornwall, that Lawrence finally gave up the struggle, relinquishing the tenancy at Higher Tregerthen. Abandoning England in 1919, Lawrence travelled to Italy, to the places he had enjoyed before the war. But, as Jane Costin has argued, his response was now very different, 'characterised by restlessness and disappointment'.[6] Behind it all, she contends, was Lawrence's intense yearning, an 'anguish of nostalgia for Cornwall' as he put it in *Kangaroo*.[7]

'It was all so like Cornwall'

Lawrence had remained in touch with Irene Whittley, daughter of Captain Short, from whom he had rented Higher Tregerthen, and they corresponded for several years. Writing to Irene from Italy, he reminisced about Cornwall and asked for the latest news, sighing, 'Ah well, but I was mostly happy at Tregerthen, and shall always remember gratefully'.[8] Having moved from one place to another on the Italian mainland, Lawrence went on to Sicily, at once dubbing it 'the Celtic land of Italy', an attempt perhaps to compare its semi-detached status with the relationship between Cornwall and England.[9] From there, it was on to Sardinia, a visit that led to his travel book *Sea and Sardinia*, published in 1921. A sense of loss and homelessness pervades the volume, which Costin has attributed to Lawrence's continued mourning for Cornwall. At Mandas, in southern Sardinia, he recognized an immediate affinity with Cornwall, a similarity he found energizing as well as nostalgic: 'It is like Cornwall, like the Land's End Region ... This is very different from the Italian landscape. Italy is almost always dramatic ... Perhaps it is the natural floridity of limestone formations ... Sardinia is another thing ...

'So on to Australia!'

a wide, almost Celtic landscape of hills'.[10] It was granite, so unlike Italian limestone, that made Mandas feel Cornish:

> I could hardly believe my eyes it was ... like Cornwall in the bleak parts ... There were several forlorn-looking out-buildings, very like Cornwall. And then the wide, forlorn country road stretched away between borders of grass and low, drystone walls, towards a farm with a tuft of trees, and a naked stone village in the distance ... it was all so like Cornwall ... that old nostalgia for the Celtic regions began to spring up in me. Ah, those old drystone walls dividing the fields—pale and granite-bleached! Strange is a Celtic landscape ... Granite is my favourite. It is so live under the feet, it has a deep sparkle of its own.[11]

At root, however, Lawrence knew that this was not 'a Celtic landscape'. It was not, of course, Cornwall either—despite the bleakness and the profusion of granite. As he admitted to himself and to his readers: 'It might almost be Cornwall: not quite.'[12]

Lawrence's restlessness eventually took him to Australia, the destination of many Cornish emigrants, mainly (but not exclusively) miners and their families, especially in the nineteenth century. Copper in South Australia, tin in Tasmania, gold in Victoria and Western Australia, silver-lead at Broken Hill, and a multiplicity of other metals in destinations scattered across the continent, had brought the Cornish to most areas of the country where there were minerals to be had. Like Lawrence, many of these Cornish emigrants had acquired a certain restlessness, a mobility encouraged by the growth of the international mining frontier during the nineteenth century, in which Cornish skills were constantly in demand around the globe. The Cornish boasted their supposed superiority as hard-rock miners—the myth of 'Cousin Jack'—as they moved within and sometimes between continents, creating a transnational identity centred on their distinctive ethno-occupational identity. They were central in the mining history of the United States, Latin America, South Africa, New Zealand and elsewhere.[13]

'Pard country'

Zennor was part of this story, a mining area and a source of emigrants for destinations worldwide. The St Ives Consolidated mine had been abandoned in 1915 but in Lawrence's time there was still mining in the locality, notably at Geevor and Levant, further down the coast towards St Just. In Zennor itself there were numerous visible remains of the mining industry, such as the majestic twin engine-houses at Carn Galver (or Galva) and the imposing ruins at Gurnard's Head. Although the products of modernity, their evident decay and weathered granite construction lent them a timeless quality, like 'remnants of some by-gone civilization' as Lawrence put it.[14]

Moreover, many Zennor families still had connections with the mining industry. James Stevens, for example, local farmer and diarist, who was born in Zennor and died in 1918 (see p. 93), recalled working as a young lad under Captain Dunstan at Wheal Grylls, a tin mine at Churchtown cliff. Dunstan had built a new count-house, where Stevens spent many evenings, reading copies of the *Christian World* newspaper lent by Dunstan. Later, Stevens was employed driving adits (drainage tunnels) and sinking shafts at adjoining Wheal Sherriffs, and also worked as a tin-dresser at the stamps, where ore was crushed. Also nearby was the Vear Mine (or Wheal Veor) run by Captain John Roach. By the early twentieth century, there were three remaining mines in Zennor: Trevail, Trewey (or Gavers Mine) and Rose Vale Mine in Foage Valley. Harry Semmens was put in charge of the horse at Trevail Mine when he was only four years old, the horse being led to and from the shaft's mouth, hauling ore brought up from underground. The mine was closed in 1913. Rose Vale Mine was driven into the hillside in the Foage Valley, the stamps worked by a large waterwheel on the Zennor river, with Dick Osborn as supervisor. By 1913 there were forty-seven men employed at the mine. The miners worked in 'pares' or syndicates, such as that comprising Tom Berryman, Tom Nankervis and Tom Berryman's father.[15] Despite its apparent promise, the mine was abandoned during the Great War, although locals continued to insist that 'Zennor tin ore is the richest in Cornwall'.[16] They also asserted that there was plenty of ore left in the old mines; one above Eagle's Nest was said to be 'as full as she can stick'.[17]

As Alison Symons observed, in larger farming families in Zennor, several of the sons would often find work in the mines when there was not enough to keep them occupied on the farms, and in this way the occupational boundaries between mining and farming became blurred.[18] Lawrence was acquainted with local families such as the Berrymans and the Nankervises, and would have met some of those who had been employed only recently in the mines. He would have known too that many Zennor folk had emigrated overseas in the last half century or more, taking their mining (and farming) skills to distant lands. Many families were still in touch with their kin overseas, with

'So on to Australia!'

emigrant stories and experiences woven into local lore. The St Just mining area, of which Zennor was a component, was nicknamed 'pard country', a reflection of the district's American connections, especially to Mineral Point in Wisconsin, where the mining settlement of Linden was known as 'pard town' after the Cornish-American practice of calling a colleague 'pard' or 'pardner'.[19]

The inherently paradoxical nature of Cornish emigration was encapsulated in the telling if apocryphal story of the young St Just girl who was asked if she had ever been to Land's End, just a few miles down the coast. The girl replied, 'Aw, no ... We St Just people don't travel much, only to South Africa.'[20] There was, too, an element of tragedy in the emigrant experience, mining accidents overseas taking a persistent toll. In July 1888, for example, a dreadful underground fire in the De Beers diamond mine in Kimberley, South Africa, led to the death of 178 Africans and twenty-four Europeans. Among the latter were four men from the St Just mining district, including Thomas Nankervis, a member of that local extended family.[21]

In the 1870s, the closure of two small tin mines at Zennor had led to a mini exodus from the parish, accounting for a drop in its population from 600 to 500 in a decade (with a further decline to 332 by 1901) and forging local family links with overseas communities as far distant as America and New Zealand.[22] Earlier, in the 1850s, Cornish emigrants from Zennor had participated in the gold rush to Victoria in Australia. As one of them noted in a letter home, on the Creswick diggings in the Victorian goldfields in 1854 he had encountered 'Richard Eddy from Treen and Matthew Thomas from Treen and David Eddy from Bosigran ... Matthew White ... Richard Eddy from Bosigran, John Hosking from Treveal and Arthur Chellew from Zennor Church Town'.[23] In their new lands, such people remembered their Zennor origins. In 1874, for example, the *Yorke's Peninsula Advertiser*, published in the copper-mining district of northern Yorke Peninsula in South Australia, carried this wistfully nostalgic ditty:

> The morn was fair at Trewey Mill,
>   And the glorious summer sun,
> Was shining out o'er Zennor Hill,
>   As if to crown the fun.
>
> The girls were cheerful, blithe and gay,
>   For all their beaus were there,

> To take them off without delay
> To Corpus Christi fair.[24]

James Stevens' elder brothers, William and Abraham, both miners, each emigrated to America. In March 1863, Abraham married Elizabeth Eddy of Churchtown, and in October they left for the United States, never to return. In the following year, William, who had married Ann White of St Just in 1854, went to America for twelve months before returning to Zennor and then emigrating to the United States for good. James Stevens learnt in March 1905 that William had died, writing in his diary: 'Had a letter from California of the death of my eldest brother William aged 75 years'. He recalled how forty years before, he had driven 'him with his wife and family and luggage to Hayle in a cart and saw them leave in a steamer'.[25] Earlier, in October 1903, James had recorded: 'Tis 40 years today since I drove my brother Abraham and his wife from Zennor to Hayle to leave there in the steamer ... to sail to America, and we have written each other regular ever since'.[26] The American families of William and Abraham remained in contact with their relations in Zennor until at least the late 1920s. James Stevens' sister Mary Jane, who had married John Thomas of Boswednack, Zennor, in 1871, emigrated with her husband and four children to New Zealand in 1890—her grandson was still corresponding with their Zennor family in the mid-1970s.

'Been in furren parts p'raps?'

Such enduring intimacy, conducted across the globe over several decades and generations, helped mould Cornwall's 'emigration culture', as it has been termed, not least in the realms of literature. The Hocking brothers from St Stephen-in-Brannel, near St Austell, and their sister Salome, were enormously popular authors in late nineteenth- and early twentieth-century Cornwall, their Cornish tales (often overlaid with Methodist morality) designed to appeal to their readerships' interests. One such theme was emigration, especially the emigrant miner returning to Cornwall after many years' absence. In Joseph Hocking's classic tale *What Shall It Profit a Man?*, for example, the hero is the splendidly named Granville Poldhu, who has returned to Cornwall from South Africa where he has 'worked under one of the ablest mining engineers in that continent'.[27]

In Silas K. Hocking's *The Lost Lode*, it is Jasper Blake who returns to Cornwall, to the fictional village of his birth, Pengowan. With the £40 his father had given him, Blake had made his way to Quebec and from there across North America, taking some eleven years all told to reach the Yukon where at last he struck it rich. But:

> To other fortunate ones gold had spelt Seattle, or 'Frisco, or Los Angeles, or the cities back east; Toronto, or Chicago, or Washington, or New York. To him it spelt Pengowan. There was only one thought in his mind, one desire in his heart—he must get back home. His Cornish hills called him across the ocean and mountain and plain; the lure of his native land was in his blood; it had never left him during all the years of his absence. Nothing would ever satisfy him until he had seen again the little grey town lying in the lap of the hills, it was a home-sickness that only the sight of home would cure.[28]

Jasper Blake does indeed return to Pengowan but he is not recognized in the local inn, where he is eyed as a stranger who has 'Been in furren parts, p'raps?', and feels depressed and disappointed:

> Till a few hours ago, Pengowan had been the paradise of his dreams, the climax of his ambitions, the sum of his desires; and yet an hour's ramble through its streets and lanes had convinced him that he had been entirely out in his reckoning. Pengowan was not an end in itself, it was only another stage on the journey. Once more he was up against the constantly recurring question, 'What next?'[29]

The theme of the returned emigrant who finds things much altered, and who is unrecognized in his hitherto familiar environment, is a common one in Cornish literature of the period. J. Henry Harris's short story 'Cousin Jacky', published in 1901, for instance, tells the tale of a Cornish miner who returns from Chile to a village near Redruth. He finds the village locked in desolation and despair, his father dead, his brothers in South Africa, and his sweetheart married to another and gone away: 'Now that he had returned with his welcome in his hand, there was no one to rejoice with him.' As he meanders with an increasingly heavy heart through the village, everyone he meets is a stranger: 'He wandered as one living with ghostly memories, and no one in the deserted village in which he was born to say "How are 'ee?". His dream of a joyous homecoming was thus wiped out and he went again into voluntary exile.'[30]

Homecoming as anticlimax was a fear that underpinned many a return journey to Cornwall, especially after years abroad, a lurking apprehension that so much would have altered, that the returnee would be rendered invisible, even irrelevant. Yet returned migrants were often determined to have their moment of triumph, to assert their success in overseas ventures and to stake their claim to their homeland. Such a response is captured in Charles Lee's novel, *Paul Carah, Cornishman*, first published in 1898, where the eponymous hero comes home after many years overseas. In marked contrast to Jasper Blake's disappointment at Pengowan, Paul Carah is exultant on his return:

> There edn' no smell on earth like the smell of Cornish ground. An' there edn' no kingdom on earth to come up to Cornwall; nor no nation fit to stand up in the sight o' the Cornish nation. 'Wan n' all' agin the world. That's we, brothers all! Hoorah for home an' a lovin' welcome, an' pilchers an' saffern an' true friends and pasties![31]

Such stories, however, whether of dejection or triumph, or both, are generally told from the perspective of the returning migrant. They also reflect the overwhelmingly masculine narrative of 'Cousin Jack': the much-in-demand skills of the Cornish miner, and the usual male-oriented cultural signifiers overseas, from Cornish wrestling contests to the performance of male voice choirs and brass bands. Insofar as women were allowed a role in the emigrant story, it was as a supporting cast, the 'Cousin Jennys', bringing domesticity and order to the otherwise rough and ready mining frontiers of the New World. As for the women who had remained in Cornwall when their menfolk had ventured overseas, there was broadly silence.

However, Lesley Trotter has investigated the fortunes of such women who, for various reasons, remained in Cornwall when husbands or other male relatives went abroad. Although some found themselves abandoned and destitute, many others (spared the exhausting drudgery of continual childbirth and domestic servitude) forged vigorous and rewarding lives, often as heads of households, displaying energy, initiative and self-confidence. Stereotypical depictions of 'left behind' wives as abandoned and often destitute were at best just a small part of the story. There were those who managed households successfully on the remittances sent home from abroad by absent husbands, and others who took on paid or even unpaid work to make ends meet. Sometimes help was accepted from family, friends and neighbours, and the financially astute made the best use of whatever credit was available and rationalized or minimized their accommodation costs, often by taking in lodgers. Only occasionally did such women turn to the Poor Law Guardians for relief.[32]

There were, inevitably, cases where remittances dried up, and there were instances where husbands overseas, tired of maintaining the links with home, built new lives and new families. Wives 'left behind' could also make similar decisions, although this was much more difficult when living in close-knit communities, and there were cases of bigamy, adultery, illegitimacy and even divorce. Yet there is much evidence that, even if abandoned by husbands overseas or otherwise losing contact, wives left behind in Cornwall could be remarkably successful in rebuilding their lives, even to the extent of running their own businesses—as in the case of Mrs Nankervis and 'The Tinners' Rest' in D.H. Lawrence's short story 'Samson and Delilah'.

'Samson and Delilah'

Lawrence knew now, from his own experience, the pull Cornwall exerted on its emigrant sons and daughters, and he appreciated the mixed feelings many of these people had towards their homeland—for their going away and for their return. An astute if sometimes ambivalent observer of the Cornish, Lawrence understood the complicated relationship between Cornwall and the distant lands of its diaspora, including the literary genre of the returned miner—to which he was shortly to contribute. In his short story 'Samson and Delilah', first published in October 1922, Lawrence writes of a Cornish miner who has come home to St Just-in-Penwith from Butte, Montana, in America, arriving late one night and making his way to the 'Tinners' Rest', the local inn. The 'Tinners' Rest' is clearly the Tinners' Arms, the public house at Zennor, while St Just is a convenient surrogate for Zennor itself. Nankervis was, of course, a local name; indeed, in reality the Tinners' Arms was run by a Mr Nankervis—such was Lawrence's propensity for peppering his fiction with thinly disguised characters and allusions chosen from real life.[33]

'Samson and Delilah' reveals the extent to which Lawrence had immersed himself in Cornish life; it is also another powerful example of Lawrence's intense nostalgia for Cornwall in the aftermath of his expulsion. The story conjures up the Cornish milieu in intimate and precise detail, from the 'motor-omnibus that runs from Penzance to St Just-in-Penwith' to the 'many miners' cottages scattered on the hilly darkness' whose lights 'twinkled desolate in their disorder, yet twinkled with the lonely homeliness of the Celtic night'. There were also the lights out to sea, 'vessels veering round in sight of the Longships Lighthouse, the whole of the Atlantic Ocean in darkness'. The returned migrant 'spoke with the west-Cornish intonation' and bid goodnight to the 'short, stump, thick-legged figures of Cornish miners [who] passed him by ... as if to insist that he was on his own ground'. He was 'a little excited and pleased with himself, watchful, thrilled, veering along in a sense of mastery and of power in conflict'.[34]

Arriving at 'The 'Tinners' Rest', the returned miner was instantly regarded by the landlady, Mrs Nankervis: 'She had noticed the man: a big fine fellow, well-dressed, a stranger. But he spoke with that Cornish-Yankee accent she accepted as the natural twang among the miners ... He was handsome, well coloured, with well-drawn Cornish eyebrows, and the usual dark, bright, mindless Cornish eyes.' He watched as the landlady joined a game of cards: 'The woman was buxom and healthy, with dark hair and small, quick brown eyes. She was bursting with life and vigour, and the energy she threw into the game excited all the men, they shouted, and laughed, and the woman held her breast, shrieking with laughter.' Shortly, she was joined by Maryann, her daughter, 'a girl of about sixteen ... tall and fresh, with dark, young, expressionless eyes, and well-drawn brows, and the immature softness and mindlessness of the sensuous Celtic type'.[35]

Still Mrs Nankervis did not see that the miner was her husband, home from America after fifteen years. Having called 'closing time', she made to bolt the door but he refused to leave: '"I'm stopping here tonight", he said, in his laconic Cornish-Yankee accent.' As she bristled with anger, the miner told her: 'You're my Missus, you are ... And you know it, as well as I do.' As he went on to explain, 'I'm Willie Nankervis', home from abroad. Refusing at first to accept this revelation, she turned to the sergeant and three young soldiers in the bar who had been about to go. Bursting into tears, she cried: 'He left me when Maryann was a baby, went mining to America, and after about six months never wrote a line nor sent me a penny bit. I can't say whether he's alive or dead, the villain. All I've heard of him is to the bad— and I've heard nothing for years an' all, now.' As she sobbed, the 'men, one and all [the Cornish motto], were overcome'.[36]

Accepting now that perhaps the returned miner was her long-lost husband, Mrs Nankervis turned to the sergeant for support, declaring that her husband was 'a scoundrel and a bully as has led a life beyond *mention*, in those American mining-camps, and then wants to come back and make

'So on to Australia!'

havoc of a poor woman's life and savings, after having left her with a baby in arms to struggle as best she might'. The sergeant and the three soldiers, suitably enraged, bundled the miner into the street, having bound him with a rope, leaving him to try to free himself in due course. Eventually untied, he crept back into the pub, surprised to find the kitchen door open. Seated there was Mrs Nankervis, evidently waiting for him, ready to berate him for his long and unseemly absence 'in Butte City and elsewhere'. Aroused by his wife's feisty manner, he reached forward, 'tentatively touching her between her full, warm, breasts, quietly'. Their confrontation of violence and passion had somehow brought them together in a strange intimacy born of separate lives: 'his hand insinuated itself between her breasts … "And don't think I've come back here a-begging", he said, "I've more than one thousand pounds to my name, I have. And a bit of fight for a how-de-do pleases me, that it do. But that doesn't mean as you're going to deny as you're my Missis …"'.[37]

The unresolved tensions of emigration would colour the rest of Lawrence's life. Restlessness in Italy prompted a desire to abandon Europe altogether, the intention being to revive the American dream but this time the preferred destination being Taos, New Mexico. Yet he decided that he wanted to travel 'east' rather than 'west', and although he insisted that America would remain the ultimate goal, he and Frieda headed for Ceylon (modern Sri Lanka) in early 1922. Lawrence was impressed by Ceylon—especially the strange jungle noises that pierced the night—but instantly he knew that the steamy climate was bad for his health. It was already time to move on again. 'So on to Australia!', as Richard Aldington put it.[38]

Lawrence was well aware of Australia as a Cornish destination, demonstrated, for example, in his novel *Kangaroo*, where William James 'Jaz' Trewhella and his brother are both emigrants from Cornwall (see p. 74). Australia, like America and South Africa, was still on the lips of Zennor folk in Lawrence's day. As David Game has shown, however, Lawrence's personal interest in Australia pre-dated his Cornish episode, including an early story 'The Vicar's Garden' in 1907 and various mentions in *The White Peacock*, first published in 1911, together with references in *The Daughter-in-Law* (1913), and 'The Primrose Path' (written in 1913 but not published until 1922). Further works, *The Lost Girl* (1920), *Aaron's Rod* (1922) and *Mr Noon* (abandoned by 1922 and not published until 1984), all pre-dated Lawrence's arrival in Australia but include Australian material. Intriguingly, as David Game has also pointed out, in both 'The Vicar's Garden' and *The White Peacock*, Australia is portrayed 'as profoundly "other" … as fundamentally oppositional to England, remote, dangerous'.[39] Here was an 'otherness' and 'difference' from England which reflected Lawrence's own estimation of Cornwall at that very moment. Cornwall and Australia, it turns out, are both peripheral places. Moreover, with the onset of the Great War, Lawrence himself became an emigrant, 'desperate to leave England, eventually undergoing a kind of self-imposed exile', an exile which would encompass both Cornwall and Australia.[40]

'The blood knowledge of the kangaroo'

Lawrence had never given an explicit opinion about Australia as a potential location for Rananim, yet in his contemplation of Australia there was more than a hint of his unrelenting search for a utopian society. David Game has noted, for example, that in *The Boy in the Bush*, the novel that Lawrence co-wrote with Mollie Skinner, the character Jack Grant has been sent by his parents to Western Australia from England in the 1880s to make a new life for himself. In carving out his own future, Grant's idealized 'quest for community in the remote north-west of Australia ... suggests that Lawrence was alive to the possibility—and impossibility—of establishing his Rananim in Australia'.[41] Indeed, according to Game, not only is Grant's striving 'strongly suggestive of Lawrence's quest for Rananim', but 'it is notable that Lawrence's wide reading included literary and anthropological works, many of which contained regenerative or utopian visions of Australia'. As Game concludes, these 'works constitute an important foundation for Lawrence's ideas about Australia'.[42]

Alongside references in his own work to Australia, Lawrence had long immersed himself in books *about* Australia. In 1912 he recorded that he was reading *Bush Stories*, probably a reference to Henry Lawson's *Children of the Bush* or possibly, as Paul Eggert has suggested, Barbara Baynton's *Bush Studies*.[43] The following year Lawrence was reading Jane Harrison's *Ancient Art and Ritual*, learning to his delight that when Aboriginal people danced as kangaroos, they *were* kangaroos, because they were members of the Kangaroo tribe. Lawrence pondered the nature of such 'primitive' societies, reflecting on what he supposed to be their underlying characteristics, and, as David Game has observed, it is 'significant that Lawrence revisited Australian anthropology after he had conceived of Rananim', his interest rekindled anew by his dreams of utopia.[44] In Lawrence's mind, Rananim and primitive simplicity were somehow entwined, in Aboriginal society as much as Celtic.

'So on to Australia!'

Just weeks before moving to Cornwall, for example, Lawrence had written to Bertrand Russell, telling him about 'the blood knowledge of the kangaroo' and its relevance to Aboriginal society, where those Aborigines 'related' to kangaroos had acquired, he said, the marsupials' innate 'blood consciousness'.[45] As Game has observed, the timing was remarkable. On the eve of relocating to Cornwall, and 'seven years before Lawrence had set foot in Australia his reading of Australian anthropology had shaped not only his early conception of Australia and its Aboriginal inhabitants but also his own idiosyncratic metaphysics'. Significantly, this included Lawrence's new-found belief in the 'conception of human physical or "blood consciousness" as separate from the intellectual consciousness'.[46]

Lawrence had gone to Cornwall mulling over the idea of 'blood consciousness' and, as Jane Costin has argued (p. 64), it was at Zennor that for him the concept crystallized. The granite-strewn moors and rocky outcrops, Lawrence decided, had the power to awaken blood consciousness, as had all primitive landscapes, the Celtic and the Australian. Meanwhile, the fascination with Australia continued. After a fortnight in Cornwall, Lawrence noted that he had been reading the novel *Where Bonds Are Loosed* by E.L. Grant Watson, set in the north-west of Western Australia. Here were portends of *The Boy in the Bush* and an awakening understanding of the myriad possibilities of Australia, including, perhaps, the potential for Rananim.[47]

'Like a fantasy seemed the Pacific'

In *Kangaroo*, with its explicit link between Cornwall and Australia, Richard Lovat Somers recalls a conversation in Cornwall with John Thomas (for which read William Henry Hocking) in which he speculates that he might eventually go to Australia: 'One day, when the war ends ... we'll go across the sea—to Mexico—to Australia—and try living there. You must come too, and we will have a farm.'[48] This may have been a case of constructive hindsight, or 'back-filling' as Game has called it. Certainly, there is no other indication that during his time in Cornwall Lawrence was contemplating an Australian adventure (although he did think William Henry a possible recruit for his fleetingly imagined utopian community in 'the Andes').[49] Yet David Game has suggested that William James 'Jaz' Trewhella—one of the key characters in *Kangaroo*—may be modelled in part on William Henry Hocking. As he has explained, it 'seems likely that Trewhella, although not a farmer, is at least partly inspired by Hocking, and if we read the above [conversational] passage autobiographically, it appears that Lawrence, in 1916, may briefly have considered Australia as one of the many possibilities for Rananim'.[50] As Game has concluded:

> In the early months of 1916, therefore, while Lawrence was settling into Cornwall, and having recently thought that 'Florida' might be a possible destination, a regenerative vision of Australia appears to have also begun to take root in Lawrence's mind, inspired by and informing his early conception of Rananim. And it is the emergence of Australia in Lawrence's vision at this time which helps to explain his introduction of Australian characters into his later novels, *The Lost Girl* and *Aaron's Rod*, before his visit to Australia.[51]

One might also add that, if Lawrence had indeed discussed the possibilities of Australia with William Henry Hocking, his intimate friend, then the cathartic quality of *Kangaroo* is doubly poignant, an example par excellence of Lawrence's deep nostalgia and yearning for Cornwall, especially as the novel was written in Australia.

Lawrence and Frieda arrived at Fremantle, Perth, in Western Australia on 4 May 1922. With its sheds, wharfs and railway yards, the docks at Fremantle seemed a 'godforsaken place', according to Lawrence's first impressions, a contrast emerging already in his mind between the breathtaking beauty of the natural landscape and an indifferent built environment.[52] Society, too, seemed dull, derivative, and uninspiring, despite—or perhaps, because of—its democratic credentials. It was the bush that captivated him, and although he did not go very far into the interior, he saw enough to be deeply affected. Somewhat scathingly, Richard Aldington scoffed, 'Of course, Lawrence never went far enough into either Western Australia or New South Wales to catch even a glimpse of the real wild bush'. But, as Aldington admitted, Lawrence 'with his uncannily quick intuition ... instantly perceived "the strange and empty and primeval" quality of Australia. It was very beautiful ... but it rather scared him. He went a mile or two into the bush under the bright Australian moonlight, and the silence and mystery of the night turned to terror for him'.[53] Frieda, too, was moved: she and Lawrence 'went a long way into that strange vague bush, everything so vague and dim, as before the days of creation'.[54]

It was in Western Australia that Lawrence met Mollie Skinner, with whom he would collaborate in rewriting her manuscript *The Boy in the Bush*.

'*So on to Australia!*'

The bush as a literary device excited and intrigued Lawrence, especially after his brief introduction to the country around Perth, his enthusiasm an antidote to the more pervasive disappointment he had felt on arrival. After two weeks in Western Australia, he and Frieda set sail for Sydney. From there, they travelled south to Thirroul, a coal-mining town on the coast of New South Wales, where they rented a bungalow with the not entirely appealing name 'Wyewurk'.

Perhaps Thirroul reminded Lawrence of Eastwood, his birthplace in the Nottinghamshire coalfield, an irony not lost on Richard Aldington who exclaimed, 'how curious to come thirteen thousand miles and reject the bush in order to settle into an Australian Eastwood!'.[55] Yet the identification was superficial, and if there were comparisons to be made, then Cornwall might have been a better choice. Frieda described their house as 'a beautiful bungalow right on the sea', with 'a stretch of grass going right down to the Pacific'.[56] She and Lawrence 'took long walks along the coast, lonely and remote and unborn. The weather was mild and full of life, we never got tired of the shore, finding shells for hours that the Pacific had rolled gently on to the sand.'[57] But sometimes the Pacific was anything but gentle, and on such occasions Lawrence and Frieda 'watched the huge blue foam-crested Pacific rollers, so huge and so near that they seemed each time as if they must swirl right through into the house'.[58] Yet when conditions allowed, they went swimming in the sea, the water warm enough, even though it was winter. Frieda waxed lyrical about the ocean:

> Like a fantasy seemed the Pacific, pellucid and radiant, melting into the sky, so fresh and new always; then this primal radiance was gone one day and another primeval sea appeared. A storm was throwing the waves high into the air, they rose on the abrupt shore, high as in an enormous window. I could see strange sea-creatures thrown up from the deep: swordfish and fantastic phenomena of undreamt of deep-sea beasts I saw in these waves, frightening and never to be forgotten.[59]

Sometimes Lawrence and Frieda ventured into the hinterland, hiring a pony cart which they drove through the bush, finding 'golden woods of mimosa ... or wattle, as the Australians call it'. There were 'red flowers and yellow mimosa, many varieties, red and gold ... strange fern trees, delicately leaved'. They found 'a wide river and followed it. It became a wide waterfall and then it disappeared into the earth. Disappeared and left us gaping.

Why should it have disappeared, where had it gone?'[60] Like Lawrence, Frieda contrasted the fascination of the bush with the ordinariness of the townscape. 'Thirroul itself was a new little bungalow town', she wrote, 'and the most elegant thing in it was a German gun [a war trophy, no doubt] that glistened steely and out of place there near the Pacific.'[61]

Despite its aesthetic shortcomings, Thirroul was a friendly town. The local farmers were especially generous. When Lawrence and Frieda asked for a pound of butter, they were given a large chunk of almost two pounds; when they requested two pints of milk, they were handed three. Food was delivered to the house, an unexpected luxury—the fish cart was a particular source of interest and amusement, the fishmonger selling a wide variety of exotic species that the Lawrences had not seen before or heard of. As Frieda remembered it, 'everything was lavish'.[62] Lawrence spent time reading the Sydney *Bulletin*, a weekly periodical with extensive coverage of contemporary politics and political opinion. For Lawrence this was an important means of steeping himself in Australian current affairs and gaining an understanding of the country's ethos, vital background material for his new novel *Kangaroo*.

Lawrence wrote most of *Kangaroo* at Thirroul, the last chapter being finished in America. The plot involves a recently arrived Englishman, Richard Lovat Somers, and his German wife Harriet. Somers is drawn into the dubious world of political extremism, first the right-wing 'Digger' movement led by Benjamin Cooley (aka 'Kangaroo'), and then Willie Struthers' socialists. He rejects both groups, criticizing Australian society in general, which he finds culturally philistine and overtly materialistic. This, of course, reflects Lawrence's own views. Like Somers, Lawrence is in awe of the bush but is disappointed to find that Australia is dominated by urban-industrial modernity, just like the England he has so recently rejected and in marked contrast to his earlier, idealized imaginings of Australia. *Kangaroo* is strongly autobiographical, as we have seen, most obviously the 'Nightmare' chapter where Somers' expulsion from Cornwall is discussed at length. Somers looks back on his time in Cornwall with mixed feelings, but he knows now that coming to Australia offers no permanent resolution.

Lawrence wrote some 3,100 words a day to (almost) complete *Kangaroo* at Thirroul, an astonishing feat, especially given his other daily activities from writing letters and reading to domestic chores and explorations of the locality. Suggestions that Lawrence may have based his political characters in *Kangaroo* on real contacts in clandestine organizations, a thesis put forward by Robert Darroch, have been disputed by most commentators,

'So on to Australia!'

not least as Lawrence would simply not have had time to meet them.[63] As Richard Aldington observed in 1950, the Australian characters were entirely invented, and 'yet seeing so little, by sheer intuition he felt and recorded more of Australia, its magic and mystery, than any other foreign writer'.[64] There is, however, an intriguing view that Cooley/Kangaroo was based on Kot—Samuel Koteliansky—the Ukrainian Jew befriended by Lawrence and who unwittingly suggested the name Rananim for Lawrence's proposed utopian community. At first glance an unlikely theory, it has been advocated by Galya Diment (among others) who has pointed to the uncanny physical resemblance between the real-life Kot and the fictional Cooley, as well as the personal relationship between Cooley/Kangaroo and Somers, which she argues mirrors that between Kot and Lawrence.[65] Perhaps Kot was the model for Kangaroo; perhaps not.

Ultimately, Lawrence was in two minds about Australia. As Richard Aldington put it, Lawrence 'loved Australia and its delicate beauty with a strange almost heart-broken intensity' but he 'would not yield himself to Australia'.[66] Any thoughts that there might be scope for Rananim in Australia had been dashed on the rocks of his disillusion. His initial impressions of Fremantle had steeled him for disappointment, and his continuing restlessness was already evident on the sea journey from Western Australia to Sydney, where in a letter to Kot, he had predicted: 'I think from Sydney we shall visit the South Sea Islands—think of our "Rananim"'.[67] From this perspective, Australia was only ever a stepping-stone on the relentless journey 'east'. Perhaps significantly, Richard Lovat Somers had been given the same initials as Robert Louis Stevenson, whose own incessant travelling took him eventually to Tahiti and to Samoa.

Frieda would have welcomed the opportunity to settle in Australia. 'I would have liked to stay in Australia', she wrote, 'and lose myself, as it were, in this unborn country, but Lawrence wanted to go to America.'[68] Taos, in New Mexico, it transpired, remained the stated destination, the preferred end result of going 'east'. Lawrence, said Frieda, was convinced that he 'must know the Pueblo Indians ... the Indians say that the heart of the world beats there in New Mexico'. Given this 'definite aim', as Frieda described it, they began to pack in preparation for their departure.[69] They had first arrived in Sydney on 27 May or thereabouts, and were to sail for San Francisco on 11 August 1922. As the date grew closer, Lawrence became more nostalgic. In his short time in Australia, he had got the measure of the country, according to his own lights at least. He delighted in the 'age-unbroken silence of the Australian bush ... the perfume in the air that might be heaven ... strange bright birds and flocks of parrots ... the bush flowering at the gates of heaven'.[70] Now that it was time to go, he 'felt a deep pang in his heart', as Somers expressed it, 'leaving Australia, that strange country that a man might love so hopelessly'.[71]

Jaz's wife had come to see them off, in Lawrence's imagining of his departure, the ship little by little slipping away from the jetty in Sydney harbour. Somers, wrote Lawrence, 'watched the Observatory go by: then the Circular Quay, with all its ferry wharves ... and the Governor's Palace, and the castellated Conservatorium of Music ... the blue inlet where the Australian "Fleet" lay comfortably rusting'.[72] Ahead of them, for Lawrence as well as for Somers, 'was the open gate of the harbour', with the South Lighthouse, the Heads guarding the entrance, and the Pacific beyond, 'breaking white'.[73] On the port side was Manly, where Somers and Harriet had caught the tram to Narrabeen, where they had first met Jaz Trewhella, the Cornish emigrant. 'It was midday before they got out of the Heads, out of the harbour into the open sea',[74] the Sydney Heads standing sentinel as the beginning and end of Australia, as did the Longships Lighthouse off Land's End for Cornwall. 'Farewell ... farewell Australia, farewell Britain ... Farewell! Farewell!'[75]

Epilogue

P.A.S. Pool presumed to speak for Cornish people, or so it seemed, when he pronounced that Zennor 'parish has more reason to be proud of him [Henry Quick, the droll-teller] than of its fleeting and unhappy association with D.H. Lawrence' (see p. 4). Yet from the earliest days, Cornish opinions of Lawrence were more varied than Pool appreciated, from the reactions of those whom Lawrence had met while living in Cornwall during the Great War, to the estimations of contemporary writers who liked to claim some kind of personal or artistic affinity.

'An unknown, unrecognised, younger brother'

Alison Symons, for example, in *Tremedda Days* recalled that at Zennor her 'mother knew him slightly but did not take to him very well'. Similarly, she observed, 'Hilda Jelbert from Carnellow, when only fourteen worked for them [Lawrence and Frieda] … Hilda was not very struck on D.H. Lawrence; she thought him moody and sarcastic'. Frieda, by contrast, according to Hilda, was 'jokey, stout and fair'.[1] However, in a telling aside that says much about the cultural gap between Lawrence and his Cornish neighbours, 'Hilda was asked one day to make pasties for their dinner and to her horror was provided with mutton instead of beef'—an almost unforgivable sin in Cornwall.[2] Unversed as he was in Cornish fare, Lawrence proved marginally more successful as a Cornish farm labourer, his efforts smiled upon by his neighbours, and, as we have seen, he became socially close to the Hocking family at Lower Tregerthen, especially his intimate friend William Henry Hocking. Only latterly, as the submarine menace multiplied, did Lawrence come under serious suspicion by elements of the local community.

D.H. Lawrence and Cornwall

A.L. Rowse, the Cornish historian, offered his own considered assessment of D.H. Lawrence. Born in 1903, Rowse was a schoolboy at St Austell during the Great War, and as he grew to know more about the writer, so he imagined himself 'an unknown, unrecognised, younger brother'.[3] Like Lawrence's mother, Rowse's own mother had married beneath her, socially and intellectually, a comparison that Rowse relished. Once, when still a young man, Rowse sought out the coal-mining village of Eastwood in Nottinghamshire, Lawrence's birthplace, identifying with Lawrence's working-class origins and making further comparisons between Eastwood and his own clay-mining district about St Austell. He was surprised to find, he said, that, 'allowing for differences in colour and accent, it might have been a clay-village at home in Cornwall ... the chapels in evidence: a working-class and petty-bourgeois community'.[4] Continuing his self-confessed affinity with Lawrence, Rowse also compared his life with that of Paul Morel, the principal character in Lawrence's semi-autobiographical *Sons and Lovers*, imagining his close friend Noreen Sweet to be his own 'Miriam', a comparison that he let slip in his collection *The English Past* in 1951—much to Noreen's annoyance.[5]

Such was A.L. Rowse's interest in and admiration for D.H. Lawrence, that at one time he considered writing a book on 'Lawrence and Cornwall'.[6] However, as Rowse admitted, one has more books in one's head than one would ever have time to write—so Lawrence's Cornish saga went unchronicled. But that did not prevent him from applauding Lawrence's short story 'Samson and Delilah', about a Cornish miner returning home to St Just after many years' absence in America (see pp. 133–5), which Rowse thought the 'most authentic of Cornish themes'.[7] An ardent student of Cornwall's 'Great Emigration' (his *The Cornish in America* was published in 1969), Rowse offered his own version of Lawrence's story, a real-life tale, he insisted, which he had heard on good authority from his own mother. In Rowse's telling, it is the abandoned wife who confronts her errant husband, travelling from Cornwall to America to seek him out. Her husband, Rowse explained, had

> left her and went to America, but for many years sent her a decent living. She saved on it, a good bit of money. Then he stopped sending for several years, and she lost touch with him. One day, somebody returning from America told her where he was, keeping a pub with another woman, by whom he had a family of young children. Mrs Hore

144

[the wife] drew out her money, sold her things, and went out to him. She went straight to his address, knocked at the door, which, as luck would have it, was opened by him: 'So I've got 'ee now', she said. The husband died of fright on the spot.[8]

Jack Clemo, the blind and deaf poet of Cornwall's clay-country, a near-contemporary of Rowse, also claimed common cause with Lawrence. His mother too had married beneath her; she from a respectable God-fearing family, her husband a rough clay-worker who, like the returned miner in Lawrence's 'Samson and Delilah', had also been out in Butte City for a time (where he had contracted the syphilis that accounted for his son's disabilities).[9] As Clemo put it: 'My foundations were roughly similar to D.H. Lawrence's, brutality and refinement warring in me through the conflicting natures of my parents, sharpened towards primitivism by the working-class Nonconformist background.'[10]

Moreover, Clemo admitted his own 'gravitation towards a dark, primitive lust of the blood, similar to D.H. Lawrence's', and confessed that 'I was driven to protect myself by the same sort of irrational fanaticism as D.H. Lawrence exhibited'.[11] Indeed, 'I had sometimes been fascinated to think of the granite cottage near Zennor, in west Cornwall, where D.H. Lawrence had suffered agonies during my infancy'.[12] But, he added, 'Lawrence's complete rejection of Christian values prevented my response from being deep and enduring'.[13] Nonetheless, Jack Clemo dedicated his poem 'The Two Beds' to D.H. Lawrence, with its acknowledgement that 'You were a child of the black pit' (as opposed to Clemo's white pit, presumably), one who 'sought always: all around the world'.[14] Like Rowse, Clemo recognized a shared working-class, mining-village background, and saw in Lawrence's global wanderings a reflection of the ubiquitous Cornish emigrant experience.

H.J. Willmott, sometime editor of the *Cornish Guardian* newspaper, also detected a degree of similarity, even sympathy, between Clemo and Lawrence. In the late 1940s, Willmott wrote to his long-standing friend and correspondent, Cornish author and theatre critic J.C. Trewin, suggesting that there 'is, I think, some common ground between D.H. Lawrence and Clemo. Both sprang from working-class roots; like Lawrence, Clemo has struggled with illness and adversity and, like him, he has a message to deliver; both are in some sense prophets, however different, almost conflicting, their prophecies.'[15]

'Sensible people like you go to live in Cornwall'

As the testimonies of A.L. Rowse and Jack Clemo attest, the multidimensional story of D.H. Lawrence in Cornwall is not so easily dismissed as P.A.S. Pool had blithely imagined. On the contrary, the impact of Lawrence was widespread and enduring, for Lawrence himself and for Cornwall too. His utopian dreams—his quest for Rananim—may have come to little but his influence lived on, not least in Zennor itself. Paul Newman, for example, in his ingenious (but chaotic and not entirely reliable) synthesis *The Tregerthen Horror*, traces a controversial yet not entirely tenuous continuity between Lawrence's sojourn and the death at Zennor in mysterious circumstances of Katherine 'Ka' Arnold-Forster in 1938. She and her husband had acquired Eagle's Nest (aka Tregerthen Cottage) in 1918 (see p. 53), not long after Lawrence's departure. Rumours of her fatal entwinement with the occult and neo-paganism somehow fitted the Lawrentian inheritance, in Newman's interpretation at least, marking Zennor as permanently outlandish and exotic in the (English) public imagination, and perhaps not a little dangerous too.[16]

Lawrence's literary net likewise extends to Virginia Woolf: it seems she had been all but persuaded to move to Zennor by Ka Arnold-Forster. In January 1919, Virginia Woolf had spent much of her time in bed ill, and envied her friend Ka's recent relocation to Cornwall. Remembering, perhaps, her happy childhood days at St Ives, she wrote to Ka, exclaiming that all 'sensible people like you go to live in Cornwall'.[17] She had heard that there was a cottage to let at Gurnard's Head, Zennor, and asked Ka to investigate. In fact, it was another of Virginia Woolf's literary associates, none other than Katherine Mansfield, who reported that the cottage at Higher Tregerthen, previously occupied by Lawrence, was now empty and available for rent. Virginia leapt at the idea, immediately taking the cottage, but it seems unlikely that she ever visited her new acquisition. Instead, she and her husband Leonard thought twice and decided that they should remain in Sussex, closer to London and their literary circle.[18] Post-Rananim in far-flung Cornwall was not for them.

The poet John Heath-Stubbs, however, was one of those literary types drawn to Zennor by the Lawrence inheritance, living there for a time in the 1940s. Perhaps unintentionally, he conjured up the pungent, oft-forbidding atmosphere of the landscape in his poem 'For the Mermaid of Zennor', evoking the lingering quixotic spirit of D.H. Lawrence:

Epilogue

This is a hideous and a wicked country,
Sloping to hateful sunsets and the end of time,
Hollow with mine-shafts, naked with granite, fanatic
With sorrow.[19]

Summing up Lawrence's time in Cornwall has never been easy. Its sheer complexity and its contradictions make generalizations difficult, and interpretations vary, sometimes widely, even wildly. For example, according to Louise Wright, 'Cornish xenophobia' is an important ingredient in any explanation for Lawrence's traumatic experiences, the result of an ingrained ethnic hostility to outsiders—to Lawrence as an interloper, to his German wife Frieda and to the German nation as a whole.[20] 'War hysteria infected the Cornish as much as it did any other people', thought Wright, 'perhaps even more so.'[21] In such a reading, any newcomer was bound to come under suspicion, particularly in wartime, especially an unusual personality such as Lawrence. It is an assessment echoed by Shelley Trower, who acknowledged Lawrence's sometimes hostile attitude towards the Cornish and yet identified him with what she imagined to be the underlying motivations of Cornish nationalism: 'If Lawrence puts forward a form of raving English colonialism he also mirrors the claims made by Cornish nationalists … in his identification with the stones and its [sic] spirits, and the desire to exclude others'.[22]

We might object that the Cornish are not the parochial reactionaries that their detractors sometimes suspect, and that the historical evidence indicates that only reluctantly did the Cornish come to embrace the more universal 'war spirit' during the Great War. We might add that Lawrence's complex attitude to the Cornish fluctuated considerably over time, quite literally from one extreme to the other, from abject (but fleeting) hate at Porthcothan to a mature and possibly homosexual love at Zennor. Here, as in so much of Lawrence's life, is a paradox that needs to be understood and considered in careful and balanced detail. We might suggest, too, that the primary aim of Cornish nationalism is not a 'desire to exclude others' (indeed civic inclusivity is a hallmark of Mebyon Kernow, the Cornish party), a preoccupation with the 'stones and its spirits' hardly central to nationalist ideology or policy.

Lawrence's contrary make-up no doubt exacerbated his predicament. But at root there was Cornwall's own predicament, its liminal space giving rise to ambiguity and uncertainty. Cornwall was ostensibly 'in England' but was plainly not 'of England'. Modernity—industrial growth and decline, emigration, Celtic revivalism, tourism—had only served to exaggerate this liminality, with Cornwall increasingly a contested space for competing imaginings. The Great War brought this liminality to a head, at least as far as Lawrence was concerned. As we have seen, he sought a Cornwall that was 'beyond England'—ethically as well as ethnically—and which he had hoped, therefore, would be beyond England's reach. In the absence of other options, this would be his Rananim, his utopia.

But, to Lawrence's horror and dismay, the war spirit did eventually encroach upon Cornwall, and he became its victim. Anger at Cornish passivity in the face of this intrusion gave way to pity as local men were conscripted to the armed forces against their will, and even when he fell under suspicion, Lawrence hoped against hope that he could remain in Cornwall. When, finally, he was banished, he was convinced that it was only a temporary measure, and that he would return. Cornwall would continue to be his home. Alas, it was not to be, and after a brief stay in England, Lawrence moved on to what proved to be for him other liminal spaces, including Australia, where he wrote his cathartic Cornish passages in *Kangaroo*.

'That older, dark, sumptuous living'

Later, in Mexico and New Mexico, Lawrence's experiences in Cornwall continued to shape his outlook and preoccupations. As Margaret Storch has observed, the 'developments in Lawrence's philosophy and religious views that began in Cornwall and Australia evolved further in the American Southwest and in Mexico'.[23] In this way, he absorbed aspects of the Pueblo culture of New Mexico, 'that timeless, primeval passion of the prehistoric races', as he put it in his novel *The Plumed Serpent*.[24]

Lawrence's view of the essential common ground between disparate 'prehistoric races'—the Celtic as much as the Pueblo, and indeed the Aboriginal Australian—is made plain when, in *The Plumed Serpent*, the protagonist Kate Leslie, an Anglo-Irish widow, visits Mexico. Here the similarities in character become clear: 'Ah, the dark races! Kate's own Irish were near enough, for her to have glimpsed some of the mystery ... Kate was more Irish than anything, and the almost deathly mysticism of the aboriginal Celtic or Iberian people lay at the bottom of her soul.' Kate herself might be only dimly aware of this blood influence. But no matter; 'Ireland would not and could not forget that older, dark, sumptuous living. The Tuatha

Epilogue

Dé Danann might be under the western sea. But they are under the living blood too, never quite to be silenced.'[25]

So for the Irish, so too for the Cornish. Ultimately, in his attempts to unshackle all such peoples from their 'fettered past' (as Julian Moynahan described it; see p. 7), Lawrence had contributed to the growing twentieth-century contestation of Cornwall's liminal space, a controversy even more apparent today. His lived experience as well as his pen pinpointed and amplified the ambiguities and uncertainties of Cornwall's existence. Then as now, there was a strong English proprietorial sense of ownership, insisting that Cornwall be considered an integral part of England, even if one recognized the 'foreign' attributes of its inhabitants. To admit otherwise was fraught with difficulties and danger, psychological and practical as well as political, especially in the Great War years, not only subverting an imagined England but also prompting the rewriting of Britain's 'national story' by constructing it as a conditional amalgam of separate places.

As James Vernon has observed, 'Cornwall has always existed on the margins of Englishness, both a county of England and a foreign country'. He has warned: 'Crossing the border to Cornwall threatens to unpick not only English history, but British history as well'.[26] It was a subversive journey that D.H. Lawrence undertook in 1915–17. In doing so, he altered his own life irrevocably but also underscored and made starkly apparent the deep paradoxes of Cornwall's existence. For him, Cornwall was not England; but it was not utopia, either.

Notes and References

Prologue

1. P.A.S. Pool, *The Life and Progress of Henry Quick of Zennor* (Redruth: Truran, 1984).
2. Pool, 1984, p. 26.
3. Pool, 1984, p. 43.
4. Ronald M. James, *The Folklore of Cornwall: The Oral Tradition of a Celtic Nation* (Exeter: University of Exeter Press, 2018), p. 33.
5. James, 2018, p. 33.
6. Pool, 1984, p. 8.
7. *Irish Times*, 5 June 2021.
8. Cited in Heather Clark, *Red Comet: The Short Life and Blazing Art of Sylvia Plath* (London: Vintage, 2020), p. 490.
9. John Bayley, *The Iris Trilogy: Memoirs of Irish Murdoch* (London: Duckworth, 2020), p. 61.
10. Anne Smith (ed.), *Lawrence and Women* (London: Vision, 1978), p. 7.
11. Faith Pullin, 'Lawrence's Treatment of Women in *Sons and Lovers*', in Anne Smith (ed.), *Lawrence and Women* (London: Vision, 1978), pp. 49–50.
12. Pullin, 1978, p. 50.
13. Mark Spilka, 'On Lawrence's Hostility to Wilful Women: The Chatterley Solution', in Anne Smith (ed.), *Lawrence and Women* (London: Vision, 1978), p. 189.
14. Lydia Blanchard, 'Mothers and Daughters in D.H. Lawrence: *The Rainbow* and Selected Shorter Works', in Anne Smith (ed.), *Lawrence and Women* (London: Vision, 1978), p. 97.
15. Smith (ed.), 1978, p. 9.
16. Julian Moynahan, 'Lawrence, Woman, and the Celtic Fringe', in Anne Smith (ed.), *Lawrence and Women* (London: Vision, 1978), pp. 122–35.
17. Moynahan, 1978, p. 122.
18. Moynahan, 1978, p. 123.
19. Matthew Arnold, 'On the Study of Celtic Literature', in *The Complete Prose Works of Matthew Arnold* (1962), ed. by R.H. Super, III, pp. 299–300, cited in Moynahan, 1978, p. 127.

Notes to pages 6–9

20 George J. Zytaruk and James T. Boulton (eds), *The Letters of D.H. Lawrence*, Vol. II: *1913–16* (Cambridge: Cambridge University Press, 2002), p. 625, Letter to Catherine Carswell, 9 July 1916.
21 Cited in Moynahan, 1978, p. 129.
22 Moynahan, 1978, p. 132.
23 Cited in Moynahan, 1978, p. 133.
24 Moynahan, 1978, p. 134.
25 Carol Siegel, *Lawrence Among the Women: Wavering Boundaries in Women's Literary Traditions* (Charlottesville: University of Virginia Press, 1991).
26 Jonathan Long, 'Murray vs Carswell: Conflicting Versions of D.H. Lawrence During His Time in Cornwall', *Journal of D.H. Lawrence Studies*, Vol. 4, No. 3 (2017), p. 47.
27 Andrew Harrison, *The Life of D.H. Lawrence: A Critical Biography* (London: Wiley-Blackwell, 2016).
28 *Irish Times*, 5 June 2021.
29 Frances Wilson, *Burning Man: The Ascent of D.H. Lawrence* (Bloomsbury: London, 2021), p. 2.
30 Wilson, 2021, p. 3.
31 Jonathan Long, Review of Frances Wilson, *Burning Man: The Ascent of D.H. Lawrence* (Bloomsbury: London, 2021), *Journal of D.H. Lawrence Studies*, Vol. 6, No. 1 (2021), pp. 236–43.
32 Mark Stoyle, *West Britons: Cornish Identities and the Early Modern British State* (Exeter: University of Exeter Press, 2002); Philip Payton (ed.), *Cornwall in the Age of Rebellion 1490–1690* (Exeter: University of Exeter Press, 2021).
33 Philip Payton, *The Making of Modern Cornwall: Historical Experience and the Persistence of Difference* (Redruth: Dyllansow Truran, 1992); Bernard Deacon, *Cornwall: A Concise History* (Cardiff: University of Wales Press, 2007); Bernard Deacon, *Industrial Celts: Making the Modern Cornish Identity 1750–1870* (Redruth: Cornish Social and Economic Research Group, 2018); Philip Payton, *Cornwall: A History* (Exeter: University of Exeter Press, new edn 2017); Ella Westland (ed.), *Cornwall: The Cultural Construction of Place* (Penzance: Patten Press, 1997); Alan M. Kent, *The Literature of Cornwall: Continuity, Identity, Difference 1000–2000* (Redcliffe: Bristol, 2000).
34 Rachel Moseley, *Picturing Cornwall: Landscape, Region and the Moving Image* (Exeter: University of Exeter Press, 2018); Gemma Goodman, *Alternative Cornwalls: Literature and the Invention of Place* (Exeter: University of Exeter Press, 2024).
35 Philip Payton, *The Cornish Overseas: A History of Cornwall's Great Emigration* (Exeter: University of Exeter Press, new edn 2020).
36 Philip Payton, *A.L. Rowse and Cornwall: A Paradoxical Patriot* (Exeter: University of Exeter Press, 2005); Philip Payton, *John Betjeman and Cornwall: 'The Celebrated Cornish Nationalist'* (Exeter: University of Exeter Press, 2010).
37 Jane Costin, 'The Legacy of D.H. Lawrence's Time in Cornwall', *Journal of the D.H. Lawrence Society*, Vol. 4, No. 3 (2017), pp. 130–52.

Notes to pages 9–14

38 Ella Westland, 'D.H. Lawrence's Cornwall: Dwelling in a Precarious Age', *Cultural Geographies*, Vol. 9, No. 3 (July 2002), pp. 266–85; C.J. Stevens, *Lawrence at Tregarthen: D.H. Lawrence in Cornwall* (Albany NY: Whitston, 1988; C.J. Stevens, *The Cornish Nightmare* (Phillips, ME: John Wade, 1996).
39 Philip Payton, *D.H. Lawrence and Cornwall* (St Agnes: Truran, 2009).

Chapter 1: Dreaming of Rananim

1 George J. Zytaruk and James T. Boulton (eds), *The Letters of D.H. Lawrence*, Vol. II: *1913–16* (Cambridge: Cambridge University Press, 2002), pp. 488–90, Letter to Ottoline Morrell, 27 December 1915 [hereafter referenced as *Letters II*].
2 Robert Gathorne-Hardy (ed.), *Ottoline at Garsington: Memoirs of Lady Ottoline Morrell 1915–1918* (London: Faber & Faber, 1974), pp. 38–39.
3 *Letters II*, To Ottoline Morrell, 27 December 1915.
4 *Letters II*, To Ottoline Morrell, 27 December 1915.
5 Richard Aldington, *Portrait of a Genius, but ... The Life of D.H. Lawrence 1885–1930* (London: Heinemann, 1950), p. 7.
6 The Ruskin Museum (website).
7 Jane Drake, *William Morris: An Illustrated Life* (Norwich: History Press, 1997), p. 1.
8 Philip Payton, *A History of Sussex* (Lancaster: Carnegie, 2017), pp. 168–69.
9 A.N. Wilson, *Hilaire Belloc: A Biography* (Singapore: Mandarin, 1997), p. 299.
10 Payton, 2017, p. 176; Wilson, 1997.
11 John Baxendale, *Priestley's England: J.B. Priestly and English Culture* (Manchester: Manchester University Press, 2007), p. 80.
12 *Saturday Review*, 27 March 1926.
13 H.V. Morton, *In Search of England* (London: Folio Society, 2002 [original edn 1927]), p. xx.
14 Simon Jenkins, 'Introduction', in Morton, 2002, p. viii.
15 Morton, 2002, p. 13.
16 Morton, 2002, p. xx.
17 John Betjeman, 'Coming Home, or England Revisited', BBC Home Service, 25 February 1943; see also Stephen Games (ed.), *Trains and Buttered Toast* (London: John Murray, 2006), pp. 138–39.
18 A.L. Rowse, *Memories and Glimpses* (London: Methuen, 1986), p. 476.
19 Philip Payton, *John Betjeman and Cornwall: 'The Celebrated Cornish Nationalist'* (Exeter: University of Exeter Press, 2010).
20 Morton, 2002, p. 83.
21 Morton, 2002, p. 113.
22 Morton, 2002, p. 113.
23 John Betjeman, *Guide to English Parish Churches*, ed. by Nigel Kerr (London: Collins, 1958, new edn 1993), p. 125.

152

24 *Evening Standard*, 8 May 1936; see also Stephen Games (ed.), *Tennis Whites and Tea Cakes* (London: John Murray, 2007), p. 186.
25 *Manchester Guardian*, 18 August 1914.
26 *Manchester Guardian*, 18 August 1914.
27 *Manchester Guardian*, 18 August 1914.
28 D.H. Lawrence, *Kangaroo* (Penguin: London, 1950), p. 140.
29 *Letters II*, To Lady Cynthia Asquith, 31 January 1915.
30 Galya Diment, *A Russian Jew of Bloomsbury: The Life and Times of Samuel Koteliansky* (Montreal & Kingston: McGill-Queens University Press, 2013), p. 75.
31 Diment, 2013, p. 76.
32 John Turner and John Worthen, 'Ideas of Community: Lawrence and "Rananim"', *D.H. Lawrence Studies* (The D.H. Lawrence Society of Korea), Vol. 8 (July 1999), pp. 135–71.
33 *Letters II*, To John Middleton Murry and Katherine Mansfield, 5 March 1916.
34 Rosie Jackson, *Frieda Lawrence: Including Not I, but the Wind and Other Autobiographical Writings* (London: Pandora, 1994), p. 145.
35 C.J. Stevens, *The Cornish Nightmare: D.H. Lawrence in Cornwall* (Phillips, ME: John Wade, 1996), pp. 53–54.
36 Diment, 2013, p. 75.
37 Paul Delany, *D.H. Lawrence's Nightmare: The Writer and His Circle in the Years of the Great War* (Hassocks: Harvester, 1979), p. 57.
38 Delany, 1979, p. 64.
39 *Letters II*, To Samuel Koteliansky, 5 February 1915.
40 Delany, 1979, p. 84.
41 Miranda Seymour, *Ottoline Morrell: Life on the Grand Scale* (London: Sceptre, 1992), p. 296.
42 *Letters II*, To Bertrand Russell, 29 April 1915.
43 *Letters II*, To Cynthia Asquith, 21 October 1915.
44 Gathorne-Hardy (ed.), 1974, p. 39.
45 Delany, 1979, p. 147.
46 Delany, 1979, p. 147.
47 Delany, 1979, p. 162.
48 Aldington, 1950, p. 172.
49 Delany, 1979, p. 169.
50 Delany, 1979, p. 177.
51 *Letters II*, To Ottoline Morrell, 27 December 1915.

Chapter 2: Dreaming of Cornwall

1 Cited in Jane Costin, 'Lawrence's "Best Adventure": Blood Consciousness and Cornwall', *Études Lawrenciennes*, Vol. 43 (2012), p. 95.

Notes to pages 23–27

2 Ella Westland, 'D.H. Lawrence's Cornwall: Dwelling in a Precarious Age', *Cultural Geographies*, Vol. 9, No. 3 (July 2002), pp. 266–85.
3 Cited in D.M. Thomas (ed.), *The Granite Kingdom: Poems of Cornwall* (Truro: Bradford Barton, 1970), p. 24.
4 Patrick Hutton, *I Would Not Be Forgotten: The Life and Work of Robert Stephen Hawker 1803–1875* (Padstow: Tabb House, 2004), p. 142.
5 Hutton, 2004, p. 175.
6 Hutton, 2004, p. 196.
7 John Betjeman, 'Hawker of Morwenstowe [sic]', BBC West of England broadcast, 7 October 1945; see also Candida Lycett Green (ed.), *Coming Home: An Anthology of Prose* (London: Methuen, 1997), p. 189; Candida Lycett Green (ed.), *Betjeman's Britain* (London: Folio Society, 1999), p. 77.
8 John Betjeman, *Cornwall: Shell Guide* (London: Murray, 1964), p. 7.
9 Philip Payton, 'Paralysis and Revival: The Reconstruction of Celtic-Catholic Cornwall, 1890–1945', in Ella Westland (ed.), *Cornwall: The Cultural Construction of Place* (Newmill: Patten Press, 1997), pp. 25–39.
10 Robert Hunt, *Popular Romances of the West of England: The Drolls, Traditions and Superstitions of Old Cornwall* (London: Chatto & Windus, 3rd edn 1881), p. 216.
11 Amy Hale, 'Genesis of the Celto-Cornish Revival? L.C. Duncombe-Jewell and the Cowethas Kelto-Kernuak', in Philip Payton (ed.), *Cornish Studies: Five* (Exeter: University of Exeter Press, 1997), pp. 100–11.
12 L.C. Duncombe-Jewell, 'About Myself and the Cornish-Celtic Movement', *Candid Friend and Traveller*, 5 July 1902.
13 *Old Cornwall*, Vol. 11, No. 8 (1934).
14 Henry Jenner, *A Handbook of the Cornish Language* (London: David Nutt, 1904), pp. v–vi.
15 Hugh Miners and Treve Crago, *Tolzethan: The Life and Times of Joseph Hambley Rowe* (Bude: Gorseth Kernow, 2002), p. 16.
16 Cited in A.L. Rowse, *The Little Land of Cornwall* (Gloucester: Alan Sutton, 1986), p. 264.
17 Cited in Barry Cunliffe, *Bretons and Britons: The Fight for Identity* (Oxford: Oxford University Press, 2021), p. 349.
18 Cited in Cunliffe, 2021, p. 356.
19 Cunliffe, 2021, pp. 369–73.
20 Cunliffe, 2021, p. 378.
21 Cunliffe, 2021, p. 378.
22 A.L. Rowse, *Matthew Arnold: Poet and Prophet* (London: Thames & Hudson, 1976), p. 12.
23 Herbert S. Vaughan, *The British Road Book* (London: E.R. Shrimpton, 1898), cited in Philip Payton (ed.), *Cornwall For Ever! Kernow Bys Vyken!* (Lostwithiel: Cornwall Heritage Trust, 2000), p. 90.

Notes to pages 27–32

24 Simon Trezise, 'The Celt, the Saxon and the Cornishman: Stereotypes and Counter-Stereotypes of the Victorian Period', in Philip Payton (ed.), *Cornish Studies: Eight* (Exeter: University of Exeter Press, 2000), p. 60.
25 Trezise, 2000, p. 60.
26 W.H. Hudson, *The Land's End: A Naturalist's Impressions in West Cornwall* (London: Wildwood, 1908), p. 175.
27 Hudson, 1908, p. 142.
28 Hudson, 1908, p. 32.
29 Hudson, 1908, pp. 95–96.
30 Hudson, 1908, p. 96.
31 Hudson, 1908, p. 97.
32 Hudson, 1908, p. 97.
33 Hudson, 1908, p. 100.
34 Hudson, 1908, pp. 106–07.
35 Hudson, 1908, p. 34.
36 Hudson, 1908, p. 129.
37 Hudson, 1908, p. 133.
38 Hudson, 1908, pp. 134–35.
39 Hudson, 1908, p. 144.
40 Hudson, 1908, p. 145.
41 Hudson, 1908, p. 146.
42 Hudson, 1908, p. 150.
43 Hudson, 1908, pp. 179–80.
44 Hudson, 1908, p. 181.
45 Hudson, 1908, pp. 173–74.
46 Hudson, 1908, p. 174.
47 John Betjeman, 'Victorian Provincial Life', BBC West of England Home Service broadcast, 24 May 1949; see also Stephen Games (ed.), *Trains and Buttered Toast* (London: Murray, 2006), p. 37.
48 Philip Payton, *Cornwall: A History* (Exeter: University of Exeter Press, 2018), pp. 278–79; Caroline Fox, *Painting in Newlyn 1900–1930* (Penzance: Newlyn Orion, 1985); Michael Jacobs and Malcolm Warner, *Art in the West Country* (Oxford: Phaidon Press, 1980); David Brown (ed.), *St Ives 1939–64* (London: Tate Gallery, 1985); Edward Mullins, *Alfred Wallis: Cornish Primitive Painter* (London: Macdonald, 1967); Marion Whybrow, *St Ives 1883–1993: Portrait of an Art Colony* (Woodbridge: Antique Collectors' Club, 1994).
49 Mary Elizabeth Braddon, *Wyllard's Weird: A Novel*, in *The Complete Works of Mary Elizabeth Braddon* (1885; repr. [n.p.]: e-artnow, 2019), p. 8250; I am grateful to Gemma Goodman for drawing my attention to this work.
50 Roger Burdett Wilson, *Go Great Western: A History of GWR Publicity* (Newton Abbot: David & Charles, 1970, repub. 1987).
51 A.M. Broadley, *The Cornish Riviera* (London: Great Western Railway, 1904).
52 Payton, 2018, pp. 280–81.

Notes to pages 33–38

53 Beverly Cole and Richard Durak, *Railway Posters 1923–1947* (London: Science Museum, 1992), p. 31.
54 Lyonesse (ed.), *Legend Land: Being a Collection of Some of the Old Tales Told in the Western Parts of Britain Served by the Great Western Railway* (London: Great Western Railway, 1922).
55 Lyonesse (ed.), 1922, p. 14.
56 Lyonesse (ed.), 1922, p. 53.
57 *Cornish Magazine*, Vol. 1 (1895), p. 236.
58 Philip Payton and Paul Thornton, 'The Great Western Railway and the Cornish-Celtic Revival', in Philip Payton (ed.), *Cornish Studies: Three* (Exeter: University of Exeter Press, 1995), pp. 83–103.
59 S.P.B. Mais, *The Cornish Riviera* (London: Great Western Railway, 3rd edn 1934), p. 7.
60 Anon., *Through the Window* (London: Great Western Railway, 1924, repub. Newton Abbot: Peninsula Press, 1994), p. 7.
61 Mais, 1934, pp. 3 and 9.
62 A.G. Folliott-Stokes, *The Cornish Coast and Moors* (London: Greening, 1912), p. 16.
63 Folliott-Stokes, 1912, pp. 16–17.
64 Folliott-Stokes, 1912, p. 18.
65 Folliott-Stokes, 1912, p. 21.
66 Folliott-Stokes, 1912, pp. 21–22.
67 Cited in Alan Bennett, *Southern Holiday Lines in North Cornwall and West Devon* (Cheltenham: Runpast, 1995), endnote.
68 Bennett, 1995, p. 44.
69 Cited in Bennett, 1995, p. 56.
70 See Kenneth Phelps, *The Wormwood Cup: Thomas Hardy in Cornwall* (Padstow: Lodenek Press, 1975).
71 Thomas Hardy, *The Complete Poems*, ed. by James Gibson (Basingstoke: Palgrave, 2001), p. 312.
72 Thomas Hardy, *Satires of Circumstance* (London: Macmillan, 1914).
73 Hardy, 1914, p. 56.
74 Hardy, 1914, pp. 51–52.
75 Hardy, 1914, pp. 58–59.
76 Hardy, 1914, pp. 62–63.
77 Adrian Tait, '"Primeval Darkness" and "Chasmal Beauty": An Ecocritical Rereading of Cornwall in the Work of D.H. Lawrence and Thomas Hardy', *Journal of D.H. Lawrence Studies*, Vol. 4, No. 3 (2017), p. 102.
78 Simon Tresize, '"Off Wessex", or a Place in the Mind', in Melissa Hardie (ed.), *A Mere Interlude: Some Literary Visitors in Lyonnesse* (Penzance: Patten, 1992), p. 35.
79 Cited in Michael Millgate, *Thomas Hardy: A Biography Revisited* (Oxford: Oxford University Press, 2004), p. 379.

Notes to pages 38–44

80 George J. Zytaruk and James T. Boulton (eds), *The Letters of D.H. Lawrence*, Vol. II: *1913–16* (Cambridge: Cambridge University Press, 2002), p. 212, Letter to J.B. Pinker, 5 September 1914.

Chapter 3: Rananim Found and Lost: Lawrence at Porthcothan

1 George J. Zytaruk and James T. Boulton (eds), *The Letters of D.H. Lawrence*, Vol II: *1913–16* (Cambridge: Cambridge University Press, 2002), Letter to Cynthia Asquith, 24 December 1915 [hereafter referenced as *Letters II*].
2 A.G. Folliott-Stokes, *The Cornish Coast and Moors* (London: Greening, 1912), p. 90.
3 *Letters II*, To Dollie Radford, 31 December 1915.
4 *Letters II*, To Edith Eder, 30 December 1915.
5 Robert Gathorne-Hardy (ed.), *Ottoline at Garsington: Memoirs of Lady Ottoline Morrell 1915–1918* (London: Faber & Faber, 1974), p. 141.
6 *Letters II*, To Catherine Carswell, 11 January 1916.
7 *Letters II*, To J.B. Pinker, 1 January 1916.
8 *Letters II*, To S.S. Koteliansky, 30 December 1915.
9 *Letters II*, To J.D. Beresford, 3 January 1916.
10 *Letters II*, To J.D. Beresford, 3 January 1916.
11 *Letters II*, To S.S. Koteliansky, 6 January 1916.
12 *Letters II*, To Katherine Mansfield, 7 January 1916.
13 *Letters II*, To Ottoline Morrell, 9 January 1916.
14 *Letters II*, To Catherine Carswell, 11 January 1916.
15 *Letters II*, To John Middleton Murry and Katherine Mansfield, 17 January 1916.
16 *Letters II*, To Barbara Low, 5 January 1916.
17 *Letters II*, To Bertrand Russell, 13 January 1916.
18 *Letters II*, To Mark Gertler, 20 January 1916.
19 *Letters II*, To Ottoline Morrell, 9 January 1916.
20 *Letters II*, To J.D. Beresford, 5 January 1916.
21 *Letters II*, To Ottoline Morrell, 21 January 1916.
22 Cecil Gray, *Peter Warlock: A Memoir of Philip Heseltine* (London: Jonathan Cape, 1934).
23 Gray, 1934, pp. 33 and 38.
24 Gray, 1934, p. 103.
25 Cited in Gray, 1934, p. 98.
26 Cited in Gray, 1934, p. 105.
27 Cited in Gray, 1934, p. 105.
28 *Letters II*, To Philip Heseltine, 18? December 1915.
29 Cited in Gray, 1934, p. 109.
30 *Letters II*, To Ottoline Morrell, 9 January 1916.

Notes to pages 45–52

31 Beryl Kington, 'Alec Rowley and Recollections of Peter Warlock', in David Cox and John Bishop (eds), *Peter Warlock: A Centenary Celebration* (London: Thames, 1994), p. 216.
32 Ian Parrott, 'The Jolly Shepherd', in Cox and Bishop (eds), 1994, p. 139.
33 Cited in Gray, 1934, p. 45.
34 Henry Jenner, *A Handbook of the Cornish Language: Chiefly in its Latest Stages with Some Account of its History and Literature* (London: David Nutt, 1904).
35 Alan M. Kent, '"Song of Our Motherland": Making Meaning of the Life of Katharine Lee Jenner 1853–1936', in Derek R. Williams (ed.), *Henry and Katharine Jenner: A Celebration of Cornwall's Culture, Language and Identity* (London: Francis Boutle, 2004), p. 124.
36 Cited in Kent, 2004, p. 128.
37 Cited in Kent, 2004, p. 128.
38 Cited in Kent, 2004, p. 129.
39 Sharon Lowenna, '"Noscitur A Sociis": Jenner, Duncombe-Jewell and their Milieu', in Philip Payton (ed.), *Cornish Studies: Twelve* (Exeter: University of Exeter Press, 2004).
40 *Letters II*, To Gordon Campbell, 20 December 1914.
41 *Letters II*, To Gordon Campbell, 20 December 1914.
42 *Letters II*, To S.S. Koteliansky, 5 January 1915.
43 Mrs Henry Jenner, *Celtic Symbolism* (London: Methuen, 1910), p. 150.
44 Jenner, 1904, p. iv.
45 *Letters II*, To Ottoline Morrell, 22 January 1916.
46 I.A. Copley, 'Peter Warlock's Choral Music', *Music and Letters*, Vol. 45, No. 4 (October 1964), pp. 318–36.
47 Gray, 1934, pp. 161–62.
48 Cited in Gray, 1934, p. 162.
49 Cited in Gray, 1934, p. 162.
50 Gray, 1934, p. 158.
51 Cited in Gray, 1934, p. 158.
52 Cited in Gray, 1934, p. 170.
53 Cited in Gray, 1934, p. 182.
54 Paul Ladmirault, 'Peter Warlock: A Great English Composer', in Cox and Bishop (eds), 1994, pp. 59 and 62.
55 Ladmirault, 1994, p. 62.
56 Donald R. Rawe, 'The Poetry of Henry Jenner', in Williams (ed.), 2004, p. 212.
57 Rawe, 2004, pp. 213–14.
58 I am grateful to Jane Costin for this suggestion.
59 Philip Payton, *John Betjeman and Cornwall: 'The Celebrated Cornish Nationalist'* (Exeter: University of Exeter Press, 2010), pp. 77–91.
60 Lowenna, 2014.
61 Paul Newman, *The Tregerthen Horror: Aleister Crowley, D.H. Lawrence and Peter Warlock in Cornwall* (n.p.: Abraxas & DGR, 2005), p. 65.

Notes to pages 53–63

62 Gray, 1934, p. 122.
63 Cited in Robert Beckhard, 'Notes from an American on a 1950s Warlock Odyssey', in Cox and Bishop (eds), 1994, pp. 204–05.
64 *Letters II*, To Ottoline Morrell, 13 January 1916.
65 *Letters II*, To Ottoline Morrell, 15 January 1916.
66 *Letters II*, To Ottoline Morrell, 13 January 1916.
67 *Letters II*, To John Middleton Murry and Katherine Mansfield, 17 January 1916.
68 *Letters II*, To Ottoline Morrell, 25 February 1916.
69 *Letters II*, To Barbara Low, 5 January 1916.
70 *Letters II*, To J.D. Beresford, 5 January 1916.
71 James T. Boulton and Andrew Robertson (eds), *The Letters of D.H. Lawrence*, Vol. III, Part 1: *1916–21* (Cambridge: Cambridge University Press, 1984), Letter to Amy Lowell, 7 December 1916.
72 *Letters II*, To Bertrand Russell, 13 January 1916.
73 *Letters II*, To Bertrand Russell, 13 January 1916.
74 *Letters II*, To Barbara Low, 5 January 1916.
75 *Letters II*, To J.D. Beresford, 5 January 1916.
76 *Letters II*, To J.D. Beresford, 1 February 1916.
77 *Letters II*, To J.D. Beresford, 1 February 1916.
78 *Letters II*, To J.D. Beresford, 1 February 1916.
79 *Letters II*, To J.D. Beresford, 1 February 1916.
80 *Letters II*, To J.D. Beresford, 24 February 1916.
81 *Letters II*, To J.D. Beresford, 24 February 1916.
82 *Letters II*, To Beatrice Beresford, 28 February 1916.
83 Cited in Gray, 1934, p. 110.
84 Cited in Gray, 1934, p. 109.
85 Cited in Gray, 1934, pp. 111–12.
86 Cited in Gray, 1934, p. 116.
87 Andrew Harrison, '"A New Continent of the Soul": D.H. Lawrence, Porthcothan and the Necessary Fiction of Cornwall', *Journal of D.H. Lawrence Studies*, Vol. 4, No. 3 (2017), pp. 35 and 39.

Chapter 4: Rananim Regained? Lawrence at Zennor

1 George J. Zytaruk and James Boulton (eds), *The Letters of D.H. Lawrence*, Vol. II: *1913–16* (Cambridge: Cambridge University Press, 2002), Letter to J.D. Beresford, 1 February 1916 [hereafter referenced as *Letters II*].
2 *Letters II*, To John Middleton Murry and Katherine Mansfield, 24 February 1916.
3 *Letters II*, To John Middleton Murry and Katherine Mansfield, 24 February 1916.
4 *Letters II*, To Ottoline Morrell, 25 February 1916.
5 *Letters II*, To John Middleton Murry and Katherine Mansfield, 5 March 1916.
6 D.H. Lawrence, *Kangaroo* (London: Penguin, 1950), p. 263.

Notes to pages 63–72

7 Lawrence, 1950, p. 265.
8 Lawrence, 1950, p. 263.
9 Lawrence, 1950, pp. 250–51.
10 Jane Costin, 'Lawrence's "Best Adventure": Blood Consciousness and Cornwall', *Études Lawrenciennes*, Vol. 43 (2012), pp. 1–12.
11 Costin, 2012, pp. 2–3.
12 Lawrence, 1950, p. 264.
13 John Hobson Matthews, *History of St Ives, Lelant, Towednack, and Zennor* (London: Eliot Stock, 1892), frontispiece.
14 W.H. Hudson, *The Land's End: A Naturalist's Impression of West Cornwall* (London: Hutchinson, 1908), pp. 220–21.
15 A.G. Folliott-Stokes, *The Cornish Coast and Moors* (London: Greening, 1912), p. 19.
16 Folliott-Stokes, 1912, p. 22.
17 Folliott-Stokes, 1912, p. 23.
18 Folliott-Stokes, 1912, p. 23.
19 Folliott-Stokes, 1912, p. 146.
20 Folliott-Stokes, 1912, p. 147.
21 Folliott-Stokes, 1912, p. 149.
22 P.A.S. Pool, *The Place-names of West Penwith* (St Austell: Federation of Old Cornwall Societies, 1973), pp. 40, 45, 46.
23 P.A.S. Pool, *The Field-names of West Penwith* (Hayle: Pool, 1990), pp. 39, 63, 45.
24 Henry Jenner, *A Handbook of the Cornish Language* (London: David Nutt, 1904), p. 12.
25 Jenner, 1904, p. 16.
26 Matthews, 1892, p. 404.
27 Matthews, 1892, p. 404.
28 Jenner, 1904, p. 16.
29 P.A.S. Pool, 'An Address Given at Zennor Church on 28 September 1991 at a Service Held to Mark the Centenary of the Death of John Davey'.
30 Jenner, 1904, p. 16.
31 Matthews, 1892, p. 405.
32 Robert Morton Nance, 'John Davey of Boswednack and His Cornish Rhyme', *Journal of the Royal Institution of Cornwall*, Vol. 22 (1922–25), pp. 146–53; Pool, 28 September 1991.
33 R. Trevelyan Lyon, *Cornish: The Struggle for Survival* (n.p.: Tavas an Weryn, 2001), p. 14.
34 *Letters II*, To Catherine Carswell, 16 April 1916.
35 Costin, 2012, p. 7.
36 Costin, 2002, p. 7. Pool, 1973, p. 80, offers no explanation for the place name Wicca, other than to suggest a derivation from Old English *wic*, a dwelling, as in Gweek and Week St Mary in other parts of Cornwall. Likewise, Pool offers no translation of Tregerthen (other than the common Cornish prefix 'Tre-'), although noting (p. 72) that in 1361 the hamlet was spelt Tregeuran or Tregauran. The Bible

Notes to pages 73–77

Christians, like other Methodist denominations in Cornwall, sometimes erected their chapels in remote spots near footpaths to enable their congregations to attend from various scattered locations.

37 Robert Hunt, *Popular Romances of the West of England: The Drolls, Traditions and Superstitions of Old Cornwall* (London: Chatto & Windus, 1908), pp. 52, 83–85, 118, 120–26, 321, 328, 335.
38 Ronald M. James, *The Folklore of Cornwall: The Oral Tradition of a Celtic Nation* (Exeter: University of Exeter Press, 2018), pp. 99, 101.
39 James, 2018, p. 99.
40 Lyonesse (ed.), *Legend Land: Being a Collection of Some of the Old Tales Told in Those Western Parts of Britain Served by the Great Western Railway* (London: Great Western Railway, 1922), p. 5.
41 J.B. Cotter, *Zennor Church* (Zennor: Zennor Parochial Church Council, n.d. c.1980), p. 1.
42 Claire Tomalin, *The Young H.G. Wells: Changing the World* (London: Penguin, 2022), p. 117.
43 I am grateful to Elise Ruthenbeck for this insight.
44 Lawrence, 1950, p. 68.
45 Lawrence, 1950, pp. 68–69.
46 Lawrence, 1950, p. 69.
47 Lawrence, 1950, p. 69.
48 Lawrence, 1950, p. 69.
49 Lawrence, 1950, p. 69.
50 Lawrence, 1950, p. 69.
51 David Game, *D.H. Lawrence's Australia: Anxiety on the Edge of Empire* (London: Routledge, 2015), p. 115.
52 Lawrence, 1950, p. 73.
53 Lawrence, 1950, p. 81.
54 Alison Symons, *Tremedda Days: A View of Zennor, 1900–1944* (Padstow: Tabb House, 1992), p. 139.
55 Brenda Maddox, *The Married Man: A Life of D.H. Lawrence* (London: Minerva, 1995), p. 227.
56 Symons, 1992, p. 142.
57 Alfred Munnings, *An Artist's Life* (London: Museum Press, 1950), p. 298.
58 Munnings, 1950, p. 276.
59 Munnings, 1950, p. 275.
60 Munnings, 1950, p. 271.
61 Symons, 1992, pp. 142–44.
62 Guy Thorne, *The Secret Service Submarine: A Story of the Present War* (New York: Sully and Kleinteich, 1915).
63 John Fischer Williams (ed.), *Memories of John Westlake* (London: Smith, Elder & Co., 1914).
64 Williams (ed.), 1914, p. 110.

Notes to pages 77–86

65 Williams (ed.), 1914, p. 99.
66 Williams (ed.), 1914, p. 138.
67 Williams (ed.), 1914, pp. 138–39.
68 Williams (ed.), 1914, p. 140.
69 Williams (ed.), 1914, p. 141.
70 Williams (ed.), 1914, pp. 141–42.
71 Williams (ed.), 1914, p. 140.
72 *Letters II*, To Katherine Mansfield, 16 July 1916.
73 Paul Newman, *The Tregerthen Horror: Aleister Crowley, D.H. Lawrence and Peter Warlock in Cornwall* (n.p.: Abraxas & DGR, 2005), p. 25.
74 James T. Boulton and Andrew Robertson (eds), *The Letters of D.H. Lawrence*, Vol. III, Part 1: *1916–21* (Cambridge: Cambridge University Press, 1984), Letter to Cynthia Asquith, 3 September 1917 [hereafter referenced as *Letters III*].
75 Newman, 2005, p. 25; *St Ives Times*, 24 August 1917; 31 August 1917.
76 *Letters II*, To John Middleton Murry and Katherine Mansfield, 5 March 1916.
77 *Letters II*, To John Middleton Murry and Katherine Mansfield, 5 March 1916.
78 *Letters II*, To John Middleton Murry and Katherine Mansfield, 5 March 1916.
79 *Letters II*, To John Middleton Murry and Katherine Mansfield, 8 March 1916.
80 Lawrence, 1950, p. 264.
81 Lawrence, 1950, p. 264.
82 *Letters II*, To John Middleton Murry and Katherine Mansfield, 8 March 1916.
83 *Letters II*, To Katherine Mansfield, 11 March 1918.
84 *Letters II*, To Ottoline Morrell, 7 April 1916.
85 Rosie Jackson, *Frieda Lawrence: Including Not I, but the Wind and Other Autobiographical Writings* (London: Pandora, 1994), p. 145.
86 Jackson, 1994, pp. 145–46.
87 Cited in Richard Aldington, *Portrait of a Genius, but ... The Life of D.H. Lawrence, 1885–1930* (London: Heinemann, 1950), p. 182.
88 Cited in Norman Page (ed.), *D.H. Lawrence: Interviews and Recollections*, Vol. I (London: Macmillan, 1981), p. 131.
89 Page (ed.), 1981, p. 131.
90 Page (ed.), 1981, p. 132.
91 Page (ed.), 1981, p. 132.
92 Vincent O'Sullivan and Margaret Scott (eds), *Letters of Katherine Mansfield*, Vol. I (Oxford: Clarendon Press, 1984), p. 268; see also Claire Tomalin, *Katherine Mansfield: A Secret Life* (London: Penguin, 1988).
93 O'Sullivan and Scott (eds), 1984, p. 268.
94 O'Sullivan and Scott (eds), 1984, p. 268.
95 Page (ed.), 1981, p. 132.
96 *Letters II*, To Ottoline Morrell, 24 May 1916.
97 *Letters II*, To Barbara Low, 30 May 1916.
98 *Letters II*, To Samuel Koteliansky, 7 November 1916.
99 Page (ed.), 1981, p. 133.

100 Page (ed.), 1981, p. 137.
101 Page (ed.), 1981, pp. 140–41.
102 Page (ed.), 1981, p. 139.
103 Page (ed.), 1981, p. 139.
104 Jonathan Long, 'Murry vs Carswell: Conflicting Versions of D.H. Lawrence During His Time in Cornwall', *Journal of D.H. Lawrence Studies*, Vol. 4, No. 3 (2017), p. 45.
105 Long, 2017, p. 61.
106 Long, 2017, p. 61.
107 Cited in Cecil Gray, *Peter Warlock: A Memoir of Philip Heseltine* (London: Jonathan Cape, 1934), p. 146.
108 Gray, 1934, p. 148.
109 Gray, 1934, p. 149.
110 Gray, 1934, pp. 234–35.
111 Gray, 1934, p. 154.
112 Gray, 1934, p. 153.
113 Gray, 1934, p. 163.
114 Gray, 1934, p. 152.
115 Gray, 1934, p. 152.
116 J.C. Trewin and H.J. Willmott, *London–Bodmin: An Exchange of Letters* (London: Westaway, 1950), p. 85.
117 Gray, 1934, p. 156.
118 Gray, 1934, p. 162.
119 Gray, 1934, p. 214.
120 Gray, 1934, p. 163.
121 Cited in Maddox, 1995, p. 245.
122 Cecil Gray, *Musical Chairs: Or, Between Two Stools* (London: Hogarth Press, 1948), p. 138.
123 Gray, 1934, p. 157.
124 *Letters II*, To Dollie Radford, 5 September 1916.
125 *Letters II*, To Dollie Radford, 11 October 1916.
126 James Stevens, *A Cornish Farmer's Diary*, ed. P.A.S. Pool (Penzance: Pool, 1977), frontispiece.
127 Symons, 1992, p. 145.
128 Jackson, 1994, p. 147.
129 Symons, 1992, p. 149.
130 Symons, 1992, pp. 149–50.
131 C.J. Stevens, *The Cornish Nightmare: D.H. Lawrence in Cornwall* (Phillips, ME: John Wade, 1996), p. 65.
132 Stevens, 1996, pp. 63–64.
133 Maddox, 1995, p. 143.
134 C.J. Stevens, *Lawrence at Tregerthen: D.H. Lawrence in Cornwall* (Albany, NY: Whitson, 1988), pp. 32–33.
135 Stevens, 1996, p. 66.

Notes to pages 96–100

136 Maddox, 1995, p. 231.
137 Maddox, 1995, p. 243.
138 Aldington, 1950, p. 195.
139 *Letters III*, To John Middleton Murry, 5 May 1917.
140 Frances Wilson, *Burning Man: The Ascent of D.H. Lawrence* (London: Bloomsbury, 2021), p. 126.
141 Gray, 1948, p. 122.
142 Gray, 1948, p. 478; Stevens, 1988, p. 105.
143 Stevens, 1988, p. 105.
144 Richard Aldington, *Death of a Hero* (London: Sphere, 1968), p. 149.
145 Ella Westland, 'D.H. Lawrence's Cornwall: Dwelling in a Precarious Age', *Cultural Geographies*, Vol. 9, No. 3 (July 2002), p. 270.
146 Hilda Doolittle, *Bid Me to Live* (London: Virago, 1984), p. 143.
147 Doolittle, 1984, p. 145.
148 Doolittle, 1984, p. 182.
149 Cited in Wilson, 2021, p. 141.

Chapter 5: War in Cornwall: 'The Nightmare'

1 George J. Zytaruk and James T. Boulton (eds), *The Letters of D.H. Lawrence*, Vol. II: *1913–16* (Cambridge: Cambridge University Press, 2002), Letter to Eddie Marsh, 25 August 1914 [hereafter referenced as *Letters II*].
2 Paul Delany, *D.H. Lawrence's Nightmare: The Writer and His Circle of Friends in the Years of the Great War* (Hassocks: Harvester Press, 1979), p. 186.
3 E.C. Axford, *Bodmin Moor* (Newton Abbot: David & Charles, 1975), p. 10.
4 Cited in Pete London, *Cornwall in the First World War* (Redruth: Truran, 2013), p. 7.
5 London, 2013, p. 7.
6 Stuart Dalley, 'The Response in Cornwall to the Outbreak of the First World War', in Philip Payton (ed.), *Cornish Studies: Eleven* (Exeter: University of Exeter Press, 2003), p. 86.
7 *West Briton*, 1 August 1914.
8 Dalley, 2003, p. 86.
9 Melanie James, 'Indifferent or Just Different? The Cornish Response to the Declaration of War in August 1914', in Garry Tregidga and Thomas Fidler (eds), *Cornwall and the Great War: Perspectives on Conflict and Place* (Penryn: Institute of Cornish Studies, 2018), p. 18.
10 James, 2018, p. 19.
11 Kresen Kernow, *Elsie Stephens' War Diary*, cited in Dalley, 2003, p. 86.
12 *Cornish Guardian*, 7 August 1914.
13 Philip Payton, *The Cornish Overseas: A History of Cornwall's Great Emigration* (Exeter: University of Exeter Press, 2020), pp. 390–97.

Notes to pages 100–105

14 Garry Magee and Andrew Thompson, 'Remittances Revisited: A Case Study of South Africa and the Cornish Migrant, c.1870–1914', in Philip Payton (ed.), *Cornish Studies: Thirteen* (Exeter: University of Exeter Press, 2005), p. 296.
15 Bernard Walke, *Twenty Years at St Hilary* (London: Methuen, 1935, repub. London: Anthony Mott, 1982), p. 104.
16 Walke, 1982, p. 106.
17 Walke, 1982, p. 106
18 Pamela Richardson, 'A Quaker Record of Maritime Falmouth in World War One', *Troze*, Vol. 1, No. 2 (December 2008), p. 6.
19 Walke, 1982, pp. 109–10.
20 Walke, 1982, p. 111.
21 *Cornish Guardian*, 7 August 1914.
22 *Cornish Echo*, 7 August 1914.
23 Dalley, 2003, pp. 98, 100–01.
24 Jack Clemo, *Confession of a Rebel* (London: Chatto & Windus, 1975), p. 18.
25 John Rowe, 'The Declining Years of Cornish Tin Mining', in Jeffery Porter (ed.), *Education and Labour in the South West* (Exeter: University of Exeter, 1975), p. 66.
26 James, 2018, pp. 19–20.
27 Dalley, 2003, p. 102.
28 Arthur Quiller-Couch, *Nicky-Nan Reservist* (London: J.M. Dent, 1915, repub. 1929), pp. v–vi.
29 *West Briton*, 7 September 1914, 14 September 1914.
30 *West Briton*, 17 September 1914.
31 *West Briton*, 20 May 1915.
32 Dalley, 2003, pp. 86–7.
33 Alan M. Kent, 'From *Meeting the Kaiser* to *An Tankow*: Imagining the First World War in Cornish and Anglo-Cornish Literature and Theatre', in Tregidga and Fidler (eds), 2018, pp. 59–63.
34 Quiller-Couch, 1929, p. 1.
35 Quiller-Couch, 1929, p. 1.
36 Quiller-Couch, 1929, p. 56.
37 A.L. Rowse, *Quiller Couch: A Portrait of Q* (Methuen: London, 1988), p. 132; see also F. Brittain, *Arthur Quiller-Couch: A Biographical Study of Q* (Cambridge: Cambridge University Press, 1948), p. 78.
38 D.H. Lawrence, *Kangaroo* (London: Martin Secker, 1923, repub. London: Penguin, 1950), p. 251.
39 Philip Payton, Alston Kennerley and Helen Doe, '"Window to a Wider World": Early and Medieval Cornwall', in Philip Payton, Alston Kennerley and Helen Doe (eds), *The Maritime History of Cornwall* (Exeter: University of Exeter Press, 2014), p. 13.
40 G.H. and R. Bennett, 'Maritime Cornwall in the Era of Two World Wars', in Payton, Kennerley and Doe (eds), 2014, p. 379.
41 Bennett and Bennett, 2014, p. 377.

Notes to pages 105–112

42 *Haverfordwest and Milford Haven Telegraph*, 21 February 1917.
43 London, 2013, pp. 48–49.
44 Cyril Noall and Graham Farr, *Wreck and Rescue Round the Cornish Coast: The Story of the Land's End Lifeboats* (Truro: D. Bradford Barton, 1965), pp. 27–28.
45 Maritime Archaeology Trust, *Forgotten Wrecks of the First World War—Site Report: Pendennis U-Boats* (London: Imperial War Museum, 2018), pp. 8–14.
46 Maritime Archaeology Trust, 2018, pp. 8–14.
47 Exeter University Library (EUL), Rowse Collection, MS113/2 Journals and notebooks/5/3 Easter 1949; see also Philip Payton, *A.L. Rowse and Cornwall: A Paradoxical Patriot* (Exeter: University of Exeter Press, 2005), p. 206.
48 Walke, 1982, pp. 111–12.
49 Walke, 1982, p. 112.
50 Walke, 1982, p. 113.
51 London, 2013, p. 49.
52 Bennett and Bennett, 2014, pp. 379–80.
53 London, 2013, pp. 61–62.
54 John Carey, *William Golding: The Man Who Wrote Lord of the Flies* (London: Faber & Faber, 2009), p. 19.
55 Kent, 2018, p. 54.
56 G. Le Q. Martel, 'Foreword', in C.J.H. Mead, *Cornwall's Royal Engineers* (Plymouth: Underhill, n.d.), p. x.
57 Lawrence, 1950, p. 241.
58 *Letters II*, To J.D. Beresford, 5 January 1916.
59 *Letters II*, To J.D. Beresford, 5 January 1916.
60 *Letters II*, To J.D. Beresford, 1 February 1916.
61 *The Times*, 3 November 1915.
62 *Letters II*, To Catherine Carswell, 9 July 1916.
63 Lawrence, 1950, p. 262.
64 C.J. Stevens, *The Cornish Nightmare: D.H. Lawrence in Cornwall* (Phillips, ME: John Wade, 1996), pp. 39–40.
65 James T. Boulton and Andrew Robertson (eds), *The Letters of D.H. Lawrence*, Vol. III, Part 1: *1916–21* (Cambridge: Cambridge University Press, 1984), Letter to Cynthia Asquith, 11 December 1916 [hereafter referenced as *Letters III*].
66 *Letters II*, To Dollie Radford, 29 June 1916.
67 Lawrence, 1950, p. 239.
68 Lawrence, 1950, p. 239.
69 *Letters III*, To Catherine Carswell, 9 July 1916.
70 *Letters III*, To Cynthia Asquith, 1 September 1916.
71 Stevens, 1996, pp. 78–79.
72 Stevens, 1996, p. 80.
73 *Letters III*, To Robert Mountsier, 7 February 1917.
74 Stevens, 1996, p. 78.
75 Lawrence, 1950, p. 265.

Notes to pages 113–122

76 Stevens, 1996, p. 79.
77 Kent History and Library Centre, U2246/9/Z/19/44, Poster: Rewards to Coast Watchers and Civilians on Shore.
78 Walke, 1982, pp. 82–83.
79 Walke, 1982, p. 83.
80 Walke, 1982, pp. 83–84.
81 Guy Thorne, *The Secret Service Submarine: A Story of the Submarine Service: A Study of the Present War* (New York: Sully & Kleinstein, 1915), p. 2.
82 Thorne, 1915, p. 9.
83 Thorne, 1915, p. 33.
84 Thorne, 1915, p. 33.
85 Rosie Jackson, *Frieda Lawrence: Including Not I, but the Wind and Other Biographical Writings* (London: Pandora, 1994), p. 146.
86 Lawrence, 1950, p. 242.
87 Lawrence, 1950, p. 274.
88 *St Ives Times*, 5 October 1917.
89 Cecil Gray, *Musical Chairs or Between Two Stools* (London: Home & Van Thal, 1948), p. 130.
90 Stevens, 1996, p. 47.
91 C.J. Stevens, *Lawrence at Tregerthen*, p. 100.
92 Alison Symons, *Tremedda Days: A View of Zennor—1900–1944* (Padstow: Tabb House, 1992), p. 142.
93 *Letters III*, To S.S. Koteliansky, 12 June 1916.
94 Symons, 1992, p. 122.
95 Lawrence, 1950, p. 253.
96 Louise E. Wright, 'D.H. Lawrence, Robert Mountsier and the Journalist Spy Controversy', *Journal of the D.H. Lawrence Society* (1992–93), pp. 7–21.
97 Cited in Wright, 1992–93, p. 15.
98 Cited in Wright, 1992–93, p. 15.
99 Cited in Wright, 1992–93, p. 15.
100 Stevens, 1996, p. 46.
101 *Letters III*, To Robert Mountsier, 9 December 1920.
102 Stevens, 1996, p. 88.
103 Stevens, 1996, p. 95.
104 *Letters III*, To Cynthia Asquith, 12 October 1917.
105 Richard Aldington, *Portrait of a Genius, but … The Life of D.H. Lawrence 1885–1930* (London: Heinemann, 1950), pp. 198–99.
106 Jackson, 1994, p. 149.
107 Lawrence, 1950, p. 251.
108 Lawrence, 1950, p. 251.
109 Lawrence, 1950, p. 251.
110 Lawrence, 1950, p. 268.

111 Brenda Maddox, *The Married Man: A Life of D.H. Lawrence* (London: Minerva, 1995), p. 247; Stevens, 1996, p. 100.
112 Stevens, 1996, p. 99.
113 Stevens, 1996, pp. 53–54.
114 Stevens, 1996, p. 84.
115 Frances Wilson, *Burning Man: The Ascent of D.H. Lawrence* (London: Bloomsbury, 2021), p. 127.
116 *Letters III*, To Montague Shearman, 29 October 1917.
117 *Letters III*, To Cecil Gray, 29 October 1917.
118 Lawrence, 1950, p. 275.
119 *Letters III*, To Catherine Carswell, 20 December 1916.
120 *Letters III*, To Cynthia Asquith, 8 January 1917.
121 *Letters III*, To Catherine Carswell, 5 September 1917.
122 *Letters III*, To S.S. Koteliansky, 9 February 1917.
123 Stevens, 1988, pp. 1–2.
124 Jane Costin, 'The Legacy of D.H. Lawrence's Time in Cornwall', *Journal of D.H. Lawrence Studies*, Vol. 4, No. 3 (2017), p. 148.

Chapter 6: 'So on to Australia!'

1 Richard Aldington, 'Farewell to Europe', *The Atlantic*, November 1940, ch. 11–15.
2 D.H. Lawrence, *Lady Chatterley's Lover* (London: Penguin, 1960, repub. 2008), p. 5.
3 Jane Costin, 'The Legacy of D.H. Lawrence's Time in Cornwall', *Journal of D.H. Lawrence Studies*, Vol. 4, No. 3 (2017), p. 131.
4 Cited in Costin, 2017, p. 135.
5 James T. Boulton and Andrew Robertson (eds), *The Letters of D.H. Lawrence*, Vol. III, Part 1: *1916–21* (Cambridge: Cambridge University Press, 1984), Letter to Catherine Carswell, 16 October 1917 [hereafter referenced as *Letters III*].
6 Costin, 2017, p. 138.
7 D.H. Lawrence, *Kangaroo* (London: Penguin, 1950), p. 275.
8 Cited in Costin, 2017, p. 139.
9 Cited in Costin, 2017, p. 140.
10 Cited in Costin, 2017, p. 141.
11 Cited in Costin, 2017, p. 142.
12 Cited in Costin, 2017, p. 142.
13 Philip Payton, *The Cornish Overseas: A History of Cornwall's Great Emigration* (Exeter: University of Exeter Press, revised edn 2020).
14 D.H. Lawrence, 'Samson and Delilah', in *England, My England* (London: Penguin, 1974), p. 125.
15 James Stevens, *A Cornish Farmer's Diary* (Penzance: P.A.S. Pool, 1977), pp. 33–34; Alison Symons, *Tremedda Days: A View of Zennor, 1900–1944* (Padstow: Tabb House, 1992), pp. 129–33.

Notes to pages 128–137

16 Symons, 1992, p. 129.
17 Symons, 1992, p. 130.
18 Symons, 1992, p. 129.
19 Frank Ruhrmund, *About St Just-in-Penwith* (St Teath: Bossiney Books, 1979), p. 5; Jim Jewell, *Cornish in America: Linden, Wisconsin* (Linden: Cornish Miner Press, 1990), p. 11.
20 Claude Berry, *Cornwall* (London: Robert Hale, 1949), pp. 4–5.
21 *Cornishman*, 19 July 1888.
22 William A. Morris, 'An Investigation into Migration Patterns from the Parish of Zennor in Cornwall During the Second Half of the Nineteenth Century', in Philip Payton (ed.), *Cornish Studies: Seven* (Exeter: University of Exeter Press, 1999), p. 36.
23 State Library of South Australia (SLSA), D6029/68/69(L), Letters written home by Cornish folk who emigrated to Australia in the nineteenth century collected by Dr J.M. Tregenza; Henry Giles to his parents, 15 November 1854.
24 *Yorke's Peninsula Advertiser* (South Australia), 1 May 1874.
25 Stevens, 1977, p. 189.
26 Stevens, 1977, p. 177.
27 Joseph Hocking, *What Shall It Profit a Man?* (London: Horace Marshall, n.d.), p. 21.
28 Silas K. Hocking, *The Lost Lode* (London: Sampson Low, Maiston & Co., n.d.), p. 13.
29 Silas K. Hocking, n.d., pp. 14–15.
30 J. Henry Harris, *The Luck of Wheal Vor and Other Stories* (Truro: Pollard, 1901), pp. 85–91.
31 Charles Lee, *Paul Carah, Cornishman* (London: James Bowden, 1898), pp. 13–14.
32 Lesley Trotter, *The Married Widows of Cornwall: The Story of Wives 'Left Behind' by Emigration* (St Day: Humble Press, 2018).
33 Lawrence, 1974.
34 Lawrence, 1974, p. 125.
35 Lawrence, 1974, pp. 126–27.
36 Lawrence, 1974, pp. 129–34.
37 Lawrence, 1974, pp. 134–41.
38 Richard Aldington, *Portrait of a Genius, but … The Life of D.H. Lawrence, 1885–1930* (London: Heinemann, 1950), p. 249.
39 David Game, *D.H. Lawrence's Australia: Anxiety at the Edge of Empire* (London: Routledge, 2019), pp. 75–76.
40 Game, 2019, p. 83.
41 Game, 2019, p. 2.
42 Game, 2019, p. 54.
43 Game, 2019, p. 56.
44 Game, 2019. p. 57.
45 Cited in Game, 2019, p. 57.
46 Game, 2019, p. 164.
47 Game, 2019, pp. 57–58.

Notes to pages 137–144

48 Lawrence, *Kangaroo* (London: Penguin, 1950), p. 265.
49 Game, 2019, p. 60.
50 Game, 2019, p. 60.
51 Game, 2019, pp. 60–61.
52 Cited in Game, 2019, p. 69.
53 Aldington, 1950, p. 250.
54 Rosie Jackson, *Frieda Lawrence: Including Not I, but the Wind and Other Autobiographical Writings* (London: Pandora, 1995), p. 161.
55 Aldington, 1950, p. 251.
56 Jackson, 1995, p. 161.
57 Jackson, 1995, p. 162.
58 Aldington, 1950, p. 252.
59 Jackson, 1995, p. 162.
60 Jackson, 1995, pp. 162–63.
61 Jackson, 1995, p. 163.
62 Jackson, 1995, p. 162.
63 Game, 2019, p. 126.
64 Aldington, 1950,
65 Galya Diment, *A Russian Jew of Bloomsbury: The Life and Times of Samuel Koteliansky* (Montreal & Kingston: McGill-Queens University Press, 2011), pp. 71–75.
66 Aldington, 1950, p. 253.
67 Cited in Game, 2019, p. 69.
68 Jackson, 1995, p. 163.
69 Jackson, 1995, p. 163.
70 Lawrence, 1950, p. 390.
71 Lawrence, 1950, pp. 392–93.
72 Lawrence, 1950, p. 393.
73 Lawrence, 1950, p. 394.
74 Lawrence, 1950, p. 394.
75 Lawrence, 1950, p. 393.

Epilogue

1 Alison Symons, *Temedda Days: A View of Zennor, 1900–1944* (Padstow: Tabb House, 1992), pp. 141–42.
2 Symons, 1992, p. 142.
3 A.L. Rowse, *Times, Persons, Places: Essays in Literature* (London: Macmillan, 1965), pp. 1–2.
4 Rowse, 1965, p. 5.
5 Exeter University Library (EUL), Rowse Collection, MS 113 Correspondence/Sweet to Rowse, n.d. c.December 1951; see also Philip Payton, *A.L. Rowse and Cornwall: A Paradoxical Patriot* (Exeter: University of Exeter Press, 2005), pp. 96–97.

Notes to pages 144–149

6 Richard Ollard, *A Man of Contradictions: A Life of A.L. Rowse* (London: Allen Lane, 1999), p. 388.
7 A.L. Rowse, *A Man of the Thirties* (London: Weidenfeld and Nicholson, 1979), p. 119.
8 Rowse, 1979, p. 120.
9 Luke Thompson, *Clay Phoenix: A Biography of Jack Clemo* (London: Ally, 2016), pp. 53–54.
10 Jack Clemo, *Confession of a Rebel* (London: Chatto & Windus, 1975), p. 16.
11 Clemo, 1975, pp. 96, 111.
12 Clemo, 1975, pp. 137–38.
13 Clemo, 1975, p. 138.
14 Jack Clemo, 'The Two Beds', in *Penguin Modern Poets 6* (London: Penguin, 1964), pp. 26–27.
15 J.C. Trewin and H.J. Willmott, *London–Bodmin: An Exchange of Letters* (London: Westaway, 1950), pp. 89–90.
16 Paul Newman, *The Tregerthen Horror: Aleister Crowley, D.H. Lawrence and Peter Warlock in Cornwall* (n.p.: Abraxas & DGR, 2005).
17 Quentin Bell, *Virginia Woolf: A Biography*, Vol. II: *Mrs Woolf, 1912–1941* (London: Hogarth, 1972), p. 65.
18 Philip Payton, *A History of Sussex* (Lancaster: Carnegie, 2017), p. 163; Bell, 1972, p. 65.
19 John Heath-Stubbs, 'To the Mermaid at Zennor', in John Clegg (ed.), *Selected Poems* (Manchester: Carcanet Press, 2018), p. 46.
20 Louise E. Wright, 'D.H. Lawrence, Robert Mountsier and the Journalist Spy Controversy', *Journal of the D.H. Lawrence Society* (1992–93), p. 6.
21 Wright, 1992–93, p. 9.
22 Shelley Trower, *Rocks of Nations: The Imagination of Celtic Cornwall* (Manchester: Manchester University Press, 2015), p. 155.
23 Margaret Storch, 'From Cornwall to New Mexico: Primal Cultures and Belief in Lawrence', *Journal of D.H. Lawrence Studies*, Vol. 4, No. 3 (2017), p. 122.
24 Cited in Storch, 2017, p. 122.
25 Cited in Storch, 2017, p. 123.
26 James Vernon, 'Border Crossing: Cornwall and the English (Imagi)nation', in Geoffrey Cubitt (ed.), *Imagining Nations* (Manchester: Manchester University Press, 1998), p. 169.

Select Bibliography

Aldington, Richard, 'Farewell Europe', *The Atlantic*, November 1940.
Aldington, Richard, *Portrait of a Genius, but ... The Life of D.H. Lawrence 1885–1930* (London: Heinemann, 1950).
Aldington, Richard, *Death of a Hero* (London: Sphere, 1968).
Anon., *Through the Window* (London: Great Western Railway, 1924, repub. Newton Abbot: Peninsula Press, 1994).
Arnold, Matthew, 'On the Study of Celtic Literature', in R.H. Super (ed.), *The Complete Prose Works of Matthew Arnold*, Vol. III (Ann Arbor: University of Michigan Press, 1962).
Axford, E.C., *Bodmin Moor* (Newton Abbot: David & Charles, 1975).
Baxendale, John, *Priestley's England: J.B. Priestley and English Culture* (Manchester: Manchester University Press, 2007).
Bayley, John, *The Iris Trilogy* (London: Duckworth, 2020).
Beckhard, Robert, 'Notes from an American on a 1950s Warlock Odyssey', in David Cox and John Bishop (eds), *Peter Warlock: A Centenary Celebration* (London: Thames, 1994).
Bell, Quentin, *Virginia Woolf: A Biography*, Vol. II: *Mrs Woolf, 1912–1941* (London: Hogarth, 1972).
Bennett, Alan, *Southern Holiday Lines in North Cornwall and West Devon* (Cheltenham: Runpast, 1995).
Bennett, G.H. and R., 'Maritime Cornwall in the Era of Two World Wars', in Philip Payton, Alston Kennerley and Helen Doe (eds), *The Maritime History of Cornwall* (Exeter: University of Exeter Press, 2014).
Berry, Claude, *Cornwall* (London: Robert Hale, 1949).
Betjeman, John, *Cornwall: Shell Guide* (London: Murray, 1964).
Betjeman, John, *Guide to English Parish Churches* (London: Collins, new edn 1993).
Blanchard, Lydia, 'Mothers and Daughters in D.H. Lawrence: *The Rainbow* and Selected Shorter Works', in Anne Smith (ed.), *Lawrence and Women* (London: Vision, 1978).
Boulton, James T. and Robertson, Andrew (eds), *The Letters of D.H. Lawrence*, Vol. III, Part I: *1916–21* (Cambridge: University of Cambridge Press, 1984).

Select Bibliography

Brittain, F., *A Biographical Study of Q* (Cambridge: Cambridge University Press, 1948).
Broadley, A.M., *The Cornish Riviera* (London: Great Western Railway, 1904).
Brown, David (ed.), *St Ives 1939–1964* (London: Tate Gallery, 1985).
Burdett Wilson, Roger, *Go Great Western: A History of GWR Publicity* (Newton Abbot: David & Charles, 1970, repub. 1987).
Carey, John, *William Golding: The Man Who Wrote Lord of the Flies* (London: Faber & Faber, 2009).
Clark, Heather, *Red Comet: The Short Life and Blazing Art of Sylvia Plath* (London: Vintage, 2020).
Clemo, Jack, 'The Two Beds', in *Penguin Modern Poets* 6 (London: Penguin, 1964).
Clemo, Jack, *Confession of a Rebel* (London: Chatto & Windus, 1975).
Cole, Beverly and Durak, Richard, *Railway Posters 1923–1947* (London: Science Museum, 1992).
Copley, L.A. 'Peter Warlock's Choral Music', *Music and Letters*, Vol. 45, No. 4 (October 1964), pp. 318–36.
Costin, Jane, 'Lawrence's "Best Adventure": Blood Consciousness and Cornwall', *Études Lawrenciennes*, Vol. 43 (2012), pp. 151–72.
Costin, Jane, 'The Legacy of D.H. Lawrence's Time in Cornwall', *Journal of D.H. Lawrence Studies*, Vol. 4, No. 3 (2017), pp. 130–52.
Cotter, J.B., *Zennor Church* (Zennor: Zennor Parochial Church Council, n.d. c.1980).
Cox, David and Bishop, John (eds), *Peter Warlock: A Centenary Celebration* (London: Thames, 1994).
Cunliffe, Barry, *Bretons and Britons: The Fight for Identity* (Oxford: Oxford University Press, 2021).
Dalley, Stuart, 'The Response in Cornwall to the Outbreak of the First World War', in Philip Payton (ed.), *Cornish Studies: Eleven* (Exeter: University of Exeter Press, 2003).
Darroch, Robert, *D.H. Lawrence in Australia* (Melbourne: Macmillan, 1981).
Deacon, Bernard, *Cornwall: A Concise History* (Cardiff: University of Wales Press, 2007).
Deacon, Bernard, *Industrial Celts: Making the Modern Cornish Identity 1750–1870* (Redruth: Cornish Social and Economic Research Group, 2018).
Delany, Paul, *D.H. Lawrence's Nightmare: The Writer and His Circle in the Years of the Great War* (Hassocks: Harvester, 1979).
Diment, Galya, *A Russian Jew in Bloomsbury: The Life and Times of Samuel Koteliansky* (Montreal & Kingston: McGill-Queens University Press, 2013).
Doolittle, Hilda, *Bid Me to Live* (London: Virago, 1984).
Drake, Jane, *William Morris: An Illustrated Life* (Norwich: History Press, 1997).
Duncombe-Jewell, L.C., 'About Myself and the Cornish-Celtic Movement', *Candid Friend and Traveller*, 5 July 1902.
Folliott-Stokes, A.G., *The Cornish Coast and Moors* (London: Greening, 1912).
Fox, Caroline, *Painting in Newlyn* (Penzance: Newlyn Orion, 1985).

Game, David, *D.H. Lawrence's Australia: Anxiety on the Edge of Empire* (London: Routledge, 2015).

Games, Stephen (ed.), *Trains and Buttered Toast* (London: John Murray, 2006).

Games, Stephen (ed.), *Tennis Whites and Tea Cakes* (London: John Murray, 2007).

Gathorne-Hardy, Robert (ed.), *Ottoline at Garsington: Memoirs of Lady Ottoline Morrell 1915–1918* (London: Faber & Faber, 1974).

Goodman, Gemma, *Alternative Cornwalls: Literature and the Invention of Place* (Exeter: University of Exeter Press, 2024).

Gray, Cecil, *Peter Warlock: A Memoir of Philip Heseltine* (London: Jonathan Cape, 1934).

Gray, Cecil, *Musical Chairs: Or, Between Two Stools* (London: Hogarth Press, 1948).

Hale, Amy, 'Genesis of the Celto-Cornish Revival? L.C. Duncombe-Jewell and the Cowethas Kelto-Kernuak', in Philip Payton (ed.), *Cornish Studies: Five* (Exeter: University of Exeter Press, 1997).

Hardy, Thomas, *Satires of Circumstance* (London: Macmillan, 1914).

Hardy, Thomas, *The Complete Poems*, ed. James Gibson (Basingstoke: Palgrave, 2001).

Harris, J. Henry, *The Luck of Wheal Vor and Other Stories* (Truro: Pollard, 1901).

Harrison, Andrew, *The Life of D.H. Lawrence: A Critical Biography* (London: Wiley-Blackwell, 2016).

Harrison, Andrew, '"A New Continent of the Soul": D.H. Lawrence, Porthcothan and the Necessary Fiction of Cornwall', *Journal of D.H. Lawrence Studies*, Vol. 4, No. 3 (2017), pp. 33–43.

Heath-Stubbs, John, 'To the Mermaid at Zennor', in John Clegg (ed.), *Selected Poems* (Manchester: Carcanet Press, 2018).

Hocking, Joseph, *What Shall It Profit a Man?* (London: Horace Marshall, n.d.).

Hocking, Silas K., *The Lost Lode* (London: Sampson Low, Maiston & Co., n.d.).

Hudson, W.H., *The Land's End: A Naturalist's Impressions of West Cornwall* (London: Wildwood, 1908).

Hunt, Robert, *Popular Romances of the West of England: The Drolls, Traditions and Superstitions of Old Cornwall* (London: Chatto & Windus, 3rd edn 1881 and 1908).

Hutton, Patrick, *I Would Not Be Forgotten: The Life and Work of Robert Stephen Hawker 1803–1875* (Padstow: Tabb House, 2004).

Jackson, Rosie, *Frieda Lawrence: Including Not I, but the Wind and Other Autobiographical Writings* (London: Pandora, 1994).

Jacobs, Michael and Warner, Malcolm, *Art in the West Country* (Oxford: Phaidon Press, 1980).

James, Melanie, 'Indifferent or Just Different? The Cornish Response to the Declaration of War in August 1914', in Garry Tregidga and Thomas Fidler (eds), *Cornwall and the Great War: Perspectives on Conflict and Place* (Penryn: Institute of Cornish Studies, 2018).

James, Ronald M., *The Folklore of Cornwall: The Oral Tradition of a Celtic Nation* (Exeter: University of Exeter Press, 2018).

Select Bibliography

Jenkins, Simon, 'Introduction', in H.V. Morton, *In Search of England* (London: Folio Society, 2002).
Jenner, Henry, *A Handbook of the Cornish Language: Chiefly in Its Late Stages with Some Account of Its History and Literature* (London: David Nutt, 1904).
Jenner, Mrs Henry, *Celtic Symbolism* (London: Methuen, 1910).
Jewell, Jim, *Cornish in America: Linden, Wisconsin* (Linden: Cornish Miner Press, 1990).
Kent, Alan M., *The Literature of Cornwall: Continuity, Identity, Difference 1000–2000* (Bristol: Redcliffe, 2000).
Kent, Alan M., '"Song of Our Motherland": Making Meaning of the Life of Katharine Lee Jenner 1853–1936', in Derek R. Williams (ed.), *Henry and Katharine Jenner: A Celebration of Cornwall's Culture, Language and Identity* (London: Francis Boutle, 2004).
Kent, Alan M., 'From *Meeting the Kaiser* to *An Tankow*: Imagining the First World War in Cornish and Anglo-Cornish Literature and Theatre', Garry Tregidga and Thomas Fidler (eds), *Cornwall and the Great War: Perspectives on Conflict and Space* (Penryn: Institute of Cornish Studies, 2018).
Kington, Beryl, 'Alec Rowley and Recollections of Peter Warlock', in David Cox and John Bishop (eds), *Peter Warlock: A Centenary Celebration* (London: Thames, 1994).
Ladmirault, Paul, 'Peter Warlock: A Great English Composer', in David Cox and John Bishop (eds), *Peter Warlock: A Centenary Celebration* (London: Thames, 1994).
Lawrence, D.H., *Kangaroo* (London: Penguin, 1950).
Lawrence, D.H., 'Samson and Delilah', in *England, My England* (London: Penguin, 1974).
Lawrence, D.H., *Lady Chatterley's Lover* (London: Penguin, 1960, repub. 2008).
Lee, Charles, *Paul Carah, Cornishman* (London: James Bowden, 1898).
London, Pete, *Cornwall in the First World War* (Redruth: Truran, 2013).
Long, Jonathan, Review of Frances Wilson, *Burning Man: The Ascent of D.H. Lawrence* (London: Bloomsbury, 2021), *Journal of D.H. Lawrence Studies*, Vol. 6, No. 1 (2002), pp. 236–43.
Long, Jonathan, 'Murry vs Carswell: Conflicting Versions of D.H. Lawrence During His Time in Cornwall', *Journal of D.H. Lawrence Studies*, Vol. 4, No. 3 (2017), pp. 45–70.
Lowenna, Sharon, '"Noscitur A Sociis": Jenner, Duncombe-Jewell and their Milieu', in Philip Payton (ed.), *Cornish Studies: Twelve* (Exeter: University of Exeter Press, 2004).
Lycett Green, Candida (ed.), *Coming Home: An Anthology of Prose* (London: Methuen, 1997).
Lycett Green, Candida (ed.), *Betjeman's Britain* (London: Folio Society, 1999).
Lyon, Rod Trevelyan, *Cornish: The Struggle for Survival* (n.p.: Tavas an Weryn, 2001).

Lyonesse (ed.), *Legend Land: Being a Collection of Some of the Old Tales Told in the Western Parts of Britain Served by the Great Western Railway* (London: Great Western Railway, 1923).

Maddox, Brenda, *The Married Man: A Life of D.H. Lawrence* (London: Minerva, 1995).

Magee, Gary and Thompson, Andrew, 'Remittances Revisited: A Case Study of South Africa and the Cornish Migrant, c.1870–1914', in Philip Payton (ed.), *Cornish Studies: Thirteen* (Exeter: University of Exeter Press, 2005).

Mais, S.P.B., *The Cornish Riviera* (London: Great Western Railway, 3rd edn, 1934).

Maritime Archaeology Trust, *Forgotten Wrecks of the First World War—Site Report: Pendennis U-Boats* (London: Imperial War Museum, 2018).

Matthews, John Hobson, *History of St Ives, Lelant, Towednack and Zennor* (London: Eliot Stock, 1892).

Mead, C.J.H., *Cornwall's Royal Engineers* (Plymouth: Underhill, n.d.).

Millgate, Michael, *Thomas Hardy: A Biography Revisited* (Oxford: Oxford University Press, 2004).

Miners, Hugh and Crago, Treve, *Tolzethan: The Life and Times of Joseph Hambley Rowe* (Bude: Gorseth Kernow, 2002).

Morris, William A., 'An Investigation into Migration Patterns from the Parish of Zennor in Cornwall During the Second Half of the Nineteenth Century', in Philip Payton (ed.), *Cornish Studies: Seven* (Exeter: University of Exeter Press, 1999).

Morton, H.V., *In Search of England* (London: Folio Society, 2002 [original edn 1927]).

Moseley, Rachel, *Picturing Cornwall: Landscape, Region and the Moving Image* (Exeter: University of Exeter Press, 2018).

Moynahan, Julian, 'Lawrence, Woman, and the Celtic Fringe', in Anne Smith (ed.), *Lawrence and Women* (London: Vision, 1978).

Mullins, Edward, *Alfred Wallis: Cornish Primitive Painter* (London: Macdonald, 1967).

Munnings, Alfred, *An Artist's Life* (London: Museum Press, 1950).

Nance, Robert Morton, 'John Davey of Boswednack and his Cornish Rhyme', *Journal of the Royal Institution of Cornwall*, Vol. 22 (1922–25), pp. 146–53.

Newman, Paul, *The Tregerthen Horror: Aleister Crowley, D.H. Lawrence and Peter Warlock in Cornwall* (n.p.: Abraxas & DGR, 2005).

Noall, Cyril and Farr, Graham, *Wreck and Rescue Round the Cornish Coast: The Story of the Land's End Lifeboats* (Truro: D. Bradford Barton, 1965).

Ollard, Richard, *A Man of Contradictions: A Life of A.L. Rowse* (London: Allen Lane, 1999).

O'Sullivan, Vincent and Scott, Margaret (eds), *Letters of Katherine Mansfield*, Vol. I (Oxford: Clarendon Press, 1984).

Page, Norman (ed.), *D.H. Lawrence: Interviews and Recollections*, Vol. I (London: Macmillan, 1981).

Parrott, Ian, 'The Jolly Shepherd', in David Cox and John Bishop (eds), *Peter Warlock: A Centenary Celebration* (London: Thames, 1994).

Payton, Philip, *The Making of Modern Cornwall: Historical Experience and the Persistence of Difference* (Redruth: Dyllansow Truran, 1992).

Select Bibliography

Payton, Philip, 'Paralysis and Revival: The Reconstruction of Celtic-Catholic Cornwall, 1880–1945', in Ella Westland (ed.), *Cornwall: The Cultural Construction of Place* (Penzance: Patten Press, 1997).

Payton, Philip, *A.L. Rowse and Cornwall: A Paradoxical Patriot* (Exeter: University of Exeter Press, 2005).

Payton, Philip, *D.H. Lawrence and Cornwall* (St Agnes: Truran, 2009).

Payton, Philip, *John Betjeman and Cornwall: 'The Celebrated Cornish Nationalist'* (Exeter: University of Exeter Press, 2010).

Payton, Philip, *A History of Sussex* (Lancaster: Carnegie, 2017).

Payton, Philip, *Cornwall: A History* (Exeter: University of Exeter Press, new edn 2017).

Payton, Philip, *The Cornish Overseas: A History of Cornwall's Great Emigration* (Exeter: University of Exeter Press, new edn 2020).

Payton, Philip (ed.), *Cornwall For Ever! Kernow Bys Vyken!* (Lostwithiel: Cornwall Heritage Trust, 2000).

Payton, Philip (ed.), *Cornwall in the Age of Rebellion, 1490–1690* (Exeter: University of Exeter Press, 2021).

Payton, Philip and Thornton, Paul, 'The Great Western Railway and the Cornish-Celtic Revival', in Philip Payton (ed.), *Cornish Studies: Three* (Exeter: University of Exeter Press, 1995).

Payton, Philip, Kennerley, Alston and Doe, Helen (eds), *The Maritime History of Cornwall* (Exeter: University of Exeter Press, 2014).

Phelps, Kenneth, *The Wormwood Cup: Thomas Hardy in Cornwall* (Padstow: Lodenek Press, 1975).

Pool, P.A.S., *The Place-names of West Penwith* (St Austell: Federation of Old Cornwall Societies, 1973).

Pool, P.A.S., *The Life and Progress of Henry Quick of Zennor* (Redruth: Truran, 1984).

Pool, P.A.S., *The Field-names of West Penwith* (Hayle: Pool, 1990).

Pool, P.A.S., 'An Address Given at Zennor Church on 28 September 1991 at a Service to Mark the Centenary of the Death of John Davey'.

Pullin, Faith, 'Lawrence's Treatment of Women in *Sons and Lovers*', in Anne Smith (ed.), *Lawrence and Women* (London: Vision, 1978).

Quiller-Couch, Arthur, *Nicky-Nan, Reservist* (London: J.M. Dent, 1915).

Rawe, Donald R., 'The Poetry of Henry Jenner', in Derek R. Williams (ed.), *Henry and Katharine Jenner: A Celebration of Cornwall's Culture, Language and Identity* (London, Francis Boutle, 2004).

Richardson, Pamela, 'A Quaker Record of Maritime Falmouth in World War One', *Troze*, Vol. 1, No. 2 (December 2008).

Rowe, John, 'The Declining Years of Cornish Mining', in Jeffery Porter (ed.), *Education and Labour in the South West* (Exeter: University of Exeter, 1975).

Rowse, A.L., *Times, Persons, Places: Essays in Literature* (London: Macmillan, 1965).

Rowse, A.L., *Matthew Arnold: Poet and Prophet* (London: Thames & Hudson, 1976).

Rowse, A.L., *A Man of The Thirties* (London: Weidenfeld and Nicholson, 1979).

Rowse, A.L., *The Little Land of Cornwall* (Gloucester: Alan Sutton, 1986).
Rowse, A.L., *Memories and Glimpses* (London: Methuen, 1986).
Rowse, A.L., *Quiller Couch: A Portrait of Q* (London: Methuen, 1988).
Ruhrmund, Frank, *About St Just-in-Penwith* (St Teath: Bossiney Books, 1979).
Seymour, Miranda, *Ottoline Morrell: Life on the Grand Scale* (London: Sceptre, 1992).
Siegel, Carol, *Lawrence Among the Women: Wavering Boundaries in Women's Literary Traditions* (Charlottesville: University of Virginia Press, 1991).
Smith, Anne (ed.), *Lawrence and Women* (London: Vision, 1978).
Spika, Mark, 'On Lawrence's Hostility to Wilful Women: The Chatterley Solution', in Anne Smith (ed.), *Lawrence and Women* (London: Vision, 1928).
Stevens, C.J., *Lawrence at Tregerthen: D.H. Lawrence in Cornwall* (Albany, NY: Whiston, 1988).
Stevens, C.J., *The Cornish Nightmare: D.H. Lawrence in Cornwall* (Phillips, ME: John Wade, 1996).
Stevens, James, *A Cornish Farmer's Diary* (Penzance: Pool, 1977).
Storch, Margaret, 'From Cornwall to New Mexico: Primal Cultures and Belief in Lawrence', *Journal of D.H. Lawrence Studies*, Vol. 4, No. 3 (2017), pp. 111–29.
Stoyle, Mark, *West Britons: Cornish Identities and the Early Modern British State* (Exeter: University of Exeter Press, 2002).
Symons, Alison, *Tremedda Days: A View of Zennor, 1900–1944* (Padstow: Tabb House, 1992).
Tait, Adrian, '"Primeval Darkness" and "Chasmal Beauty": An Ecocritical Rereading of Cornwall in the Work of D.H. Lawrence and Thomas Hardy', *Journal of D.H. Lawrence Studies*, Vol. 4, No. 3 (2017), pp. 91–110.
Thomas, D.M. (ed.), *The Granite Kingdom: Poems of Cornwall* (Truro: Bradford Barton, 1970).
Thompson, Luke, *Clay Phoenix: A Biography of Jack Clemo* (London: Ally, 2016).
Thorne, Guy, *The Secret Service Submarine: A Story of the Present War* (New York: Sully and Kleinteich, 1915).
Tomalin, Claire, *Katherine Mansfield: A Secret Life* (London: Penguin, 1988).
Tomalin, Claire, *The Young H.G. Wells: Changing the World* (Penguin: London, 2022).
Trewin, J.C. and Willmott, H.J., *London–Bodmin: An Exchange of Letters* (London: Westaway, 1950).
Trezise, Simon, '"Off Wessex", or a Place in the Mind', in Melissa Hardie (ed.), *A Mere Interlude: Some Literary Visitors in Lyonnesse* (Penzance: Patten Press, 1992).
Trezise, Simon, 'The Celt, the Saxon and the Cornishman: Stereotypes and Counter-stereotypes of the Victorian Period', in Philip Payton (ed.), *Cornish Studies: Eight* (Exeter: University of Exeter Press, 2000).
Trotter, Lesley, *The Married Widows of Cornwall: The Story of Wives 'Left Behind' by Emigration* (St Day: Humble Press, 2018).
Trower, Shelley, *Rocks of Nations: The Imagination of Celtic Cornwall* (Manchester: Manchester University Press, 2015).

Select Bibliography

Turner, John and Worthen, John, 'Ideas of Community: Lawrence and "Rananim"', *D.H. Lawrence Studies* (The D.H. Lawrence Society of Korea), Vol. 8 (July 1999), pp. 135–71.

Vaughan, Herbert S., *The British Road Book* (London: E.R. Shrimpton, 1898).

Vernon, James, 'Border Crossing: Cornwall and the English (Imagi)nation', in Geoffrey Cubitt (ed.), *Imagining Nations* (Manchester: University of Manchester Press, 1998).

Walke, Bernard, *Twenty Years at St Hilary* (London: Anthony Mott, 1982).

Westland, Ella, *Cornwall: The Cultural Construction of Place* (Penzance: Patten Press, 1997).

Westland, Ella, 'D.H. Lawrence's Cornwall: Dwelling in a Precarious Age', *Cultural Geographies*, Vol. 9, No. 3 (July 2002), pp. 266–85.

Whybrow, Marion, *St Ives 1883–1993: Portrait of an Art Colony* (Woodbridge: Art Collectors' Club, 1994).

Williams, John Fischer (ed.), *Memories of John Westlake* (London: Smith, Elder & Co., 1914).

Williams, Derek R. (ed.), *Henry and Katharine Jenner: A Celebration of Cornwall's Culture, Language and Identity* (London: Francis Boutle, 2004).

Wilson, A.N., *Hilaire Belloc: A Biography* (Singapore: Mandarin, 1997).

Wilson, Frances, *Burning Man: The Ascent of D.H. Lawrence* (Bloomsbury: London, 2021).

Wright, Louise E., 'D.H. Lawrence: Robert Mountsier and the Journalist Spy Controversy', *Journal of the D.H. Lawrence Society* (1992–93), pp. 7–21.

Zytaruk, George J. and Boulton, James T. (eds), *The Letters of D.H. Lawrence*, Vol. II: *1913–16* (Cambridge: Cambridge University Press, 2002).

Index

References to photographs appear in *italic* type.

Aaron's Rod (Lawrence) 135
Aboriginal societies 136–7
Admiralty 113
agriculture *see* farms and farming
A.L. Rowse and Cornwall (Payton) 9
Aldbaran (Swedish steamer) 106
Aldington, Richard 11, 20, 97, 121, 125, 135, 138, 139, 141
All Year Round (Dickens) 27–8
Allinson, Adrian 53
Alternative Cornwalls (Goodman) 8
America 20, 105, 130, 135, 141
'An Old Song' (Heseltine) 49
Ancient Art and Ritual (Harrison) 136
Andrews, Esther 119
Andrews, Marian 78
anti-industrialism 12
anti-submarine motor launches 107–8
anti-war views 19–20
Archaeologia Britannica (Lhuyd) 67
Archaeologia Cornu-Britannica (Pryce) 68
Arnold, Matthew 5–6, 27
Arnold-Forster, Katherine ('Ka') 53, 146
Arthurian traditions 22–3, 25, 98
artists and artists' colonies 30–1, 76
Arts and Crafts movement 11–12, 13

Asquith, Cynthia, Lady 18–19, 39, 80, 110, 120–1, 123
'Atlantic archipelago' 8
Atlantico (Portuguese sailing ship) 106
Atlantis (Norwegian steamer) 106
Australia 74–5, 127, 135–42 *see also Kangaroo* (Lawrence)
Australian anthropology 136–7
'authentic' England 13

Baillot, Mlle Juliette 54–5
Balkan wars 77
Ballarat, HMAT 105
Bamse (British merchantman) 106
Baxendale, John 12
Bayley, John 4
Baynton, Barbara 136
'Beeny Cliff, March 1870–March 1913' (Hardy) 38
Belloc, Hilaire 12
Benjamin Cooley ('Kangaroo,' *Kangaroo*) 140–1
'Benneth Nadelik ha'n Bledhen Noweth' (Heseltine) 52
Bennetts, Revd G.A. 101
Bentwich, Norman 77
Beresford, Beatrice 58–9
Beresford, J.D. 21, 39–41, 42, 55, 57–8, 109

Index

Bernard Carey (*The Secret Service Submarine*) 115
Berryman, Katie 94
Berryman, Tom 94, 128
Betjeman, John 13–14, 23–4, 30–1
Bid Me to Live (Doolittle) 98
biographies 9
Birch, John 'Lamorna' 31
blackouts 116
Blanchard, Lydia 5
'blood consciousness' 63–4, 71–2, 82, 137
'blood sacrifice' 81–2
Blutbrüderschaft 81, 85
Bodinar, William 67
Bodmin 110–11
Boer War 100
Booth, William 114
Borrow, George 45
Bosigran, Zennor 87, 91, 97–8, 116
Bosigran Castle tin mine 97
Bossiney Round, Tintagel 22
Bottrell, William 24
The Boy in the Bush (Lawrence & Skinner) 136, 137, 138–9
Braddon, Mary Elizabeth 31–2
Breton Gorsedd 27
Breton language 25
British and Irish Isles 8
The British Road Book (Vaughan) 27
Brittany 25–8, 31–2
Broadley, A.M. 32
Bruhl, Louis Burleigh 33
Buckley Jones, Walter 45
Burning Man (Wilson) 7–8
Burrows, Louie 21
Bush Studies (Baynton) 136
By the Cornish Seas and Moors (London and South Western Railway) 35

Campbell, Charles (Gordon) 2nd Baron Glenavy 47
Canadian Cavalry Brigade 76
Carn Galver, Zennor 128
Carnac, Brittany 26, 91
Carswell, Catherine 41, 71, 86–7, 110, 111, 123
Carter-Wood, Florence 76
Cefn Bryntalch, Montgomeryshire 45
Celt-woman nexus 6
Celtia magazine 50
Celtic Brittany 25
'Celtic-Catholic Cornwall' 24
Celtic Congress (Caernarfon, 1904) 25
Celtic-Cornish movement 25
Celtic Cornwall 31–2, 63–4
Celtic Literary Revival 5–6
Celtic Revival 24–5
'Celtic symbolism' 47, 71
Celtic Triad (Heseltine) 49
'Celtic Twilight' movement 55–6, 92
'Celtic vision' 70
'the Celts' 5–7, 55
Ceylon (Sri Lanka) 135
Channing, Minnie Lucy ('Puma') 53–5, 88
Charteris, Yvo 18–19
'Cherry of Zennor' 73
Chesham, Buckinghamshire 17
Children of the Bush (Lawson) 136
China-clay exports 102
Christian Symbolism ('Mrs Henry Jenner') 46–7
Clay Phoenix (Thompson) 9
Clemo, Jack (son) 9, 145
Clemo, Reginald (father) 102
coast-watching 113–14, 116
Concarneau, Brittany 26, 31
conscription 109–10
Copley, Ian 48
Cornish-Celtic Revival 25, 34, 60
Cornish-Celtic Society (Cowethas Kelto-Kernuak) 24, 52
Cornish Celts 56–7, 67
'A Cornish Christmas Carol' (Heseltine & Jenner) 49–51

181

The Cornish Coast and Moors (Folliott-Stokes) 34–5, 65–6, 80
Cornish dialect of English 68–9
Cornish emigration 127–30
Cornish Gorsedd 27
Cornish Guardian 100
Cornish humour 76, 93–4
Cornish identity 3, 9
Cornish language 25, 47–52, 67–71
'Cornish Lives' (Truran Books) 9
Cornish mining 33, 100, 127–9
Cornish nationalism 147
The Cornish Nightmare (Stevens) 9
Cornish people: as 'foreigners'/'other' 27; innate superiority 9; Lawrence's contrary feelings 56–8; negative portrayals 28–30; superiority as hard-rock miners 9, 127; as unwarlike 110
Cornish Rananim *see* Rananim utopian community
Cornish revivalists 25, 27, 33–4, 45, 53
'Cornish Riviera' 30
The Cornish Riviera (Broadley) 32
The Cornish Riviera (Mais) 34
'Cornish Riviera Limited' train 32
'The Cornish Riviera' poster (Bruhl) 33
Cornish studies 9
Cornish tourism 31–2
Cornishman newspaper 99
Cornwall: 'Atlantic archipelago' 8; and Brittany 31; Celtic past 24; 'emigration culture' 130; expulsion from 96–7, 120–4; liminal/peripheral place 136, 147–8; as a myth and fantasy 60; 'new British history' 8; as 'pagan' and 'pre-Christian' 53; responses to war 99–104, 108–9; as un-English/not England 13–14, 21, 98, 149
Cornwall (Westland) 8
'Cornwall: A Celtic Nation' (Jenner) 25

Cornwall in the Age of Rebellion (Stoyle) 8
Cornwall's Royal Engineers (Mead) 108
Costin, Jane 9, 64, 71–2, 124, 125–6, 137
Cotter, J.B. 73
'Cousin Jack' 9, 75, 127, 132
'Cousin Jacky' (Harris) 131
'Cousin Jennys' 132
Cowethas Kelto-Kernuak (Cornish-Celtic Society) 24, 52
'Crankan Rhyme' (Davey) 69–70
Creswick diggings, Victoria, Australia 129
Crowley, Aleister 52–3
'Cult of the Celt' 4–8
Cunliffe, Barry 25–6
The Curlew (Heseltine) 43

'D.H. Lawrence's Cornwall' (Westland) 9
Daily News 19
Dalley, Stuart 100
Darroch, Robert 140–1
The Daughter-in-Law (Lawrence) 135
Davey, John 68–70
De Beers diamond mine, Kimberley, South Africa 129
Death of a Hero (Aldington) 97
Defence of the Realm Act 1914 117, 118
'Delectable Duchy' 30
Delius, Frederick 20, 44, 45, 59, 91
Denbola (merchant steamer) 106
Derby Scheme 109
Dickens, Charles 27
Diment, Galya 17, 141
Doolittle, Hilda ('H.D.') 97–8
'droll-tellers' (itinerant storytellers) 2–3
Duke of Cornwall's Light Infantry 102
Duncombe-Jewell, L.C. 24, 50, 52
Dunstan, Captain 128

Index

Eagle's Nest (Tregerthen Cottage) 78, 118
East and West (play) 80
Easter Rising 1916 56, 119
Eastwood, Nottinghamshire 11, 139, 144
Eddy, Arthur 95
Eddy, Elizabeth 130
Eddy, P.O. 116
Edward Hain & Son 105
Edwardian era 12
Eggert, Paul 136
Emanual Espana (coal boat) 117
emigration 127–30
Emma (housekeeper) 55
England 13
The English Past (Rowse) 144
English prejudice 55–6
ethnic cleansing 89–90

Falmouth 101, 107
Falmouth Wesley Church 101
farms and farming: labourers enlisting 102; Lawrence working on 92, 94–5, 111, 143; and mining 128; sense of inevitable disaster 96–7
feminist critiques 4–5
Florida project 16
folkloric motifs 72–3
Folliott-Stokes, A.G. 34–5, 65–6, 80
'For the Mermaid of Zennor' (Heath-Stubbs) 146–7
Forbes, Stanhope 31, 32
Fort Myers, Florida 20
Fox family 101
The Fox (Lawrence) 6
Fremantle, Western Australia 138
'Furry Dance' 33

Game, David 17, 75, 135–8
Garsington Manor, Oxford 10, 18
Gaugin, Paul 26
Gay, Maisie 77

German folk-songs 116
German submarine officers story 106, 112
Germans 101
Gertler, Mark 42
giants 72–3
Gifford, Emma 36–8
Gill, Eric 12
Gjertrud (Norwegian ship) 106
'The Goat and Compasses' (Lawrence) 121
Golding, William 108
Goodman, Gemma 8
Gorsedds 27, 46, 68
gossip and innuendo 120
Gray, Cecil: blackouts 116, 118; cottage at Bosigran 87–8, 97–8; and Freda Lawrence 91; and Hilda Doolittle 97–8; and Philip Heseltine 43–4, 48–9, 53, 89; at Zennor 91
Great War: atmosphere of suspicion 115; attitudes to 99–104, 108–9, 148; coast-watching 113–14; debasement of humanity and industrialization 14; driving Lawrence 'out of England' 10–11; industrial warfare 3, 14; insidious influences 55, 56; low-level harassment 120; military order to leave Cornwall 96–7, 120–2; 'national honour' 44; outbreak of war 15; Philip Heseltine's attitude 44; as pointless 116; shipping losses 105–8; slaughter and destruction 12 *see also* U-boats
Great Western Railway 32–4, 73
Greatham, Sussex 17–18
Gregynog (merchant steamer) 106
Gull, Ranger (Guy Thorne) 77
Gurnard's Head, Zennor 66, 128, 146

Hall, John 70
A Handbook of the Cornish Language (Jenner) 25, 45, 47, 67–8, 70–1

Hardy, Thomas 35–8
Harris, J. Henry 131
Harrison, Andrew 7, 60
Harrison, Jane 136
Harry Chatteris (*The Sea Lady*) 73
Hawken (landowner) 57
Hawker, Robert Stephen 23–4, 25
'Hawker of Morwenstow' 30
Heath-Stubbs, John 146–7
Hebrew music 15–16
Helene (Dutch ship) 106
Helston 33
Henry, Mrs George 101
Hermetic Order of the Golden Dawn 52
Heseltine, Philip 20, 30, 42–5; avoiding conscription 91–2; Celticism 47–52; contrary views 89–91; 'A Cornish Christmas Carol' 49–51; Cornish language 71; critical of Cornish people 89–90; Jekyll and Hyde personality 89–90; love life 54; new beginning in Cornwall 44, 89; occult 53; as 'Peter Warlock' 43, 50, 52, 89; and Puma 53–4; second thoughts about Lawrence and Rananim 59–60; at Zennor 87–9
Higher Tregerthen cottage, Zennor 71–2, 72, 81, 98, 116, 120, 146 *see also* Zennor, Cornwall
History of the Parishes of St Ives, Lelant, Towednack, and Zennor (Matthews) 64, 67–8
Hocking family of Lower Tregerthen 94, 143
Hocking, Stanley (brother) 17, 94–6; interview with C.J. Stevens 110, 111–12, 124; Lawrence and Frieda's eviction from Cornwall 122; suspicions of Lawrence and Frieda 112–13, 119–20
Hocking, William Henry (brother) 92, 93; as John Thomas (*Kangaroo*) 96, 137–8; Lawrence and Frieda's eviction from Cornwall 122; relationship with Lawrence 95–6, 143
Hocking family of St Stephen-in-Brannel, St Austell 130–1
Hocking, Joseph (brother) 108, 130
Hocking, Salome (sister) 130
Hocking, Silas K. (brother) 130–1
Holiburn (giant) 72–3
holidaymaking 30–1
homosexuality 95–6, 147
Hudson, W.H. 28–30, 65
Hunt, Robert 24
Hurlers stone circle, St Cleer 33
Hy-Brasil story 88–9

'I Found Her Out There' (Hardy) 37–8
'Idylls of the King' (Tennyson) 23–4
In Search of England (Morton) 13
'Inconveniences of Being a Cornishman' (Dickens) 27
industrial warfare 3, 14 *see also* Great War
International Law (Westlake) 77
Irish question 119
Irish rebels 1916 56
'Island' project 18
Isle of Avalon 23
Italy 126

Jack Grant (*The Boy in the Bush*) 136
James, Melanie 100
James, Ronald M. 2, 3
Jasper Blake (*The Lost Lode*) 130–1
Jelbert, Charlie 94
Jenkins, Simon 13
Jenner, Henry ('Gwas Myhal') 24–5, 67–71; Celtic revivalism 52; 'A Cornish Christmas Carol' 49–51; *A Handbook of the Cornish Language* 25, 45, 47, 67–8, 70–1; and Kitty Lee 45–7; reviving Cornish 49

Index

Jenner, Katharine Lee (Kitty Lee) 45–7, 70, 71
John Betjeman and Cornwall (Payton) 9
John Carey (*The Secret Service Submarine*) 115
John Thomas (*Kangaroo*) 137
journalists 118–19

Kangaroo (Lawrence): Australian society 140–1; autobiographical 140; 'blood-consciousness' 82; changing attitude to war 109; conscription 115–16; Cornwall and Australia link 137–8; journey to Bodmin 111; military searches 120; nostalgia for Cornwall 60, 63–4, 123; old world ending 15; Richard Lovat Somers 63, 74–5, 96, 111, 112, 121, 137, 140, 141; U-boats 112, 118; war-wave 121; William James (Jaz) Trewhella 74–6, 135, 137–8 *see also* Australia
Kangaroo tribe 136
Kanow Kernow (Songs of Cornwall, Heseltine & Jenner) 52
Kate Leslie (*The Plumed Serpent*) 148–9
Katherine's tower 81, 82, 83
Kent, Alan M. 8, 46, 103, 108
'King Arthur class' locomotives 35
King Arthur legends 22–3, 25, 98
Kington, Beryl 45
Kintuck (Admiralty transport) 105
Knight, Harold and Laura 31
Kotcliansky, Samuel (Kot) 15–17, 40–1, 47, 86, 117, 123, 126, 141
Kouyoumdjian, Dikran (Michael Arlen) 54

Ladmirault, Paul 49–50
Lady Chatterley 4
Lady Chatterley's Lover (Lawrence) 125
Lady of the Lake 23
Lamorna Cove, Cornwall 31

Lampitt, Ronald 33
The Land's End (Hudson) 28–30, 65
Lawrence, D.H. 3–4; approaches to women 5; bankruptcy 18; birth and background 11; categorizing 5; 'Celtic vision' 47, 70; Cornish neighbours 143; destroying his work 121; engaged to Louie Burrows 22; expulsion from Cornwall 96–7, 120–4; farm work 92, 94–5, 111; feminist critiques 4–5; fights with Frieda 84–5, 87; homosexuality 95–6, 147; literary influences 4; literary responses to places 125; medical examinations 20–1, 110–11; opinion of the Cornish 6, 123–4, 147; post-war travels 16, 135–42, 148–9; reception and rehabilitation 7–8; as spies 117
Lawrence, D.H. **books and stories**: *Aaron's Rod* 135; *The Boy in the Bush* (with Mollie Skinner) 136, 137, 138–9; *The Daughter-in-Law* 135; *The Fox* 6; 'The Goat and Compasses' 121; *Kangaroo* see *Kangaroo* (Lawrence); *Lady Chatterley's Lover* 125; *The Lost Girl* 135; *Mr Noon* 135; *The Plumed Serpent* 148–9; 'The Primrose Path' 135; *The Rainbow* 15, 19–20, 117; *The Reality of Peace* 121; 'Samson and Delilah' 133–5, 144; *Sea and Sardinia* 126; *Sons and Lovers* 10, 144; *A Study of Thomas Hardy* 38; *The Trespasser* 10; 'The Vicar's Garden' 135–6; *The White Peacock* 10, 135–6; *Women in Love* 88, 96
Lawrence, Frieda: atmosphere of suspicion 115–16; Australia 141; background 11; and Cecil Gray 91; fights with Lawrence 84–5, 87; the 'Murrys' at Zennor 82–3; *Not I, but the Wind* 115

Lawrence Among the Women (Siegel) 7
Lawrence at Tregerthen (Stevens) 9
'Lawrence, Woman, and the Celtic Fringe' (Moynahan) 5
Lawson, Henry 136
Lee, Charles 132
Lee, Katharine (Kitty) *see* Jenner, Katharine Lee (Kitty Lee)
'left behind' wives 132–3
Legend Land (Great Western Railway) 33, 73
Levitin, Mia 4
Lhuyd, Edward 67
The Life of D.H. Lawrence (Harrison) 7
The Life and Progress of Henry Quick of Zennor (Pool) 1
Limpots, Jimmy 94, 113
Linden ('pard town' Wisconsin) 129
The Literature of Cornwall (Kent) 8
Lloyd George, David 56, 121
Loe Pool, Helston 23
London 122
London and South Western Railway 35
Long, Jonathan 7, 87
loss and homelessness 126
The Lost Girl (Lawrence) 135
The Lost Lode (Silas K. Hocking) 130–1
Low, Barbara 42, 55, 56–7, 85, 86
Luard, John 107
Lusitania, RMS 105
Lyon, Rod 70
Lyonnesse/Lyonesse (*Legend Land*) 23, 33, 35–6, 38

Machen, Arthur 52
Maddox, Brenda 95
Magee, Gary 100
Mais, S.P.B. 34
A Man of the Thirties (Rowse) 144–5
Manchester Guardian 14
Mandas, Sardinia 126–7

Mann, John 70
Mansfield, Katherine: and Dikran Kouyoumdjian 54; hatred of Cornwall 84; Higher Tregerthen cottage 146; holiday at Porthcothan 21; isolation at Zennor 83; Lawrence and Frieda's fights 84–5; Lawrence liking Cornwall 41–2, 61–2; Rananim utopian community 16, 81–6
March (*The Fox*) 6
Matthews, John Hobson 64, 67–70
McNabb, Vincent 12
Mead, C.J.H. 108
medical examinations 20–1, 110–11
'Mermaid of Zennor' 71–6, 79
'Messianic phase' (Delany) 17
Methodists 108
Methuen & Co. 20
Mexico 148
Meynell, Viola 17
Military Service Act 1916 109
military service exemptions 20–1, 110–11
Millett, Kate 4
Mineral Point, Wisconsin 129
mining 33, 100, 127–9
modernity 3
Morrell, Ottoline, Lady 10–11, 17–19, 40, 42–3, 44, 47, 53–5, 62, 82, 85
Morrell, Philip 15, 18, 20
Morris, William 11–12, 13
Morton, H.V. 12–14
Morton Nance, Robert 25, 69
Moseley, Rachel 8
Mountsier, Robert 118–20
Moynahan, Julian 5, 6–7
Mr Noon (Lawrence) 135
'Mrs Henry Jenner' *see* Jenner, Katharine Lee (Kitty Lee)
Munnings, Alfred 76–7
Murry, John Middleton ('Jack') 16; bad time at Higher Tregerthen 86;

Index

Lawrence and Dikran Kouyoumdjian 54; Lawrence liking Cornwall 41–2; at Porthcothan 21; Rananim membership 81–6; *Reminiscences of D.H. Lawrence* 83–4
'the Murrys' (Jack Murry and Katherine Mansfield) 16, 61–2, 81–6
Mylor, Falmouth 85, 86
'the myth of Cousin Jack' 9, 127

Nankervis, Mr (Tinners' Arms) 94, 133
Nankervis, Mrs ('Samson and Delilah') 133–5
Nankervis, Thomas (miner) 129
Nankervis, Tom (miner) 128
Nanna (merchant steamer) 106
'national honour' 44
naval battles 111–12
Naval Reservists 103–4
'new Cornish historiography' 8
New Mexico 16, 135, 141, 148
New York Times 119
Newlyn school of artists 31, 32, 76
Newman, Paul 80, 146
Nichols, Robert 60, 88, 89, 90
Nicky-Nan, Reservist (Quiller-Couch) 103–4
Nonconformist utilitarianism 75
North Cornwall 22, 38, 98
Not I, but the Wind (Frieda Lawrence) 115

Obscene Prints Act 1857 20
occultism 52–3
'Off Wessex' (Hardy) 35
OHMS call up papers 110
'old Mary Colineck of Zennor' 73
Olivia (Cornish ship) 105
'On the Study of Celtic Literature' (Arnold) 5–6
Orientalism 46–7
Osborn, Dick 128

Ottoman Empire 77
'outsiders' 5

Pacific Ocean 139
pacifism 101
Paddington to Penzance train 32
'pagan' Cornwall 53
painters 30
A Pair of Blue Eyes (Hardy) 36
'pard country' 127–30
'pares' (syndicates) 128
Pascoe, Mr (stonecutter) 94
Passing of Arthur 23
Paul Carah, Cornishman (Lee) 132
Paul Morel (*Sons and Lovers*) 144
Payton, Philip 9
peace meetings 107
Pendraggles ('Inconveniences of Being a Cornishman') 27–8
Pentreath, Dolly 67
Penwith, Cornwall 31, 65–6
Phillpotts, Gertrude 78–9
Phoenicians 71, 98
phoenix resurgent symbol 47, 70–1, 124
Picturing Cornwall (Moseley) 8
Pinker, J.B. 38, 40
Plath, Sylvia 4
The Plumed Serpent (Lawrence) 148–9
'The Poems of 1912–13' (Hardy) 37
Polijames (British merchantman) 106
Pollard, Emma ('Cornish Pasty') 42, 109
Pool, P.A.S. 1–4, 9, 143
Porthcothan, North Cornwall 21, 39–40, 60; domestic contentment 42; King Arthur's land 98; Philip Heseltine and Puma 53–5
Porthcothan Cove 39–40
post-industrial economy 34
post-war travels 16, 135–42, 148–9
'pre-Christian' Cornwall 53
Priestley, J.B. 12–13

'The Primrose Path' (Lawrence) 135
Pryce, William 68
Psalm 33 16
Pueblo Indians, New Mexico 141, 148
Pullin, Faith 4–5
Puma (Minnie Lucy Channing) 53–5, 88

Q-ships (decoy vessels) 107
Quakers (Society of Friends) 101
'The Quest of the Sangraal' (Hawker) 23
Quick, Henry 3–4, 9
Quiller-Couch, Arthur 24, 33–4, 103–4
Quiller Couch (Rowse) 104

R.B. Chellew of Truro 105
Radford, Dollie 21, 92, 110–11
The Rainbow (Lawrence) 15, 19–20, 117
Ranani Sadekim Badanoi (Hebrew song) 16
Rananim utopian community 3; Australia 136–8, 141; Cornwall 16–17, 38, 42–5, 59–60, 86; and the 'Murrys' 81–6; origins of name 15–17; and Philip Heseltine 53, 59–60; recruits 53–4, 80–1; South Sea Islands 141; at Zennor 61–2, 87, 146
Ranger, Gull (Guy Thorne) 114–15
Rawlings, William 45–6
The Reality of Peace (Lawrence) 121
Reminiscences of D.H. Lawrence (Murry) 83–4
remittances 133
returned emigrants 130–5
Rhein, Wilhelm 106
Richard Lovat Somers (*Kangaroo*) 63, 74–5, 96, 111, 112, 121, 137, 140, 141

Richthofen, Manfred von ('Red Baron') 11
Roach, John 128
Romantic movement 64
Rose Vale Mine, Foage Valley 128
Rowe, Hambley 25
Rowse, A.L. 13, 104, 106, 144–5
Royal Cornwall Gazette 99–100
Royal Naval Reserve 103
Royal Navy 102–3
Ruskin, John 11
Russell, Bertrand 17–18, 42, 56, 117, 137
Ruthenbeck, Elise 74

Sackville-West, Edward ('Eddy') 77
'Samson and Delilah' (Lawrence) 133–4, 144
Sardinia 126–7
Satires of Circumstance (Hardy) 37, 38
'Scene in West Cornwall, A' (Tinney) 64–5
The Sea Lady (Wells) 74
Sea and Sardinia (Lawrence) 126
The Secret Service Submarine (Ranger/Thorne) 77, 114–15, 115
Semmens, Harry 128
Sennen Cove 28
The Servile State (Belloc) 12
Sexual Politics (Millett) 4
Seymour, Miranda 18
shipping losses 105–8
Sicily 126
Sickert, Walter Richard 31
Siegel, Carol 7
Skinner, Mollie 136, 138–9
Slaughter Bridge, Camelford 22
Smith, Anne 4
Society of Friends (Quakers) 101
Sons and Lovers (Lawrence) 10, 144
South Africa 100, 129
South Sea Islands 141
spies 116–17

Index

Spilka, Mark 5
Sri Lanka (Ceylon) 135
St Austell 101
St Breward parish 22
St Hilary, West Cornwall 101
St Ives Consolidated mine 102, 127
St Ives Times 80
St Juliot, Boscastle 35–6
St Just mining area 129–30
St Just-in-Penwith 70
St Mawr (Moynahan) 6–7
Stamford, Lady Mary 80
Standard 19
Starr, Meredith 80
Stephens, Elsie 100
Stevens, Abraham 130
Stevens, C.J. 9, 110, 111, 124
Stevens family 92–3
Stevens, James 93, 128, 130
Stevens, Mary Jane 130
Stevens, William 130
Storch, Margaret 148
'The Story of the Submarine' (Booth) 114
Stoyle, Mark 8
A Study of Thomas Hardy (Lawrence) 38
submarine warfare 104–8, 112–13, 115, 118 *see also* U-boats
A Summer in Brittany (Trollope) 26
Sweet, Noreen 144
Sydney *Bulletin* 140
Symons, Alison 76, 93–4, 116–17, 128, 143

Tait, Adrian 38
Tamar Bridge 31–2
Taos, New Mexico 135, 141
Taylor, Colin 44
teaching jobs 22
Tennyson 23–4
'The Two Beds' (Clemo) 145
Thirroul, Australia 139–40

Thomas, John 130
Thompson, Andrew 100
Thompson, Luke 9
Through the Window (Great Western Railway) 34
tin mines and miners 102
Tinners' Arms, Zennor 83, 88, 94, 133
'Tinners' Rest' ('Samson and Delilah') 133–5
Tinney, J.M. 64–5
Tintagel 22
tradition versus modernity paradox 3
Trebetherick, North Cornwall 30
Tregerthen Cottage (Eagle's Nest) 78, 118
The Tregerthen Horror (Newman) 146
Tremedda Days (Symons) 76, 93–4, 143
Tresize, Simon 38
The Trespasser (Lawrence) 10
Trevail Mine 128
Trewarveneth Studio 31
Trewhella, Matthew ('Mathey') 73–6
Trewin, J.C. 90, 145
Trezise, Simon 27
Trollope, Thomas 26
Troon, Camborne 102
Trotter, Lesley 132
Trower, Shelley 147
Truran Books 9
Tuatha Dé Danann 98
tuberculosis 43
Turner, John 16
Twenty Years at St Hilary (Walke) 101

U-boats 104–8, 112–13 *see also* submarine warfare
United States *see* America
utopian dreams *see* Rananim utopian community

Vaughan, Herbert S. 27
Vear Mine (Wheal Veor) 128
Vernon, James 149

189

'The Vicar's Garden' (Lawrence) 135–6
Victoria, Australia 129
'The Voice' (Hardy) 37

Walke, Bernard 101, 106–7, 113
war 99
war machines 3, 14 see also Great War
Warlock, Peter see Heseltine, Philip
Warren, Dorothy 54
Watson, E.L. Grant 137
Wells, H.G. 74
Welsh Gorsedd 68
West Briton newspaper 100, 102
West Britons (Stoyle) 8
West Penwith 31, 66
Western Australia 138
Western occultism 52–3
A Western Wildflower ('Katharine Lee') 46
Westlake, Alice 79–80
Westlake, John 68, 77–80, 93, 118
Westland, Ella 8, 9, 22–3, 98
Westwood (merchantman) 106
What Shall It Profit a Man? (Joseph Hocking) 130
Wheal Grylls tin mine 128
Wheal Sherriffs 128
When Fortune Frowns ('Katharine Lee') 46
'When I Set Out for Lyonnesse' (Hardy) 36
Where Bonds Are Loosed (Watson) 137
Whistler, James McNeill 31
White, Ann 130
The White Peacock (Lawrence) 10, 135–6
Whittley, Irene 126

Wild Wales (Borrow) 45
William James (Jaz) Trewhella (*Kangaroo*) 74–6, 135, 137–8
Willie Nankervis ('Samson and Delilah') 134–5
Willmott, H.J. 90, 145
Wilson, Frances 7–8, 122
witches 73
women 132–3
Women in Love (Lawrence) 88, 96
Woolf, Virginia 146
Worthen, John 16
'wrecking' 117–18
Wright, Louise 118–19, 147

Yeats, William Butler 52, 92
Yorke's Peninsula Advertiser 129–30

Zennor, Cornwall 1–3; Celtic landscape 63–4; church 66, 73–4, 79; Churchtown 62, 66; Cornish dialect of English 68–9; emigration 128–9; giants 72–3; interests and anxieties of community 96; landscape and seascape 64; Lawrence's opinion of the locals 58; mermaid 71–6, 79; mining industry 128–9; nostalgic ditty 129–30; path to Higher Tregerthen 71–2; place names 67; political sensitivities 79, 118; post office 94; as the Promised Land 61–4; sense of humour 93–4; Tuatha Dé Danann and Phoenicians 98; utopian communities 16; John Westlake's community of intellectuals 79 see also Higher Tregerthen cottage, Zennor
Zennor Church (Cotter) 73

Printed in the USA
CPSIA information can be obtained
at www.ICGtesting.com
LVHW090741020824
786978LV00020B/29